FORGOTTEN SOLDIERS

The Irishmen Shot at Dawn

STEPHEN WALKER ∾

Gill & Macmillan

Gill & Macmillan Ltd
Hume Avenue, Park West, Dublin 12
with associated companies throughout the world
www.gillmacmillan.ie

© Stephen Walker 2007
978 07171 4182 1

Index compiled by Helen Litton
Typography design by Make Communication
Print origination by Carole Lynch
Printed and bound in Great Britain by
MPG Books Ltd, Bodmin, Cornwall

This book is typeset in Linotype Minion and
Neue Helvetica.

The paper used in this book comes from the wood
pulp of managed forests. For every tree felled,
at least one tree is planted, thereby renewing
natural resources.

A CIP catalogue record for this book is available
from the British Library.

5 4 3 2 1

CONTENTS

PREFACE

It was early evening in Belfast, and in the open-plan offices that housed BBC Radio Ulster's current affairs department in Broadcasting House my reporting shift had just begun. It was a frustratingly quiet news day. As the afternoon light faded outside I scanned the newspapers scattered over the desk, looking for stories that might make features for the next day's edition of 'Good Morning Ulster'.

A small item caught my eye about a Labour MP who had begun a campaign to secure pardons for First World War soldiers who had been shot for desertion or disobedience. The story intrigued me. Who were these men, and what did they do to deserve being shot at dawn? I wondered aloud, in earshot of my colleague, whether any of them were from our patch. Then I suggested optimistically that we might have at least one story for the morning. So I rang the MP, Andrew Mackinlay.

He was pleased to get the call and quickly confirmed that about two dozen Irishmen, including a number of Ulstermen, had been put before firing squads for deserting the trenches. It was a story that had me hooked and with typical black humour pleased my producer, who could at last see one item appearing on his empty running order.

That initial phone conversation in 1992 sparked a series of news stories and unwittingly marked the start of a fifteen-year journey that ultimately led to this book—an odyssey that has taken me around the battlefields of France and Flanders, to the national archives and public record offices in London and Belfast, to the homes of veterans and relatives, and to Dáil Éireann and the House of Commons.

I quickly discovered that it was the families of the executed men who were at the heart of this story, and over the past eighteen months I have been warmly received by many of those whose loved ones died at the hands of firing squads. While each case is different, all the families shared similar emotions and experiences. Many felt anger at what had happened nine decades ago; all felt they had been stigmatised for having a so-called coward in the family. I am most grateful to the relatives who came forward to share their stories with me, and I appreciate that even nine-ty years later this story still causes pain and emotional turmoil.

So why is it important to tell this story today?

For much of the last century the detail of how hundreds of British soldiers were executed has been a state secret. It is only in recent years that the details of the courts martial and the executions have become public. This story marks one of the most controversial chapters in British military history, and the emotion and pain that surround the men's deaths. The long-running campaign to obtain pardons for them has clearly pricked the national consciousness in Britain and in Ireland.

The twenty-six Irish-born soldiers who were executed during the Great War were men of all faiths and backgrounds and from all parts of Ireland. This book examines their stories: who they were, where they enlisted, and how they died. Using previously confidential court martial records, battalion war diaries, personal diaries and interviews, I have been able to compile the most complete narrative of the Irish soldiers who were executed during the First World War.

Throughout I have attempted to be impartial and objective. It is easy to judge the events of the Great War through the eyes of 2007 and to use the standards of law we expect today, so I have endeavoured to under-stand what military commanders were thinking at the time.

This work is not an apology for the behaviour of those who were shot, nor is it a condemnation of those who gave the orders. It is an attempt to tell a story that for decades has been shrouded in secrecy but in recent years has rarely been far from the headlines.

I have amassed many debts writing this story, and without the kindness of friends and family this work would not have been completed. Fergal Tobin and Susan Dalzell at Gill & Macmillan have a lot to answer for. They began the process by persuading me to write this book, and I am grateful for their encouragement and for the support of their colleague Deirdre Rennison Kunz. My employers at BBC Northern Ireland have been most generous in allowing me leave of absence to finish the work, and my BBC colleagues have been particularly supportive.

Bruce Batten unwittingly set this project in motion in 1992 when he commissioned me to present and produce a documentary about the Irish executions for BBC Radio Ulster. Since then I have reported the various twists and turns of this story in news programmes and bulletins and in 2005 I made a second BBC documentary, this time for 'Spotlight', under the expert guidance of Brian Earley. Many colleagues have shared their thoughts and ideas with me as I have tried to tell this story. My fellow-journalists Jeremy Adams, Michael Cairns, Mark Carruthers, Andrew Colman, Paul Clements, Gwyneth Jones, Hugh Jordan, Malachi O'Doherty, Vincent Kearney and Darragh MacIntyre have all contributed in different ways.

I would also like to place on record the assistance of the Arts Council of Northern Ireland, which was helpful during my leave of absence. Others have provided shelter and a quiet place to think and write, and I am particularly grateful to Ruth, Mark, Alison and George. Family friends have also been most helpful. Donna and Aaron Gooding acted as computer wizards and provided much-needed translations of French court martial papers. Allen and Fiona Cox have been loyal and supportive friends, particularly in the summer of 2006; and the hospitality of Paul and Gill Keating in London was most welcome.

The staff at the National Archives in London were always gracious, despite my long list of seemingly never-ending questions. I would also like to thank the officials at the Ministry of Defence, the Department of Foreign Affairs, the Public Record Office of Northern Ireland, and the Royal Irish Fusiliers Museum in Armagh.

The Shot at Dawn campaigners Peter Mulvany and John Hipkin have been of great assistance, as have the soldiers' families, including Muriel Davis, Christy Walsh, Sadie Malin, Eileen Hinken, John McGeehan, Derek Dunne, Paddy Byrne, Gertie Harris and Janet Booth.

Martin Brennan was most generous with information regarding John James Wishart; Timothy Bowman pointed me in helpful directions; and Ronnie Ferguson's assistance on the Crozier case was very useful. Jeremy Shields kindly did some internet searching for relatives, and Colin Bateman was full of advice regarding publishing and writing. I would also like to thank Aidan O'Hara in Paris and Lize Chielens in Ypres.

A number of British and Irish politicians were prepared to discuss their roles in this story, and I am grateful to Des Browne MP, Tom Watson MP, Don Touhig MP, Andrew Mackinlay MP, Dermot Ahern TD and Martin Mansergh TD.

I am indebted to a trio of warm-hearted historians whose hospitality and patience I have tested to breaking point over the past eighteen months. Philip Orr, author of important books on the Somme and Gallipoli, had the painful task of reading various drafts of this work and ended up acting as my punctuation tsar. Julian Putkowski, whose book *Shot at Dawn* (1989) lifted the lid on the secret world of military executions, was most generous and by spotting my schoolboy errors has hopefully saved me from much embarrassment. Dr Gerard Oram provided a similar role, and his research and guidance have proved invaluable. Any mistakes, however, remain my sole responsibility.

My family have been particularly understanding, including my parents, brothers Matthew and Geoff and sister Kate, and my children Grace, Jack and Gabriel. In particular my wife, Katrin, has spurred me on at every step, and without her love, patience and endless encouragement this book would never have happened.

I am well aware of the work of other writers in this particular area. William Moore, Judge Anthony Babington, Julian Putkowski, Julian Sykes, Cathryn Corns and John Hughes-Wilson have all touched on different aspects of this story. But this book is different from other publications. It is the first to concentrate on the Irish dead, the first to include full details of all the Irish executions, and the first to chronicle in detail the pardons campaign. Essentially, I am telling two stories in this book: the story of the Irishmen who died and the story of the campaign to pardon them. I hope I have been able to shed new light on a subject that, ninety years later, still arouses great passions.

In Ireland the Shot at Dawn campaigners and the Irish government have recognised twenty-six Irish-born soldiers who were executed during the Great War. I have investigated their stories, but I have also examined the deaths of two other soldiers who I believe should be part of this narrative. One was an American citizen and the other was English-born. Both men served with Irish regiments and, like their Irish-born counterparts, died at the hands of firing squads.

Each story is different. It is easy to assume that every executed soldier was shell-shocked and was given no chance to change his ways. Some were suffering medically when they wandered away from battle; others were simply unable to adapt to life in the trenches and could not cope with the conditions. Some were serial deserters who had been warned repeatedly about the consequences of their behaviour. A number were not model soldiers and had serious disciplinary records, including prison sentences for desertion. That does not justify their fate but simply underlines the dilemma military commanders faced when trying to deal with difficult soldiers who clearly did not want to fight.

Some of the executed Irishmen were teenagers, raw recruits who had never been away from home and were experiencing warfare for the first time; others were army veterans from such places as rural Cork or Clare. Yet despite their different backgrounds all shared a similar fate. In often hastily arranged court proceedings the men were tried, usually with no legal defence, in hearings that sometimes lasted a matter of minutes.

It was a legal lottery. The great majority of more than three thousand British and Commonwealth soldiers brought to court martial and sentenced to death were spared, but 10 per cent—some 306 soldiers—were shot for battlefield offences such as desertion or cowardice. During the past fifteen years I have been fascinated by the soldier-volunteers, some of whom were brought up, enlisted and trained for the Great War in places I know well. I wanted to know more about them, their families, their alleged crimes and the circumstances of their deaths. Although I was reminded constantly that I was stretching the definition of 'current affairs' by investigating the events of the Great War, the pardons story just would not go away.

By 2005 my interest had reached a point where I had amassed so much background material about this story that I wished I had written a book about it. It was a project I had repeatedly put off to concentrate on work and family commitments. Eventually I began writing, and then something remarkable happened. A court case brought by the daughter of a Yorkshire soldier, Private Harry Farr, resulted in the British government saying it would re-examine his case. Then, in the late summer of 2006, this story took its most dramatic twist. In the middle of August I found myself on the phone to Andrew Mackinlay MP, who was calling with the news he had been hoping for since we first began talking some fourteen years earlier. He told me that the government had agreed to a conditional pardon for Harry Farr and the other soldiers who had been executed for battlefield offences, such as desertion and cowardice.

The campaigners had won. The final chapter of this story could at last be written.

Stephen Walker
Co. Down, August 2007

The Western Front 1914—18

N

BELGIUM

○ DUNKIRK

○ CALAIS

Poperinge ●
● Passchendaele
○ YPRES

St Omer ●
Hazebrouck ●
LILLE ○

○ BOULOGNE

Bethune ●
● Neuve Chapelle

○ ETAPLES

La Bassée ●
MONS ○

Montreuil ●
Mazingarbe ● ● Loos

● Vimy
FRANCE

○ ARRAS
○ CAMBRAI

○ ABBEVILLE

Bapaume ●
LE CATEAU ○

ALBERT ○

○ AMIENS

○ HAVRE

R. Somme

PARIS
○

0   50   100 km

0   25   50 miles

Map by Design Image

Chapter 1 ∿

‖ NINETY YEARS ON

We are going to have to sort this out.
—TOM WATSON, MINISTER FOR VETERANS' AFFAIRS, 2006

L ondon, 2006. On a summer's day at the Ministry of Defence in Whitehall, 92-year-old Gertie Harris sat in one of the large-windowed rooms that overlook the Thames. The city's tourist season was in full swing, and in the bright sunshine visitors and office workers were enjoying the warm weather. Outside the building, civil servants were having a smoking break; others were chatting and sipping takeaway coffee, and in the distance the London Eye was slowly turning.

Inside the offices that house the leading personnel in Britain's military establishment it was a particularly busy time. Officials were answering phones, preparing presentations and holding meetings. With British forces on duty in Iraq and Afghanistan, there was a constant stream of enquiries to answer.

At the rear of the building, in one of the ministerial rooms, a group of people had gathered to discuss the army's behaviour in a foreign land; but it was not a modern conflict they had come to consider. As Gertie Harris, the daughter of Harry Farr, gathered her thoughts and members of her family settled into their seats she was thanked for coming, and then the man sitting beside her leaned forward and spoke. 'Now, Gertie, I am just going to listen to your story. Myself or my staff won't interrupt you; we are just here to hear your story. You take as long as you like.'[1]

For the next forty minutes the small audience listened carefully as she spoke movingly and quietly about a man she never knew. He had been a soldier, a husband and a father. She talked of how proudly he went to war, only to be killed by his own side. A survivor of the Battle of the Somme, he had been in hospital for five months with shell-shock and then later was found guilty of cowardice. He was so convinced of his innocence that at his execution he refused to wear a blindfold as he faced the firing squad.

Then Gertie Harris explained how the stigma and shame had affected her mother, how they were left penniless, with no army pension, and then made homeless. She recalled how his execution had been kept a family secret for decades, how her mother refused to talk about it, and why ninety years later it was time his name was cleared. When she finished her appeal she looked to her host, the newly appointed Minister for Veterans' Affairs, Tom Watson, who was beside her. He was so overwhelmed and emotional from what she had told him that tears welled in his eyes.

The Minister composed himself and after a few words brought the meeting to an end. He thanked the Farr family for coming and then organised tea for his guests. Afterwards, as he escorted his visitors out of the building, he promised them that he would do everything to find a resolution.

Watson's officials were shocked by what they had just witnessed. They had not expected to see their Minister in tears, and the meeting was not the one they had planned for. They had come prepared to rebut the family's arguments and had counselled the Minister to choose his words carefully during the encounter.

For months the Farr family and the Ministry of Defence had been locked in a legal battle, and Tom Watson had been warned by his legal advisers not to admit liability and to remain neutral. The tears were not part of the plan. The new Minister's response to meeting the Farr family was genuine, and he was surprised at how the encounter had affected him. He had not expected to become emotional, as he had never previously thought strongly about the issue of pardons for those shot at dawn. The meeting with Harry Farr's family changed all that. When his visitors left the building he turned to his officials and said, 'We are going to have to sort this out.'

The issue of war pardons was not a new political challenge for officials in Whitehall, and the questions running through the new minister's mind were the same that had been asked of previous government ministers.

For decades successive Conservative and Labour governments had rejected the idea of granting posthumous pardons, and officials at the Ministry of Defence were well versed in the arguments. The campaigners often argued that the original trials were unfair and badly run and that soldiers were not given fair treatment. Those against the pardons stated that it was wrong to apply the standards of today to the events of the past. Critics also suggested that such a move would be interpreted as historical revisionism, and many argued that the move was impracticable, as there simply wasn't enough evidence available to re-examine each case.

It was these arguments that were traditionally used by government ministers. In 1993 the Conservative Prime Minister John Major rejected the call for pardons, saying it would be rewriting history. Similarly in 1998, after he personally reviewed a hundred of the cases, John Reid, then a junior defence minister in the newly elected Labour government, concluded that pardons were not possible because the evidence was insufficient. He insisted that it was not possible to determine from the records who was innocent and who had deliberately deserted their colleagues.

Tom Watson's radical departure from the Whitehall script was a U-turn in government thinking and was not universally accepted by his staff. Some were not prepared to countenance a change of policy without further discussions; and one official privately challenged Gertie Harris's version of events.

Watson remained convinced that he had heard a powerful story of injustice, and he was determined that his department would bring comfort to the Farr family. Within hours his tearful reaction to Gertie Harris's story had become common knowledge throughout the corridors and offices of Whitehall. The news became a topic of conversation, and days later the new Minister was offered tea and sympathy when a member of the catering staff remarked with a knowing smile, 'I heard you had a difficult meeting with Mrs Harris the other day.'[2]

Recently promoted as a junior defence minister, the MP for West Bromwich East was enjoying the biggest job of his short political career. Elected in 2001, Watson had a typical CV that mapped out his Labour credentials. Before he was elected to Parliament he was a spokesman for Labour students and had worked as a full-time trade union official. He arrived in the department in May 2006 as part of a Cabinet reshuffle, changes that saw Des Browne take the top post of Secretary of State for Defence. Browne's predecessor, John Reid, moved to the Home Office after Charles Clarke was sacked.

At thirty-nine, Tom Watson knew that this promotion was a golden opportunity to progress up the ministerial ladder, and he was keen to make his mark. Before he arrived in the department he sought out his predecessor, Don Touhig, to get an understanding of what awaited him in his new position. As a former Minister for Veterans' Affairs, Touhig had served under the previous Secretary of State for Defence, John Reid, and would prove helpful to Watson.

Touhig was very experienced in the machinations of government, having been Parliamentary Private Secretary to the Chancellor of the Exchequer, Gordon Brown, and later a whip in the House of Commons before he became a minister in the Welsh Office. When he took up his role in 2005 as Minister for Veterans' Affairs he began to take an interest in the pardons issue and started by reading the court martial file of Private Harry Farr. When he read the notes he was alarmed at what he saw and quickly concluded that the Farr family had a good case. He realised that the Ministry of Defence needed to come up with a response that would satisfy not just the Farr relatives but all the other family members related to executed men.

He privately floated the idea that the government could simply issue a statement of regret, but after taking soundings from MPs sympathetic to the pardons campaigners he knew that would not be acceptable. Eventually he came to the conclusion that the only way to solve the issue was to bring in legislation granting a statutory pardon to all the executed men.

He knew it would be difficult to convince John Reid that a new response was needed, as Reid had originated the 1998 inquiry and would probably be against revisiting the issue. Touhig then invited his officials to discuss what steps the department should be considering, but this was not greeted with universal support:

The officials were not being wholly cooperative and were deliberately awkward. I thought they were putting barriers up. I was repeatedly told this was a complex and difficult issue.

It reminded me of that famous Gladstone quote about Ireland: that every time he came up with a solution to the Irish problem the Irish changed the problem. That was the same here: every time I suggested a solution I was told it was too difficult.[3]

Convinced that he was being thwarted, he pursued the issue with John Reid and told him that he believed the only way the pardons issue could be dealt with was through new legislation that would result in a pardon for all those guilty of battlefield offences such as desertion and disobedience. At first Reid was resistant but he eventually allowed Touhig to ask his officials to explore the idea and draft some legislation, which he would examine in detail. Although Reid endorsed this move, Touhig doesn't think he was particularly enthusiastic about it.

I don't think his heart was in it. I think I was being indulged. I am convinced that John Reid felt that such a move would bring him into conflict with the defence chiefs and former defence chiefs in the House of Lords.[4]

As the officials began drafting legislation, Touhig wanted to inform other government officials in relevant departments about their plans, but he claims he was told by one official to keep the issue secret until more work was done.

However, in May 2006, when he was sacked in the Cabinet reshuffle, Touhig felt he could at least confide in his successor. He told Tom Watson about the plans for the 'shot at dawn' cases but warned him that, as the review was confidential, officials in Whitehall would be wary if he appeared to have knowledge of it. When Watson got to the Ministry of Defence some days later he questioned one official about the pardons, and the reply was exactly as Touhig had predicted. 'Oh, you know about that, do you? That's meant to be confidential.'

Secrecy had haunted the pardons debate for decades, and campaigners had made political capital out of the fact that the original court martial papers had been hidden from public view for most of the twentieth century. The files were originally expected to be stored in government archives for a hundred years, but in the early 1990s many of the papers were made public. The court martial files for all the executed soldiers are stored in the National Archives in London, and they vary in size and content. Some are short documents that reveal little and contain only brief accounts of what the offenders were charged with and what the evidence was. Others have more detailed information, often containing summaries of what happened at the court martial and a history of the soldier's disciplinary problems. They often include medical reports and testimony from senior officers and colleagues.

Over the past ninety years the soldiers' files and the correspondence associated with them have generated filing cabinets full of paper at the Ministry of Defence. Tom Watson was keen to get a sense of what the documents revealed. He asked that briefing documents surrounding the latest government review be delivered to his office. When they arrived he was staggered when close to a thousand pieces of paper thundered down on his desk. He wondered whether his officials were trying to make a point.

> I think they were basically trying to show me how difficult this problem was and perhaps making a visual point that this is a difficult issue which I was not going to solve quickly. I looked at it and thought, somewhere in the middle of all this lies the answer. However, I did read every single piece of paper that was placed in front of me.[5]

The new Minister's reading matter included a 53-page report that had been gathering dust in the Ministry of Defence for eighteen months. The document was significant not just for its contents but because of its origins. The report had been submitted to the British government in October 2004 by the Irish government, which believed that twenty-six Irish-born soldiers had been unjustly executed and should be pardoned. The Irish investigation had started after officials had been lobbied by the Irish Shot at Dawn campaign, run by Peter Mulvany, a former merchant seaman.

In his fifties, Peter Mulvany, who had an interest in military history, was also involved in a campaign to secure compensation for Irishmen who had been taken prisoner by the Germans during the Second World War. He realised that the backgrounds and religions of the executed men meant that there was the potential to attract cross-community support, and he quickly won endorsements from all the major political parties, north and south of the border. His campaigning paid off in 2003 when the then Minister for Foreign Affairs, Brian Cowen, agreed to support the group's objectives and vowed to take the matter up with the British government. Within months Irish officials had met their British counterparts and asked for the files of the Irish-born soldiers to be copied and forwarded, so that officials in Dublin could make an assessment of the 'shot at dawn' cases. After studying the files, Irish officials wrote a damning report that condemned the executions as unjust and alleged an apparent disparity in the treatment of Irish-born soldiers.

The report's authors concluded that the men should be pardoned. Brian Cowen took the matter up at ministerial level with his British counterpart and publicly made this appeal:

As we approach the 90th anniversary of the outbreak of the Great War, and the world prepares to once again remember those who sacrificed so much during those terrible years of trench warfare, a retrospective action by the British government to redress the condemnation of those 'shot at dawn' would be widely welcomed, both in Ireland and further afield.[6]

Mulvany was amazed that the government was prepared to push the pardons campaign so forcefully, and he had not seriously expected his own government to commission a report or raise the matter with British Ministers:

I didn't think they would come across with the support that they came across with. Remember, this was a nationalist government, who would call themselves republicans with a small 'r', and they supported a campaign such as this. All I expected was a letter coming from the Irish government simply expressing support. When I was told officials were writing a report I nearly fell off the chair. I did not expect that.[7]

The Irish intervention would prove to be most timely. In Britain the Shot at Dawn campaign appeared to be flagging after John Reid's review in 1998 had rejected the introduction of pardons. Further disappointment followed when the Labour MP Andrew Mackinlay failed on several occasions to get approval for his Pardons Bill.

The involvement from Dublin proved to be both appropriate and historic. Twenty-six Irish-born soldiers were executed during the Great War, men who had different faiths and came from all parts of Ireland. They were Protestants and Catholics, unionists and nationalists, farmers' sons and city boys, raw recruits and veterans—a religious and social mix that represented a slice of Irish life from a bygone age. They were members of twelve regiments, including the Royal Irish Rifles, Royal Inniskilling Fusiliers, Royal Irish Fusiliers, Leinster Regiment, and Royal Dublin Fusiliers—famous regiments that no longer existed and whose colours had long since left the field of battle. The Irish move not only breathed new life into the pardons debate but also demonstrated how official Irish attitudes to the First World War had changed.

For decades the memory of that time appeared to be made up of two competing images, each battling for the high ground of history. Unionists saw themselves as the loyal citizens of the empire, whose 'blood sacrifice' at such places as the Somme had secured the union with Britain, and as a result for much of the twentieth century the commemoration of Ireland's First World War dead had been largely a unionist affair. In turn, nationalists had their own sacrifice to remember as they commemorated the dead of the Irish revolution of 1916. The positions cancelled each other out and left an important body of men adrift in the middle ground: the thousands of Catholic and nationalist Irishmen who had fought and died in the Great War wearing a British uniform. They had enlisted from all parts of Ireland and took the 'king's shilling' for a variety of reasons. Some joined up simply because they believed it was a just fight; some went to secure Ireland's freedom; others went to war purely for the money and the sense of adventure and comradeship. Unlike their English, Scottish and Welsh counterparts, the Irish recruits were largely volunteers, as plans to apply conscription in Ireland were never followed through.

In the years after the ending of the First World War many soldiers who had hoped Ireland would become independent felt disillusioned and let down by Britain. Thousands had supported the political leadership of John Redmond and had believed that once the hostilities with the Germans were over, Home Rule would be delivered as an acknowledgement of Irish support in the Great War. It didn't materialise, and inevitably those in nationalist Ireland who had supported the Crown felt betrayed.

When partition finally came, many unionists claimed that it was their loyalty and sacrifice at places like the Somme that had secured the link with Britain and helped found the new state of Northern Ireland. Although Catholic ex-servicemen participated in commemorations throughout Northern Ireland, the events of the Great War and

35,000 Irish men died in the Great War

particularly the Somme were quickly woven into the fabric of Ulster unionism.

If the post-war commemorations in the north were viewed as political, so were those in the south. In the new Ireland, free from the trappings of the Crown, many republicans, such as Seán Lemass, saw such occasions as 'an endeavour to use Ireland in the interests of the Empire.' Parades marking the Irish sacrifice did take place in the 1920s, and they were often well attended, but tensions existed in the background between the government and veterans' associations on the issue of how to mark Ireland's Great War contribution. When attempts were made to build a memorial in Dublin in 1927, Kevin O'Higgins, Minister for Justice in the Irish Free State, said that he had no hostility to ex-servicemen.

> No one denies the sacrifice, and no one denies the patriotic motives which induced the vast majority of these men to join the British Army to take part in the Great War, and yet it is not on their sacrifice that this state is based and I have no desire to see it suggested that it is.[8]

For much of the last century the Irish Great War experience was exclusive to one section of society, and those Catholic Irishmen who fought in the 10th and 16th (Irish) Divisions were the forgotten men. However, in the 1960s the attitude in the Republic showed signs of changing when the Taoiseach, Seán Lemass, a past critic of Remembrance parades, remarked that Irishmen who served the British Army in the Great War should be recognised.

> They were motivated by the highest purpose, and died in their tens of thousands in Flanders and Gallipoli, believing that they were giving their lives in the cause of human liberty everywhere, not excluding Ireland.[9]

Lemass's comments marked a shift in how Ireland viewed those who had died in the uniform of the Crown. It recognised that among the three-quarters of a million British servicemen who lost their lives in the Great War there were thirty-five thousand Irish-born, men who deserved the same recognition as those who had died in the Easter Rising of 1916.

Over the last twenty years Ireland's Great War experience has slowly moved from being the preserve of one culture to a shared history that both unionist and nationalist traditions can relate to. It has been a slow transition, but the 'official amnesia' that prevailed for most of the last century in southern Ireland lifted spectacularly in 1998 at the opening of the Island of Ireland Peace Tower at Messines in Belgium. On a November day the tower, made from stone exported from Ireland, was unveiled by the King of Belgium, Queen Elizabeth and President Mary McAleese, who declared that the monument should bear witness to the 'redeeming of the memory' of those Irishmen who died in the Great War.

The choice of Messines for a peace memorial was deliberate. It was in the mud in June 1917 that men from the 16th (Irish) Division fought alongside their comrades in the 36th (Ulster) Division, Irishmen of different hues united by a common cause. Belgium was also appropriate because the retreat from the town of Mons in August 1914 had an enormous impact in Ireland, both north and south.

After the British Expeditionary Force sustained heavy losses, new recruits were quickly needed, and Lord Kitchener, the Secretary of State for War, increasingly looked to Ireland for help. Government posters encouraging Irishmen to enlist featured the German invasion of Belgium and in September the pressure on Irish politicians to support the war effort intensified.

John Redmond would have a crucial role in the story of Ireland and the Great War. As the leader of the Irish Party he had significant influence over the Irish Volunteers, a nationalist army formed in 1913 to fight for Home Rule and to oppose the Ulster Volunteer Force (UVF). Although he had some reservations about Irishmen serving the Crown, when the war broke out Redmond believed the plight of Belgium could not be ignored.

> The struggle of Belgium appeals in a very special way to the senti-ments and feelings of Ireland . . . There is no sacrifice I believe which Ireland would not be willing to make to come to their assistance.[10]

A defining moment came on 20 September 1914 when Redmond used a speech at Woodenbridge, Co. Wicklow, to pledge the Irish Volunteers to the war effort. He made his call after the Better Government of Ireland Bill—popularly known as the Home Rule

Bill—became law but was suspended for the duration, and he was confident that after the war the legislation would be put into effect and Ireland would at last gain political freedom. Redmond hoped that if Irish soldiers aided the British war effort, such generosity would be reciprocated after the war. He also knew that if civil conflict broke out in Ireland after the war, having thousands of Irishmen trained in the use of firearms would aid the nationalist cause.

Redmond's arguments did not gain universal approval among the wider nationalist family. His call to support the British war effort led to a split in the ranks, and republicans who opposed him broke away to form their own Volunteer movement.

Redmond's rallying cry would do more than split the Volunteer movement. His speech signed the death warrant of his own group, the National Volunteers, as an effective nationalist voice and would set in train a series of events that would ultimately lead to the Easter Rising of 1916. Those who formed the anti-Redmond group in the Irish Volunteers worked hard to discourage young Irishmen from enlisting in the British Army. Anti-recruitment posters and leaflets were distributed that depicted Redmond as a recruiting sergeant for the British Army, and Irishmen who took the 'king's shilling' were branded as traitors to Ireland. Much political capital was made of the British government's decision to delay Home Rule for the duration of the war, and republicans argued that freedom from British rule remained a hope rather than a political certainty.

In Belfast, political manoeuvring of a different kind was going on that involved Sir Edward Carson, the Ulster Unionist leader. For most of 1914 Ireland had been holding its breath as civil war edged closer. The Ulster Volunteer Force, under Carson's leadership, was backed with men and smuggled weapons. It had threatened to use its firepower if the Liberal government proceeded with Home Rule. Ireland was now awash with guns, largely because of gun-running, and in effect contained three different armies: the British Army, the UVF, and the less well-armed Irish Volunteers. When war with Germany was declared, Carson was placed in a dilemma. He knew that as a unionist he could not ignore Britain and the empire in its time of need, yet he wanted to gain some concessions and try to keep Ulster within the union. To this end he tried first to negotiate with London by offering the services of UVF men in return for a postponement of the Home Rule Bill. His game of bluff failed as events in Belgium forced his hand, and government pressure led him to promise recruits unconditionally. On 7 September he would declare: 'We do not seek to purchase terms by selling our patriotism . . . England's difficulty is our difficulty.'[11]

From its headquarters in Wellington Place in Belfast the Ulster Division began to recruit and organise into a series of brigades and battalions. Men came forward in their thousands, now that the UVF and Carson were promising their loyalty to the Crown and to an army that they had been prepared to fight only weeks before. Throughout Ireland, north and south, men responded to Lord Kitchener's call, and volunteers packed out recruiting offices. Within a few weeks there would be three Irish divisions in the British Army: the 36th, known as the Ulster Division, and two Irish divisions, the 10th and the 16th. By the autumn of 1914 Ireland's role in the Great War had truly begun.

Chapter 2 ∿

THE CLASH OF THE CROZIERS

War is all pot-luck, some get a hero's halo, others a coward's cross.
—LIEUTENANT-COLONEL FRANK PERCY CROZIER, 9TH BATTALION, ROYAL IRISH RIFLES

As they journeyed across the English Channel on their way to France, the Ulstermen wanted to enjoy their last few hours of freedom. However, what many on board really wanted was a drink: wine, whiskey, beer—anything they could get their hands on that would lift their morale and while away the time as they went to war. Under the blackness of an autumn evening the men hatched a plan. Within minutes the door of the ship's liquor store was breached, hands quickly reached in, and dozens of bottles were removed. As the volunteers from the 9th Battalion of the Royal Irish Rifles sailed to battle they began to get drunk on stolen wine.

To avoid alerting the enemy, their sailing from Folkestone had been made without the use of lights, and the soldiers had been forbidden to smoke on deck during the crossing. The men arrived in France as they had set off, in complete darkness, and they would have to wait until daybreak to fully appreciate their new surroundings. Once ashore, by now tired and hungry, they were escorted to their rest camp and told to grab a few hours' sleep before breakfast.

When they awoke on their first day on French soil, trouble was brewing. The cross-channel binge had come with a heavy price, and it was more than a hangover.

The theft of ten pounds' worth of wine was reported to Frank Percy Crozier, the battalion's second in command, who had personally recruited many of the men and who had tried to instil in them a sense of duty and honour. Crozier felt his men had let him down on their opening day of active service. He told the battalion's colonel that the ship's owner should be compensated for the theft. 'We had I think better pay up to avoid a bad mark on arrival in the country.'[1]

To avoid further trouble, the drinks bill was settled, but not before Frank Percy Crozier attempted to discover who was responsible. Feeling groggy from a night's drinking and looking a little tired, the West Belfast recruits presented themselves for duty. As they stood in line, their overnight drink-fuelled exploits were condemned, and the offenders were asked to be honest enough to identify themselves. But the alcohol appeared to have prompted a bout of amnesia: the men remained silent; no-one stepped forward. Frank Percy Crozier later recalled the incident:

> Of course not a man moves; so the men who were on that part of the deck nearest to the bar are placed under stoppages to make good the amount. Such is war and booze.[2]

Among those under Crozier's command was a young soldier whom he had helped to enlist. James Crozier (unrelated to his namesake) had left his job at the shipyard in Belfast and had joined the Royal Irish Rifles in September 1914. His arrival in France in October 1915 was the start of a great adventure, a life-changing experience that he hoped would make him a man. It was the day he had waited for as he trained in camps in Co. Down, Hampshire, and Sussex. Crossing the twenty-two miles of water from Kent was more than a simple journey: this was a rite of passage, the moment when his boyhood ended and he began life in earnest.

The two Croziers shared a surname, a regiment and a common enemy but little else. Their lives and backgrounds could not have been more different. Frank Percy Crozier, who had recruited James in his home city of Belfast, was twenty years older than his young charge. He was a career soldier from an upper-class Anglo-Irish family that had produced a long line of army officers. Renowned as a disciplinarian, he became one of the most controversial figures to serve in the Royal Irish Rifles. Privately educated in England, like so many children of the Irish gentry, the young Frank spent his summer holidays in Dublin and every Christmas at a stately home with friends or family in Scotland. His life had been one of opportunity, privilege and wealth.

In contrast, James Crozier had been brought up in a small terrace house in Battenberg Street in the Shankill district of Belfast, one of the toughest and poorest parts of the country. Unemployment and poverty were endemic, and young James's apprenticeship at the Harland and Wolff shipyard, famous for building the ill-fated *Titanic,* brought in much-needed money to the Crozier household. The family, however, were better off than many of their neighbours, as James's parents, Elizabeth and James senior, ran a grocery shop close to their home. Even so they were difficult times.

Inner-city Belfast had all the economic problems of other pre-war industrial towns, and family life was understandably hard for those with little money and plenty of time on their hands. For the children of the Shankill the streets and fields of the district were their playgrounds. In the summer they played games in the meadows along the banks of the Farset River, where the milk-round horses were taken to graze. In the winter they built snowmen at Woodvale Park and skated on the frozen factory reservoirs.

It was a simple childhood; but for many youngsters this tranquillity was interrupted in the late summer of 1914. For boys like James Crozier, the outbreak of war ended the innocence of adolescence and opened up a new world.

The daily chore of travelling across Belfast by tram to the shipyard and the long working hours may have done little to satisfy the young apprentice's boyish sense of adventure. So when Britain declared war on Germany he rushed to join the colours, and it was only natural that he would go to the local battalion, the 9th Battalion of the Royal Irish Rifles, also known as the West Belfast Volunteers.

James Crozier and his friends were all volunteers who came from adjoining streets in West Belfast. Crozier was a Presbyterian, and the Shankill district, which was overwhelmingly Protestant and unionist, was an ideal recruiting ground for enlisting those who wanted to fight for King and country. Some men needed little encouragement to join up: they simply had a thirst for excitement and were desperate to leave the daily grind of being a weaver, a mill hand or a shipyard apprentice. Some volunteered simply to follow friends and family, while others needed the money.

To the hundreds of unemployed men in districts such as the Shankill, joining the army was a lifeline, a golden opportunity to escape the ravages of poverty and regain a personal sense of worth and purpose.

In 1914, after the outbreak of war, Frank Percy Crozier did more than simply encourage young James Crozier to join up: he claims he witnessed his enlistment. When the youngster arrived at the recruiting office he was accompanied by his mother, Elizabeth. Although records suggest that James was twenty years old when he enlisted, Frank Percy would claim that the young man's mother said he was only seventeen. She was unhappy about her son's desire to fight and had threatened to tell the authorities that he was not of age. Army rules dictated that recruits had to be at least eighteen. The regulations meant that thousands of under-age boys simply lied about their age. No birth certificates were required, and recruiting sergeants in many instances turned a blind eye to boy soldiers joining up.

Once inside the recruiting office, the now tearful Mrs Crozier at first kept her silence and simply watched as her son prepared to become a soldier. As the would-be recruit began to fill in his papers, Frank Percy Crozier was standing nearby and introduced himself to Elizabeth. He had spotted the family name and struck up a conversation with her. As her son signed the papers, Frank Percy Crozier promised her he would take good care of her son. 'Don't worry, I'll look after him, I will see no harm comes to him.' Unconvinced, Elizabeth Crozier replied, 'How can you do that? How can you stop him from being shot?' Anxious to allay her fears, Frank Crozier said: 'We shan't be going to war for a long time,' and he added, 'Untrained battalions aren't sent to war.'

Frank Percy Crozier's arguments cut little ice with James's mother. 'They'll all go sooner or later,' Elizabeth replied.[3]

She then turned and, according to Crozier, without another word walked out of the recruiting office. Eighteen months later Frank Percy Crozier's pledge to look after Elizabeth Crozier's boy would be put to the ultimate test in the mud and slaughter of the Somme. Writing in his memoirs, he claims he tried to look after his namesake:

One day in 1915 I asked him if he was going home for his final leave to say good-bye. No Sir, he replied. Why? I asked in surprise. I said good-bye sir when we left home . . . I couldn't stand it again.[4]

Both of Frank Percy's grandfathers had been in the British Army, and with his father a major in the Royal Scots Fusiliers it was no surprise that as a boy he longed for a military career. However, mother nature was not kind to him, and his physical characteristics prevented him from immediately following in the family tradition. Though he was the son of a soldier, he was considered too small and too lightweight by the army, and he had to seek adventure elsewhere. In 1898, as a nineteen-year-old, he travelled to the far edges of the British Empire and to the Crown colony of Ceylon, where he began life as an apprentice tea planter on an estate called Wana Rajah. However, life in the Indian Ocean amidst the heat and dust of the plantation did little to satisfy his lust for excitement and within months he was on the move.

With the Boer War in its infancy, Crozier at last saw a chance to follow in his father's footsteps. He boarded a ship and travelled to South Africa, where army recruiting criteria were relaxed, and, much to his delight, he was quickly accepted into a mounted infantry regiment of the British Army.

His learning curve was swift and steep, and he soon experienced fighting in Natal and the Transvaal. He served with the West African Frontier Force and saw action in Nigeria, where he claims he first ordered the execution of a local soldier.

In Kano in northern Nigeria he is believed to have sanctioned the shooting of an African soldier who had robbed and murdered a market trader. Concerned that the native marksmen might not be able to kill the offender, Crozier dramatically brought in a machine gun and had the prisoner peppered with bullets at close range. This event reveals much about his views on discipline and the practicalities of carrying out an execution, an experience that he would put to use in the battle-fields of France.

By 1905 the burden of soldiering in Africa had taken its toll on Frank Percy Crozier's health and he started to drink heavily. His dependence on alcohol increased, and when he suffered a bout of malaria his personal problems got worse. He returned to England and, using his Boer War experience, resumed his military career, but it was a short-lived affair, as he was forced to resign from the 2nd Battalion of the Manchester Regiment and the North Lancashire Regiment for dishonouring cheques. The humiliation increased when he was declared bankrupt.

Now it seemed that any hope of a long and distinguished army career had vanished. With his military life in tatters, Crozier not surprisingly chose a different vocation, and, as before, he took to the high seas. This time he ventured west across the Atlantic and decided on a new career as a farmer some three thousand miles away in the rugged terrain of Canada. He settled in North America and began working the land, but it didn't last long.

In 1912 life changed again and he retraced his steps when at the age of thirty-three he found the call of home too strong and set sail for Britain. When he arrived back Crozier found himself at the heart of the Home Rule crisis that had engulfed Ireland and was exercising the highest political minds in Belfast, London and Dublin. Keen to earn money and to put his soldiering skills to use, the Boer War veteran was drawn to Belfast, where he joined the Ulster Volunteer Force and, using his military experience, was given the task of recruiting volunteers in West Belfast.

When Carson pledged the men of the UVF to Lord Kitchener, Crozier knew he would soon be back in the uniform of the British Army.

In September the war effort had begun in earnest in Ireland. In Belfast the 36th Division was formed with men from the UVF. Its 107th Infantry Brigade was to be made up of Belfast recruits from the Royal Irish Rifles, and Frank Crozier was appointed second in command of the 9th Battalion, the West Belfast Volunteers.

Fortune favoured Crozier's re-entry into the ranks of the British Army. It seems that no-one had discovered that he had previously been forced to resign for dishonouring cheques, and so with a stroke of good luck his military career began once again. Just like the role he had with the UVF, Crozier set about the task of finding and recruiting suitable men for service. The Shankill district would be his hunting ground, but he needed more than just local recruits, and so he cast his eye over all parts of Ireland and Britain. He travelled to London to find officers and he recruited men at Horse Guards Parade and then despatched them to Belfast. He also became a regular visitor to Scotland and on one occasion enlisted a number of Orangemen who wanted to join the 36th (Ulster) Division.

On the journey to Ireland, as Crozier accompanied his new charges back to Belfast, the new recruits enjoyed their last few hours of freedom by embarking on a rowdy drinking session. Crozier would later remark that he had never witnessed such 'blasphemy and booze'. Now a recovering alcoholic, he had become a proselytising teetotaller. Such was his fervour against the evils of drink that he often lectured his charges on

the abuse of alcohol. During training he told his recruits that he wanted to 'knock the beer and politics out of them.' For the leader of a
rough-and-ready, hard-drinking Belfast battalion it proved to be a vain
hope. However, alcohol was not the only temptation that would come
the way of Crozier's men.

By the summer of 1915 the 9th Battalion of the Royal Irish Rifles,
including young James Crozier, was in Seaford, Sussex, going through
the final stages of training before travelling to France. Away from
Belfast for the first time, many men found a range of temptations in
front of them. As Frank Crozier recalled, some found the opportunity
of casual sex too hard to refuse.

In the case of the officers, London, Brighton, Eastbourne and other
resorts offered inducements of which the uninitiated boys of Belfast
had seldom heard, let alone experienced. The times were abnormal.
Who could tell, might they not all be pushing up the daisies in some
foreign field shortly? Why not have a fling and enjoy the pleasures of
sexual intercourse while the chance was there?[5]

In France the issue of sex was raised again when the battalion's
second in command routinely warned his men about the dangers of
sexual encounters with local women:

At the bases and in the towns, when boys are more on their own,
going and coming, lounging in clubs, hotels and estaminets, the
dangers of excessive drinking must be added to the toll, as drink
excites the sexual organs and makes men careless.[6]

What becomes apparent from a study of Frank Crozier's account
of the Great War is that his soldiering in France was marked by an
obsession with keeping his men sober and free of sexually transmitted
diseases. It seems that these two areas of human behaviour accounted
for much of the battalion's personnel problems. Later Crozier had to
deal with one officer who contracted gonorrhoea and later deserted,
only to have his death sentence commuted. On another occasion he
had to deal with a prostitute who was sleeping with large numbers of
his men, 'an infected girl who hops from camp to camp and ditch to
dyke like the true butterfly she is.'[7]

In October 1915, after their short stay in Boulogne, young James
Crozier and his comrades were bound for the Somme. They first went
to the historic town of Amiens in Picardy, and from there they marched
to their billets in Mailly-Maillet.

In late October most of the 36th Division had moved back from the
front line, but Crozier's battalion went in the opposite direction.
Discipline was already becoming a problem in the Ulster Division and
in particular James Crozier's brigade, the 107th. Major-General Oliver
Nugent, who was in command of the entire 36th Division, wrote to
his wife:

> I am not too happy about the Ulster Division for it cannot be denied
> that some of them have very little discipline. The Belfast Brigade is
> awful. They have absolutely no discipline and their officers are
> awful. I am very much disturbed about them.

Conscious of the importance of what he had written and its impli-
cations, he later added:

> Don't breathe one word of this to a living soul please.[8]

In November 1915 members of Crozier's battalion were transferred
to the 4th Division, a move that gave many Belfast men their first taste
of battle. This was the moment that brought James Crozier closer to the
front line and ultimately nearer to his death. Frank Percy Crozier says
that the linking with the 4th Division was a direct result of problems
with discipline. There were reports of looting by members of the
Belfast battalions, and there was a particular incident that appears to
have angered the divisional commander. Four officers from Frank
Crozier's battalion went missing and were found drunk. They had
been drinking French brandy. It was another occasion for the teetotal
officer to point out the perils of the demon drink. 'These men had no
knowledge of the narcotic power of bad brandy. They consumed it as if
they were drinking Guinness in their native land.'[9]

The four offenders were tried by court martial, demoted, and
sentenced to spells in jail. Frank Crozier believes that Major-General
Nugent sent the 9th Battalion into battle with the 4th Division as part
of that punishment.

At the start of 1916 the countdown to the Battle of the Somme had begun. Preparations were being made for an offensive that would eventually begin in July. James Crozier began the year seeing the horrors of trench warfare at first hand, and his experience coincided with the worst weather his battalion had witnessed. The rain was non-stop, and the trenches were swamped. Even when the weather improved slightly soldiers had to cope with thick mud underfoot. By late January young Crozier was stationed at a place called Redan near Serre. The area was a 'hellhole' according to Frank Percy Crozier. 'The men are up to their waists in mud and water. Rats drown and rations can not be got up.'[10]

One officer of the 9th Battalion got blood poisoning and had to be removed from the front after he was bitten on the nose by a rat. The strain of the weather, the constant enemy attacks and the death toll began to show on the faces of Frank Crozier's men. One of his youngest charges was the first to crack, and it was a familiar name.

On the last day of January, James Crozier reached breaking point. That evening he was due on sentry duty. At 7 p.m. he marched in with the rest of his platoon. At half past eight he was warned not to leave his post, as he was due to be on sentry duty in half an hour. At a quarter to nine Corporal Todd went to look for Crozier but couldn't find him, so he reported it to his superiors. A week later the Belfast man was found wandering some twenty-five miles from the 4th Division headquarters. Corporal Taylor would later tell Crozier's court martial:

> I saw the accused walking aimlessly about. He had no numerals, cap badge, pay book or rifle. I asked him his name and particulars of his regiment and he told me he was a deserter. I placed him under arrest and reported the case to my superior officers.[11]

Crozier was then brought back to headquarters and charged with desertion.

On 14 February 1916 court martial proceedings began. Crozier defended himself. He had no legal representation, nor did he have a 'prisoner's friend'—an officer who would help him defend himself. In his defence Crozier said he went into the front-line trench and that he was feeling unwell, with pains all over his body. He said he did not remember what he did but he was dazed. He did not remember being told about being on duty, and he could not recall leaving the trenches.

Questioned about whether or not there was any bombardment going on at the time he was feeling unwell, Crozier told his court martial: 'There were some rifle grenades bursting about ten yards from me.'[12] He added that his illness got worse when he began to get cold, and he said he hadn't reported sick before.

Once the evidence had been heard and the court had considered its verdict, Crozier's conduct sheet was produced. The short six-line statement in spidery black writing is in Crozier's court martial file, which today rests in the National Archives in London. The charge sheet reads:

> Rifleman Crozier, A Company 9th Battalion Royal Irish Rifles.
>   Character shown Bad
>   Charges since arrived in France 2.
>   1. Absent from working parties
>   2. Absent from his billet.[13]

The conduct sheet does not record any details of what punishment was meted out for the previous offences. It gives the last date of entry as 21 January, which was ten days before his disappearance, and it also states there is no record of his being drunk.

Worse was to come, however, from the man who had promised to look after him. As his commanding officer, it was only proper that Frank Percy Crozier was called upon to offer his official recommendations. On 5 February he wrote:

1. From a fighting point of view, this soldier is of no value. His behaviour has been that of a shirker for the past three months. He has been with the Expeditionary Force since 3/10/15.
2. I am firmly of the opinion that the crime was deliberately committed with the intention of avoiding duty in the Redan, more particularly as he absented himself shortly after the case of another soldier had been promulgated for a similar crime. The officer commanding the man's company is of the same opinion. Sentence was remitted in the case mentioned to 2 years' hard labour.[14]

Frank Percy Crozier's statement sealed young James's fate. Though Crozier pleaded not guilty, he was found guilty. Brigadier-General W. M. Withycombe, who commanded the 107th Brigade, wrote that the death sentence should take place because Crozier had deliberately avoided duty in the trenches and it should be a deterrent to others.

During the court martial Crozier had raised the issue of his health, and subsequently he was examined by a doctor. On 18 February Lt-Col Fawcett wrote that James Crozier was of sound mind and of sound body and there was no evidence that he had recently been otherwise.

Five days later Field-Marshal Haig, Commander-in-Chief of the British Expeditionary Force, confirmed that the death sentence should be carried out.

On Saturday afternoon, the day before his execution, James Crozier was told of his fate. In the square at the regimental headquarters of Mailly-Maillet he was marched to the centre of the parade ground by the sergeant-major. The charge was read out, and the death sentence was delivered. Crozier was emotionless; he continued to stand to attention and was then escorted away by the regimental police.

Watching all this was the man who helped him enlist eighteen months earlier. Frank Percy Crozier waited for the prisoner to be escorted away, then he too left the square. His own exit could not have been more different. On horseback, at the head of the battalion, he slowly rode back to his billet for breakfast, as his men marched in step behind him. In his memoirs, published after the war, Frank Percy Crozier wrote of that fateful afternoon. Bizarrely, he changed Crozier's name to Crocker; whether this was out of embarrassment or an attempt to protect Crozier's family, his reasons are not clear:

> We all feel bad but we carry out our war time pose. Crocker didn't flinch, why should we? After tea the padre comes to see me. Might I see Crocker? he asks. Of course, Padre, but don't be too long winded, I say seriously; after you have done anything you can for him tell his company commander. But I don't think his people should be told. He can go into the 'died' return. War is all pot-luck, some get a hero's halo, others a coward's cross. But this man volunteered in 14. His heart was in the right place then, even if his feet are cold in 16.[15]

On Saturday 26 February James Crozier spent the last night of his life writing letters and praying with the chaplain. Then, in an attempt to ease his suffering, Frank Crozier ordered that the prisoner be allowed to get drunk. In custody, James Crozier was plied with alcohol. In Frank Percy Crozier's words, he was given enough spirits to sink a ship.

The executioners' party would be made up of Crozier's own comrades, who understandably would find the act of killing a comrade difficult. Frank Percy Crozier explains that he made his namesake drunk to ease his 'living misery'. However, he also admits that he was worried about the firing squad's ability to kill the prisoner. As he wondered what to do, he may have been reminded of the similar dilemma he had faced in Nigeria, when he brought in a machine gun and had the prisoner shot many times at close range.

This time Crozier didn't need the back-up of a machine-gunner. Instead, he turned to a fellow-officer for help. The night before the execution he asked to see a junior officer. He told the young man:

> You will be in charge of the firing party . . . The men will be cold, nervous and excited, they may miss their mark. You are to have your revolver ready loaded and cocked; if the medical officer tells you life is not extinct you are to walk up to the victim, place the muzzle of the revolver to his heart and press the trigger. Do you understand? The officer replied, Yes Sir.[16]

That night Frank Percy Crozier insisted that the junior officer dine with him and he kept him under supervision so that he would not turn to alcohol before the execution. The next morning, at daybreak, the officer was sober and knew what lay ahead—unlike young Crozier, who was lying in a near-comatose state in his cell. The evening binge of spirits had rendered him lifeless, and, just as Frank Crozier had hoped, he was in no state to comprehend what was about to happen.

Outside the winter snow lined the ground. It was freezing. James Crozier's guards wanted him to walk the short distance to a small garden where the firing party was waiting. The young rifleman was too drunk to move, and he had to be carried out into the open space. By now he was practically unconscious. Bound with ropes, he was attached to the execution post. His battalion formed up on the open road close to the garden. Screened by a wall, they would not see the execution but would hear the shots that ended their comrade's life.

Frank Percy Crozier stood on a mound near the wall and watched as the firing squad readied themselves. The man who had recruited the prisoner and promised his mother that he would watch out for her son was now preparing to watch him die. Crozier would later recall how his namesake was secured to a stake ten yards from the firing squad.

> There are hooks on the post; we always do things thoroughly in the Rifles. He is hooked on like dead meat in a butcher's shop. His eyes are bandaged—not that it really matters, for he is already blind.[17]

Then James Crozier was shot.

> A volley rings out—a nervous volley it is true, yet a volley. Before the fatal shots are fired I had called the battalion to attention. There is a pause, I wait. I see the medical officer examining the victim. He makes a sign, the subaltern strides forward, a single shot rings out. Life is now extinct.[18]

The firing squad, made up of men from his own regiment, shot wide, so James Crozier was killed by a bullet fired by a junior officer. After the shooting, as Frank Crozier recalled, life resumed as normal.

> We march back to breakfast while the men of a certain company pay the last tribute at the graveside of an unfortunate comrade. This is war.[19]

David Starrett, Frank Percy Crozier's batman, would later recall how the men reacted:

> That evening the boys did not play housy-housy or any other games. They sat about silent or loud in argument, steadily lowering their drink. The Colonel buried himself in plans and maps of the line.[20]

Frank Crozier did not want James Crozier's family to discover how he had died. He tried to pass off his death as 'killed in action', but his plan failed. According to Julian Putkowski and Julian Sykes, James Crozier's mother was informed of the manner of her son's death. Details of the execution and the manner of Crozier's death leaked out—though the facts were never made public at the time. Some weeks later one of Frank Crozier's officers was tackled about the shooting

when he was on leave. He was asked by a civilian about the Crozier execution, and it was suggested that it had brought shame on the battalion
and on the city of Belfast. Crozier's colleague angrily replied:

> He tried and failed. He died for such as you! Isn't it time you had a
> shot at dying for your country?[21]

Frank Percy Crozier believed the killing of his namesake acted as a
deterrent and stopped others in his battalion from deserting.

> I did not regret his death at the time, nor even the circumstances
> surrounding it, for intuitively I felt that it would be the first and last
> of its kind in my regiment. That prediction was proved true by
> fact.[22]

He would add:

> Of course, theoretically, it is wrong and indefensible to kill a
> comrade in such circumstances. But what is the alternative? Loss of
> battle, of the position, or of the war.[23]

James Crozier's behaviour, his trial and execution raise a number of
fundamental questions. Firstly, he told officers that he was not well and
left his post because he was ill. Was his claim that he was medically unfit
taken seriously enough, and could that have explained his desire to
leave the trenches? Though an officer who interviewed Crozier
described his behaviour as 'peculiar', a medical examination concluded
that he was of sound body and mind, dismissing any suggestion that he
could have been suffering from what was to become known as shell-
shock.

In 2004 the Irish government study of James Crozier's death
questioned the way his medical examination had been carried out.

> The medical examination of Private Crozier on 18 February 1916 is
> interesting in that it declares him sound in mind and body not only
> at the time, but also previous to the exam itself. There is no evidence
> as to how this conclusion of being sound in mind and body *prior to
> being examined* is reached.[24]

Though having such a condition as shell-shock would not necessarily mean that a death sentence would be commuted, it is possible that some officers would have shown leniency had the young man's health problems been considered a factor in his case. As a young inexperienced soldier, Crozier clearly found the horrors of trench warfare too much, and it is of course possible that, despite the reports to the contrary, he was suffering from shell-shock.

What clearly goes against him is that he would have been fully aware that desertion carried with it the death penalty, and the Belfast teenager had a history of disappearing. It is clear that Frank Crozier saw this as a serious case: in fact he described his namesake's character as 'bad' and clearly believed an example had to be set. With a number of breaches of discipline in the past, it is apparent that senior officers in the 9th Battalion and in the 107th Brigade felt that Crozier's execution was militarily necessary to maintain a sense of order. Yet there is a contradiction here, because discipline at the time was officially considered to be good. If that was so, why was Crozier shot?

The Crozier case raises other questions. Why did Frank Percy Crozier try to mislead Elizabeth Crozier about the manner of her son's death? His motives for this are not clear. Was it that he felt guilty because some eighteen months earlier he had pledged to look after her son? Alternatively, he could have tried to pass off young Crozier's death as a 'killed in action' statistic simply because he felt the killing was wrong. After the war he wrote about the affair, and a degree of remorse can be detected.

> He was no rotter deserving to die like that. He was merely fragile. He had volunteered to fight for his country . . . He was condemned to die at the hands of his friends, brothers, with the approval of his church.[25]

Crozier later added:

> To us, what was he. He was poor Crozier. And we never made up our minds for whom we were sorrier—him, or ourselves. Such is war.[26]

David Starrett says he recalled seeing him distressed about what had become of young Crozier.

The Colonel was more upset than I had ever seen him. 'To have to shoot one of your own men,' he kept saying.[27]

When James Crozier was shot he became the youngest Irish deserter to face a firing squad; but Frank Percy Crozier's career blossomed. He saw action at the Battle of the Somme and rose up the ranks to eventually become a brigadier-general. After the war his life took a number of unexpected and controversial twists. In 1919 he was promoted to general and appointed military adviser to the newly established Lithuanian army; but his new job was not a success, and within months he resigned. He then returned to Ireland and became the commander of the Auxiliary Division of the Royal Irish Constabulary, and, as ever, controversy followed his every footstep.

Ireland was in turmoil as the IRA waged war with the 'Black and Tans' and Crozier's Auxiliaries. In 1920, as the IRA took its campaign to the streets of Dublin, a British soldier was shot by a young gunman named Kevin Barry. Barry became a Republican martyr after he was hanged for his crime. Crozier took an interest in his case, as his men were used to guard the young man in the hours before his death. He visited Barry in his cell, and the encounter reminded him of the time he went to see another Irishman, James Crozier, hours before his execution in France in 1916.

Crozier did what he did, in desperation, perhaps, to escape the cold and the wet of a fire-trench during a grim winter campaign. Barry did what he did while fired by the desire to free his Ireland from what he considered an unfair yoke; with his eyes wide open to the facts and the consequences, he was prepared to forfeit his life in combat or by execution. Neither of these lads whined. Had I the opportunity I might have given Barry the chance I gave Crozier—of getting drunk in his last few hours. But I had no such opportunity; and, in any case, I very much doubt if he would have accepted the offer if it had been placed before him, because he was a proud boy. He was proud of dying for an ideal, for the freedom of Ireland. He was not sorry to leave the earth; he was glad to die as he was dying. Crozier on the other hand, never disguised his sorrow at having to leave us.

In France I had no difficulty in finding a firing party to shoot Crozier. It was there at my instant command. But in Ireland, as no hangman could be found to hang Barry, we had to bring one all the way from England, in disguise and in great secrecy. He came three hundred miles across the sea, surreptitiously, to hang a rebel murderer. Or—he came three hundred miles across the sea, surreptitiously, to hang a soldier of Ireland. You see, so much depends on one's point of view.[28]

Frank Percy Crozier's Irish experience made him disillusioned with Britain's military and political leadership. Like his tenure in Lithuania, his role in Ireland was short-lived, and within months he was out of office. He later claimed that he resigned his position because senior military and political figures were prepared to condone the murders in Ireland and allow the 'Black and Tans' to operate unchecked.

I resigned not so much because I objected to giving the Irish assassins the tit for the tat, but because we were murdering and shooting up innocent people, burning their homes and making new and deadly enemies every day.[29]

He later added:

I resigned when I discovered the deception, for the Crown regime was nothing more or less than a Fascist dictation cloaked in righteousness.[30]

Crozier's account was disputed by his superiors, and according to documents in the National Archives he was allowed to resign before he was sacked.

For Crozier, his time in the Auxiliaries was another turning-point in a remarkable personal and political journey. Once he had been on the streets of Belfast as a UVF man, getting ready to fight Home Rule, and after his experiences in Dublin he was beginning to show enthusiasm and understanding for the Irish nationalist cause. Over the next decade his views on the military continually brought him into conflict with successive British governments, and he became active in the Peace Pledge Union. Just as controversy followed him during his days of service, in civilian life his personal behaviour continued to attract attention. He left many bills unpaid, and a series of women began legal action to recover money from him. His wife contacted the War Office and claimed she could not trace her husband, who had left her destitute. He then turned his wartime experiences and his controversial views into a series of books, which would often make headlines because of their outlandish claims.

In his writing he returned to the familiar themes of sex and alcohol. He claimed that during his time in Nigeria, British officers were often drunk and that orgies with native women were commonplace. He also wrote how officers had looted the bodies of dead Africans. He detailed his experiences in Ireland, where he condemned British rule and criticised the violent behaviour of the 'Black and Tans'.

Files in the National Archives in London show how the military and political establishment viewed Crozier's literary talents. One Home Office document from 1930 gave a blunt assessment.

No good could possibly come of raking up the past even if Crozier could be trusted to stick to the facts, and from experience we know that is the last thing he is likely to do. Fortunately I think he is by now pretty completely discredited.[31]

Another government report shows how officials considered how to respond to press coverage of one of Crozier's books.

In connection with 'A Brass Hat in No Man's Land' and 'Five Years Hard' it was decided that the best course of action was to let the books sink back into the mind from which they emerged.[32]

Eventually, Frank Percy Crozier, once viewed as a war hero and supporter of the Empire, came to be regarded as a nuisance and an embarrassment by his former employers. When he died, in 1937, his death gave the obituary-writers much to cover, and the newspapers were full of details of his past exploits on the battlefield and his later days as an author and peace campaigner. His death received much national attention, in contrast with the secret demise of his namesake two decades earlier. In 1916 James Crozier was interred in Mailly-Maillet at the Somme, where he was executed, but he was later reburied in the Commonwealth War Grave at Sucrerie, some ten miles north of the town of Albert. Today, close to the cemetery gate, his grave is like any other and is marked with the traditional white headstone and a standard inscription.

Every year in July a group from Northern Ireland, including ex-servicemen, travels to France to pay tribute to James Crozier at his graveside. They come simply to pay their respects and to remember one of their own: the Belfast boy-soldier who went to war to become a man but who found the rigours of battle too much to take.

Chapter 3 ~

THE NEW FRONT

That is a good joke, you let me enlist and then bring me out here and shoot me.
—PATRICK DOWNEY

Under a burning Mediterranean sun it was the blood of Irishmen that helped turn the ocean crimson. The water and the beach stood between the invaders and the defenders, but the contest was a mismatch of catastrophic proportions. The men of Munster and Leinster had little chance as the machine-gunners embedded on the shore picked them off by the dozen. Many Irishmen, weighed down by their 60-pound packs, drowned as they fought to get ashore; others were cut down before they even left their landing craft, and some desperately struggled through the water only to be killed as they touched Turkish soil for the first time. Their bodies would soon be everywhere: on the boats, floating in the sea and lying on the beach. This was meant to be a new dawn in warfare, a new front; instead the mistakes of the Western Front were repeated as soldiers were sent without cover to face machine guns and artillery. It could have been Flanders or France, except this time under the narrow slopes of Cape Helles; it was slaughter in a red sea.

The landings at Gallipoli in 1915 were part of the Allied plan to take control of the Turkish Straits. The objective was to seize the 38-mile channel and ultimately take the city of Constantinople. The Russians had appealed for a diversionary attack on Turkey to relieve pressure on the Caucasus, and the plan devised by the First Lord of the Admiralty, Winston Churchill, was seen at the time as a way of shortening the war. It was a bold and brave attempt to use sea power and assault forces to change the course of history, but it would end in failure and disaster.

Tommy Davis, a young Irish recruit, witnessed the carnage that April morning. The son of a shoemaker from Co. Kerry, he was one of six children brought up in a one-room stone cottage in Ennis, Co. Clare. It was a typically tough upbringing: money was scarce, but his parents, John and Margaret, worked hard to feed and clothe their children. The family grew vegetables in land behind their cottage, and Margaret, keen to earn a few extra shillings, took in washing—no mean feat when their only source of heat was the fire in the cottage's only room. Although the Davis family were poor and the army obviously provided a much-needed income, there was another reason why young Tommy was attracted to the colours of the Crown.

There was a family tradition of British military service. Tommy's grandfather had seen action with the British Army and as a young man was posted to India, an experience that would change his life. It was in the far corner of the empire that he met and fell in love with a local Muslim woman who would later become his wife. In the unenlightened days of the 1800s their relationship was frowned upon, yet, despite this clash of culture and religion, love was stronger than prejudice and the pair eloped. Davis's grandfather brought his new love back to Ireland, where they settled and raised a family.

Decades later, as France and Flanders echoed to the sound of gunfire, his grandson Tommy would carry on the family tradition of soldiering. The new recruit joined the 1st Battalion of the Royal Munster Fusiliers and in 1915 set sail for the Dardanelles.

As Davis prepared to land at Gallipoli some weeks later he was on board the *River Clyde,* a ship packed with two thousand soldiers, mainly from the Royal Dublin Fusiliers and Royal Munster Fusiliers. The plan was that the vessel would run aground and quickly let the soldiers disembark onto barges and then go ashore. The ship had been specially prepared for the assault. Exits had been cut into its sides, gangways were in position and there were machine guns sandbagged on deck. In addition to the *River Clyde* other soldiers would be landed in smaller boats, including men from the Royal Dublin Fusiliers.

The plan ran into trouble within minutes. The barges could not get close enough to the *River Clyde,* and as the vessel came into the Turkish soldiers' line of fire the ships' exits came under sustained gunfire. A series of attempts to disembark simply led to many casualties. The bodies began to pile up on board, making an immediate assault on the shore virtually impossible.

As some men on the *River Clyde* struggled to leave the ship, others were already in the water. Many had to swim ashore; some succeeded in staying afloat, while others, weighed down with their packs, drowned.

Captain David French, an officer with the Royal Munster Fusiliers, was hit by a bullet as he came ashore. He was given first aid and then watched as men from his own battalion struggled to follow him:

> I counted 42 men in one platoon, not a single man escaping. And still they came down the gangways. It was an awful sight but they were a brave lot. After a few minutes it became even harder for them to get ashore. After passing down the gangways and across the lighters under a heavy fire they had to run along about 25 yards of jagged rocks—each side of the ridge now being covered with bodies.[1]

Like David French, Tommy Davis managed to get ashore. As he began to defend the beachhead he found himself at the centre of a military disaster. Surrounded by the dead and dying, he and what was left of his battalion were outgunned and outnumbered and it was increasingly clear that the Allied forces had been outmanoeuvred. Similar difficulties were experienced at 'Anzac Cove' on the western coast of the peninsula, where the Australian and New Zealand units had landed.

In the days that followed the first landings, two facts became abundantly clear. This would not be a quick invasion because of the terrain and the determination of the Turkish army; and the casualties were much higher than anticipated. Battalions once proud and well staffed now barely existed and within days the remnants of the 1st Battalion of the Royal Dublin Fusiliers and 1st Battalion of the Royal Munster Fusiliers temporarily merged to form the 'Dubsters'. The arrangement would last until new officers arrived to boost the old battalions.

As Irish soldiers dug in on the peninsula, the first few weeks would be taken up by a series of attacks and counter-attacks. On the rocky ground and high gullies the Turks had a natural advantage and the battles and skirmishes developed a familiar pattern.

As the Allied forces fought, the reminders of the sacrifice their comrades had made were all around, as hundreds of decomposing bodies lay in the sand and on the shore. The casualties among the British and French forces and the ANZAC Corps had been high in the first month and by now the smell of rotting corpses hung in the air. Under the blazing heat, the stench of death was overpowering. The poet A. P. Herbert, who served at Gallipoli, wrote:

The Flies! Oh God, the flies
That soiled the sacred dead.
To see them swarm from dead men's eyes
And share the soldiers' bread!
Nor think I now forget
The filth and stench of war,
The corpses on the parapet
The maggots in the floor.[2]

By late May both Turkish and Allied forces needed to bury their dead. A truce was declared and men on both sides swapped their rifles for shovels and dug a series of graves. After the temporary ceasefire, trench life returned to normal and conditions remained grim. Water had to be rationed, food was in short supply and many of the soldiers fell ill, often with dysentery.

By mid-June, Tommy Davis, like many of his compatriots, was feeling the effects of the heat and battle. The young fusilier was not well and had developed stomach cramps. On 20 June he was told to be on sentry duty at headquarters for a period of two hours, beginning at 1 a.m. At 2:30 Lance-Sergeant Bradshaw, a Tipperary man, checked the position but found the young Clare man missing. He asked another soldier, Private Borleigh, if he had seen Davis, but he could not be found. Borleigh would not see the missing Irishman for a few hours, but eventually he came across him between 5 and 5:15 a.m.

Davis was charged with quitting his post without permission, and two days later he appeared before a court martial made up of two captains and a lieutenant. No other officer was available to act as president of the hearing, so Captain Taylor of the Royal Dublin Fusiliers stepped in.

Davis was not represented and said little in his defence except

Lance Sergeant Bradshaw posted me at 1 o'clock a.m. as a flying sentry around headquarters. At 2.15 I got cramps in my stomach. I went off my post to go to the latrine. I stopped there about two hours...As I was coming away I got another attack and had to return.[3]

It then emerged that Davis's disappearance was not an isolated event. The adjutant reported that he had been disciplined the previous month and after a court martial was sentenced to be shot, but that had been commuted to ten years' penal servitude, to take effect at the end of the war. Within a week Davis's problems had worsened when he left his post and as a result was given 'field punishment no. 1', whereby he was shackled and left on public view so his comrades could see that he was being disciplined.

When the court martial met to consider Tommy Davis's latest transgression, they simply did not believe his story that he was ill and had left his post to go to the latrine. He had pleaded not guilty but the hearing found him guilty and sentenced him to death. Though dysentery was a well-known illness among the soldiers, the court martial panel clearly believed that Davis had shirked his responsibilities.

That view was endorsed by General Sir Ian Hamilton, Commander-in-Chief of the Mediterranean Expeditionary Force. According to the military papers, he appears to be the only officer on record to have expressed an opinion on Davis, which is unusual. What is also worth examining is the speed with which the case was considered. Davis's case was heard and his punishment was considered in seven days.

Hamilton's recommendation came on 29 June and three days later his wishes were carried out when Tommy Davis was taken out onto 'Gully Beach' and shot by a firing squad. There is no official record of his last moments, though his death is recorded as part of the battalion war diary for early July.

> 11am July Battalion back on Gully Beach for a rest from the trenches. Four officers reported to the battalion for duty, but were sent on to the Royal Fusiliers, as we had more officers than the other battalion in 86th Brigade.
>
> Private Davis sentence promulgated.
>
> 5 a.m. July 2nd Sentence of death passed on Private Davis carried out.[4]

Tommy Davis's case, like those of the other Irishmen executed during the Great War, has been examined by the Irish government. In 2004 officials of the Department of Foreign Affairs heavily criticised the treatment meted out to him.

There is no evidence on file as to Private Davis' character as a fighting man, and there are no comments available from the confirmation process as is the norm with other files. It seems that by being missing for 45 minutes of his assigned duty, because of bad stomach cramps, Private Davis was executed without so much as a second thought by the military hierarchy. Dysentery was rampant at the time, so this would not have been an unreasonable excuse.[5]

The Irish government officials were right to draw attention to the issue of dysentery. In his book *The Great War,* Correlli Barnett states that by September 1915 (albeit after the Davis execution) '78 per cent of the Anzacs from seven battalions were suffering from dysentery and 60 per cent from skin sores.'[6]

These figures give an important insight into the state of health of the Allied troops on the Gallipoli peninsula. However, there is another issue worth exploring that may shed some light on Tommy Davis's execution and that is the question of regimental discipline.

In May 1915, two months before his execution, three members of Davis's battalion were found guilty of cowardice. Sergeant Evans, Corporal O'Mahoney and Private Quill were brought before a court martial and disciplined. The men were spared execution; instead they were sentenced to ten years' penal servitude. These incidents may well have sparked concerns in the hierarchy that discipline was becoming a problem in the battalion. Certainly they would not have helped Tommy Davis escape death. It seems likely that senior officers believed an example was necessary to address the issue of discipline; it is also apparent that in the eyes of the Commander-in-Chief, General Sir Ian Hamilton, young Davis had developed the behaviour of a serial absentee.

Tommy Davis's execution understandably shocked and shamed his family at home in Co. Clare. His mother received the news at her home in Ennis and was deeply upset about the way her son had died. She called Tommy's siblings together and told them how their brother had died, asking each one to keep the details secret.

In the autumn of 1992, during the making of a BBC Radio Ulster documentary about the Irish executions, I made contact with Tommy Davis's sister-in-law, Muriel, who had married Tommy's younger brother, Ambrose. For years the Davis family secret had remained just that: a private matter best kept quiet. Muriel Davis had been told in confidence but agreed to share her thoughts with me and Radio Ulster listeners. She explained how Tommy's death had affected his mother.

> His mother could not accept it. To her he was not a coward. She didn't want the world to class him as a coward. Her sons were all brave, and Tommy was to her very special. So she kept this hidden, and as far as I knew nobody knew the true story.[7]

After the BBC documentary was broadcast Muriel Davis wrote to me and explained that she was pleased with the programme and was glad that at last Tommy's case had been brought into the open. She explained that she had sent copies of the programme to her relatives so that everyone in the family would know about Tommy's last days. She then added what the programme had meant to her and her family:

> It left us with a feeling of profound sadness and unfortunately—in the case of my brother in law—even after all these years and the efforts and research of historians, we are faced with many unanswered questions. The truth, I am afraid, will never be known.
>
> Thank you for enabling me to share some part in your programme and we hope and pray that it will help to bring a speedy pardon to all those who lost their lives in such inhuman and unjust ways.[8]

The Davis family had every reason to feel that their name had been dishonoured when Tommy was shot in July 1915. Tommy's brother Francis also saw action during the Great War in a British uniform, but his experience could not have been more different. He was commended for his bravery during one assault when he and an officer held German snipers at bay. Francis, who would live until his eighties, was clearly proud of his part in the Great War. For decades his medal and framed citation were prominently displayed on the wall of his home in Ennis until the day he died.

The Davis family have Francis's record of service in the Great War, but their knowledge of Tommy is sadly incomplete. It is not known where he is buried, as no grave or headstone has ever been found. His name, however, is commemorated on the impressive Helles memorial to the missing that today is maintained by the Commonwealth War

Graves Commission. The memorial includes the names of many thousands who lost their lives at Gallipoli—a campaign that never recovered from its appalling beginning.

———

Within days of Tommy Davis's death other Irishmen would follow in his footsteps and land on the Gallipoli peninsula. More Irishmen landed at 'Anzac Beach' and joined forces with troops from the Australian and New Zealand Corps. Among them was a young inexperienced boy from Munster who was getting his first taste of battle on a foreign shore. Nineteen-year-old Patrick Downey was another volunteer who, like Tommy Davis, would die thousands of miles away from home in front of a firing squad.

The Downey family, consisting of five boys and one girl, all grew up in a three-roomed house in Limerick cared for by their mother, Mary Ann, who worked as a housekeeper. When war broke out in Europe two of the boys joined up. Michael, who had been working as a messenger, would see action on the Western Front. Patrick, three years younger, originally joined the ranks of the Royal Munster Fusiliers, which would have been his local regiment, but then transferred to the 6th Battalion of the Leinster Regiment. His great-nephew Christy Walsh, now living in Dublin, believes his great-uncle went to war simply to escape the poverty of Limerick.

> He would have joined simply because of the lack of work. In those days there was little to do around Limerick and he would have gone to earn a few shillings. Remember, he was very young, so I suppose joining up helped him satisfy his sense of adventure.[9]

On 9 July 1915 Patrick Downey's grand adventure into the unknown got under way. He and his comrades left the docks at Liverpool and set out for Gallipoli, arriving in the region just over three weeks later.

By August, Downey and thousands of other men from all over Ireland were fighting alongside their colleagues in the grandly titled Mediterranean Expeditionary Force in a series of battles on the peninsula. Men from the Inniskillings and the Royal Irish Fusiliers saw action at Suvla Bay along with men from Munster and Dublin.

To the south of Suvla Bay, at 'Anzac Cove', volunteers from the Royal Irish Rifles and the Connaught Rangers fought alongside soldiers from Lancashire, Wiltshire, and New Zealand and Australia. As they toiled together in the oppressive heat the conditions worsened and the piles of dead and dying grew with each passing day.

On 11 August, Lieutenant-Colonel H. F. Jourdain, who commanded the 5th Battalion of the Connaught Rangers, wrote in his diary:

> The sight of our camp at 4 a.m. this morning was terrible, wounded and dying men all over the place. Men groaning and dying without a murmur. I assisted as many as possible but it was too horrible to contemplate.[10]

For those who continued to dodge Turkish bullets and shells, daily life brought added problems. The heat sapped energy, and the lack of proper drinking water exacerbated dehydration. Dysentery caused havoc throughout the ranks and it was becoming clear that the long-desired objective of reaching Constantinople was unlikely to succeed. Attempts to push the Allied forces forward through the Turkish lines repeatedly failed and by late August more than three thousand Irish soldiers were among the dead.

The fighting carried on until late summer, but by the autumn of 1915 the Allied campaign in Gallipoli was on its last legs.

By October General Sir Ian Hamilton was replaced as Commander-in-Chief by General Sir Charles Monro, who recommended a military withdrawal. By now Bulgaria had entered the war on the side of the Germans. That resulted in Greece and Serbia both calling for Allied help, which meant that the operation in Gallipoli was no longer a priority. In November, Winston Churchill realised that his ambitious plan to get the Allies to Constantinople was not going to succeed and within weeks all the Allied forces were successfully withdrawn from 'Anzac Cove', Suvla Bay and Cape Helles. Nearly half a million British Empire and French troops served on Gallipoli; half that number were killed, wounded or evacuated through sickness. From the Allied point of view it had been a futile exercise: too ambitious, badly planned and poorly executed.

There were other casualties too, apart from the many thousands of lives lost or damaged. By the end of the campaign Winston Churchill—

the youngest person to hold the post of First Lord of the Admiralty—
had resigned. His political career was temporarily over and he sought a
posting on the Western Front. Other participants in the Gallipoli disaster also had new roles to play. Irishmen such as Patrick Downey and his
comrades were now needed elsewhere.

By early autumn at least 90 per cent of the Irish Division were dead,
injured or sick. Depleted and bloodied, the remaining soldiers were
withdrawn to Salonika in October 1915. After a short journey to their
new posting, Downey and his comrades set about helping to make a
camp and building roads. The weather in and around Salonika was at
first warm and sunny, and for the men their new home seemed much
preferable to the horror and intensity of Gallipoli.

In November the division moved to Serbia on the shores of Lake
Dorian, where fighting with the Bulgarians was shortly expected.
However, within days the weather would take a serious turn for the
worse. Rain was followed by a blizzard and then temperatures unexpectedly plummeted. Many of the men had the wrong clothes and
equipment and were unprepared for the wintry onslaught. The conditions were appalling, as one officer would later recall:

> Boots get wet then frozen. If one sits still your feet get frozen. I feel
> sorry for the men, some of them have only one blanket . . . I never
> want to see snow again.[11]

Hundreds of Irishmen suffered frostbite and exposure and dozens
had to be evacuated to hospitals in Salonika. Patrick Downey managed
to escape the ravages of winter and he remained with his division in
Serbia. As he prepared for a new battle in different surroundings the
teenager may have considered how his life had changed since he left
Ireland. His last six months had been like no other time in his life. He had
witnessed the carnage and death of Gallipoli, escaped the firepower of
the Turks; and as he waited to go into line against the Bulgarians he had
just experienced the ferocity of a Serbian blizzard.

Ironically, Patrick Downey's life would be ended not by enemy fire
but by British hands. His difficulties began in late November 1915 when
he appeared before a trial on a charge of insubordination. He was given
eighty-four days' 'field punishment no. 1', publicly tethered to a cartwheel in view of his comrades.

The day after this punishment was handed out, Downey's problems got worse. He was clearly unhappy about his treatment and was not prepared to change the way he dealt with those who had authority over him.

When an officer approached him and ordered him to fall in for duty he refused to do so. When the command was repeated he refused again. Downey was then ordered to put on his cap, but he said, 'No, I won't.' It seems clear that he was now testing the patience of his superiors, and by this time they believed he had gone too far. The Limerick man was taken away and later charged with disobedience.

Downey was not alone. Five of his comrades from the same battalion also found themselves in trouble for similar offences. On 1 December six men serving with the 6th Battalion of the Leinster Regiment were brought before a court martial. Such was the pressure on manpower that a senior officer could not be spared from duty to sit as president of the hearing, so only three officers heard the evidence, a captain and two lieutenants. This would mean that an inexperienced team of officers would consider the fate of six men—inexperience that would later have grave consequences.

Two of the Leinsters who appeared before the panel were Private Thomas McMahon and Private Michael Bergin, who were charged with using insubordinate language to an officer. The two men had been ordered on duty but had refused. Private McMahon told the court martial why he had ignored the officer's command:

> I told him I would not do it until I had finished my breakfast. The previous day I had only had two and a half biscuits, a slice of bread and a tin of corned beef and some tea.[12]

McMahon, who had a record of minor misdemeanours, pleaded not guilty to the charge but was found guilty by the court. He was sentenced to six months' hard labour and Bergin got a year's hard labour. The other soldiers were given field punishment.

If Downey was expecting similar treatment to that of his comrades he must have been shocked by the court's decision. The Limerick man bizarrely pleaded guilty to the charge of disobedience. In mitigation he said very little, except that he had previously been in the Royal Munster Fusiliers and he had never been in prison in civil life.

One of the most puzzling aspects of this case is Downey's plea of guilty. It was highly unusual. Is it possible that he was pleading guilty to a charge that he thought did not carry the death penalty? What is now clear is that his original charge was amended by Brigadier-General R. S. Vandeleur. The original charge had read:

> On active service disobeying a lawful command given personally by his superior officer in the execution of his office.

That was changed to read:

> On active service disobeying a lawful command in such a manner as to show wilful disobedience of authority given personally by his superior officer in the execution of his office.[13]

The amended charge, which was far more serious than the first, carried the death penalty. Was Patrick Downey's guilty plea referring to the original charge, which did not carry the death penalty? If so, he had pleaded guilty to the wrong charge and had in effect signed his own death warrant. Significantly, none of the charges against Downey's co-accused were altered.

What is now apparent is that Downey had become the scapegoat for the battalion's indiscipline. His plea of guilty should not have been accepted, as it contravened court martial rules. A more experienced court martial panel would have spotted this.

Cathryn Corns and John Hughes-Wilson examined Patrick Downey's case in their book *Blindfold and Alone* (2001). They concluded that the hearing was using old rules of procedure drawn up in 1914 and since then the regulations had changed.

> Downey should have been made to plead 'not guilty' and the evidence heard. When the conviction went for confirmation the finding should have been quashed and a retrial ordered.[14]

Were crucial mistakes in procedure committed in Patrick Downey's case? It is clear that his most unusual plea of guilty caused some concern with the army's hierarchy. Lieutenant-General Brian Mahon from Co. Galway, who commanded the British forces in Greece, would have a role in his fellow-Irishman's story. Mahon, from Anglo-Irish stock, was a chain-smoking veteran who had served in Sudan and South Africa, including the legendary Battle of Mafeking. He wrote to the Mediterranean Expeditionary Force headquarters on 12 December 1915:

> Under ordinary circumstances I would have hesitated to recommend that the Capital sentence awarded be put into effect as a plea of guilty has been erroneously accepted by the court, but the condition of discipline in the Battalion is such as to render an exemplary punishment highly desirable and I therefore hope that the Commander-in-Chief will see fit to approve the sentence of death in this instance.[15]

It is apparent that the issue of battalion discipline was at the forefront of senior officers' minds at this time, something that is borne out in the correspondence of Lieutenant-General Mahon. In the eyes of the divisional hierarchy Downey's execution was the very act that would stem indiscipline.

It was not just the poor conduct of his comrades that had placed Downey in difficulties and put him at the top of the execution list: his own disciplinary record was not a good one and certainly did little to help his case. In the court martial papers he is described as a soldier with a bad character and a history of minor offences, including losing equipment, refusing to comply with orders, disregarding battalion orders, and one charge of drunkenness.

As Christmas came for the troops in Salonika there was little cheer for Patrick Downey as he waited under armed guard to learn his fate. On St Stephen's Day the Commander-in-Chief, General Monro, endorsed Lieutenant-General Mahon's view and recommended that Private Downey be executed.

Within twenty-four hours that recommendation had been put into effect. Just before eight o'clock on 27 December, Patrick Downey was taken from his cell, escorted by his guards, and tethered in front of a firing squad at Eurenjik, near the port of Salonika. The firing party, which is thought to have come from the Durham Light Infantry, was under the command of Captain Charles Villiers, Assistant Provost-Marshal of the 10th (Irish) Division. The execution would be over in seconds, and Captain Villiers would later write a brief report confirming that Downey's death was instantaneous.

There would be a postscript to the execution that would remain largely hidden for decades. The story, unearthed by the historian Julian Putkowski, was contained in the memoirs of an army doctor published in 1933. K. C. Mackenzie was working in an army hospital close to Patrick Downey's camp. On 28 December 1915, the day after Downey's execution, Mackenzie wrote in his diary:

> There was a tragedy in the next camp to us yesterday. A young Irishman in the Leinsters who had been giving trouble ever since he came out here was court-martialled, the immediate charge being desertion in the face of the enemy and general insubordination. He was sentenced to be shot and the sentence was duly carried out. An officer who had command of his unit said that when he heard the sentence he began to laugh and said, 'That is a good joke, you let me enlist and then bring me out here and shoot me.'[16]

More than ninety years after his execution, debate still surrounds the last days of Patrick Downey. Cathryn Corns and John Hughes-Wilson, who examined his case, have drawn attention to the deficiencies in the procedures surrounding his court martial, though they remain convinced that a different trial, using correct procedures, might have secured the same result.

> By our standards he was treated harshly and by the legal standards of the day his conviction should not have stood, but even if a retrial had been ordered the final outcome might still have been the same.[17]

The Irish government agreed that Patrick Downey was treated unfairly. Its investigation in 2004 into his military trial and execution concluded that his case had all the hallmarks of a miscarriage of justice.

> Private Downey must not have been aware of the implications of his pleading guilty, or else he would not have done so since he was effectively signing his own death warrant. It is clear from the file that no prisoner's friend was available to assist him with his defence.[18]

Patrick Downey's death was a landmark in the history of military executions. He was the first soldier to be executed for disobedience during the First World War. At nineteen he was also one of the youngest Irishmen to be placed before a firing squad. Though the records do not confirm this, his family suspect that he may have been under age when he joined up. Christy Walsh, Patrick Downey's great-nephew, supported the Irish Shot at Dawn campaign, which successfully persuaded the Irish government to investigate the cases of the executed men. He says the changed political climate in the South meant it was easier for families to come forward and publicly talk about their ancestors.

> In the old days, no-one would have said anything about this. People would have said, 'Don't talk about this'. Today people are more relaxed. I was doing this for the family name. We owe it to the Irish executed to show that they were victims of injustice. They went to fight for freedom and they gave their lives for freedom.[19]

In 2006 Walsh met another man who knew all about his great-uncle's death, but his historical journey had been very different. Martin Mansergh TD, an Irish government adviser during the peace process, had special reason to take an interest in the case of Patrick Downey. A cousin of Martin Mansergh's grandmother was Captain Robert Otway Mansergh, who presided over Downey's court martial in Serbia in December 1915.

> When I saw the name, because it is such a rare name I knew he must be related. I could have guessed that he came from the Cork branch of the family. I went and looked it up in the Irish Family Records, and there it was. I was working as an adviser at the time to the Taoiseach, so I mentioned to him straight away and he expressed sympathy.[20]

In 2006 Martin Mansergh issued his own regrets when he spoke in the Seanad about his relative and offered an apology.

> I can only express the deepest regret to his family, including his great-nephew, for the little that it is worth.

Mansergh then spoke about how he viewed the Irish executions and why he believed the men should be pardoned.

> The executions were an awful episode in an awful war. The Irish were volunteers and this was dreadful recompense for often intrinsically minor disciplinary offences. There is no doubt that this was directed right from the top but, unfortunately, officers were not concerned to spare life in general. There is shame on all involved.[21]

As Mansergh spoke, Christy Walsh was watching from the public gallery. Afterwards the two men met and shook hands and talked about their connection with the events of nine decades ago. As they chatted, Christy Walsh told Martin Mansergh that he forgave those who shot his great-uncle and that Mansergh had no reason to apologise, as he had done nothing wrong. Mansergh said he hoped that those men who died at the hands of firing squads would soon be pardoned, and Christy Walsh agreed that official recognition was long overdue:

> Many of the men came from Republican families and they volunteered because of Redmond's appeal to go and fight. Let us not forget that many were castigated for doing so. So to go and fight for the British Army and then get executed, and then after the war their names were left off the official war memorials—it is as if they never existed.[22]

In many ways Patrick Downey did not exist, at least officially. His name does not appear in Ireland's war records or on any Irish war memorials; but the life of the young soldier is commemorated elsewhere. About five miles south of the Greek city of Thessalonika lies the British cemetery of Míkra. Cared for by the Commonwealth War Graves Commission, with its neat white headstones and trimmed grass, it serves as a reminder of the sacrifice so many people made when the Allies tried to create a new front in 1915. It is home to nearly two thousand Commonwealth war graves and hosts a memorial to those who died when their ships were lost in the Mediterranean, servicemen and women who have no graves but the sea. The cemetery also records the name of an adventurous young man from Limerick, an Irishman who wore the uniform of the British Empire and went to fight on a distant shore; a volunteer soldier, who evaded Turkish and Bulgarian firepower, escaped the twin ravages of dysentery and frostbite and ended up being shot by his own side.

Chapter 4 ～

SIDE BY SIDE

These two cases are particularly heinous ones, and I hope that the extreme penalty which has been awarded by the court will be approved.

—LIEUTENANT-GENERAL CHARLES MONRO

The two military policemen, one British, the other French, walked up the track to the farmhouse and knocked on the door. Moments later a woman greeted them; she knew exactly why the two visitors had come to see her. The gendarme enquired if she had seen two British soldiers missing from the Irish Guards. Yes, she replied; she had seen the two men, but they had left that morning to go and rejoin their regiment.

There was something unconvincing about her replies and the investigators walked on to meet one of the woman's neighbours. This time their questions were met with different answers. Slowly the story emerged. A neighbour took the policemen back onto the land they had just walked from and pointed to a nearby barn. She told the gendarme to have a look inside. They tried to get into the building but the door was locked, so they retraced their steps to talk once again to the farmer's wife. She stuck to her story that the soldiers were not on her land and defiantly refused to unlock the door of the barn. The policemen persisted and demanded that she help them. Their voices were now raised; then, worn down by argument, the woman reluctantly handed over the keys to her visitors. Corporal Thomas Brennan and his French colleague walked to the barn and stepped inside. He looked up into the loft and then saw his quarry. Side by side in the hay sat Albert Smythe and Thomas Cummings, the two missing Irish Guardsmen. The hunt was over.

It was the middle of January 1915. The war was only five months old and the heavy fighting and appalling wintry conditions had taken their toll on the soldiers. Cummings and Smythe, serving with the 1st Battalion of the Irish Guards, had gone into battle at Ypres some months earlier, in early November.

This Belgian town would play a crucial role in the geography and history of the war. In the heart of the Flanders countryside the British, French and Belgians needed to halt the advance of the German army, whose commanders wanted to seize control of the Channel ports.

The fighting in the winter of 1914 in northern Belgium in what would become known as the First Battle of Ypres was a landmark in the progress of the campaign. During the hostilities, the Allied units would eventually manage to stall the German progress towards the coast. The battle would also change the landscape for ever. The two sides would dig in and would construct a labyrinth of trenches that would eventually stretch from the Swiss border in the south to the Belgian coast in the north.

Cummings and Smythe had arrived on the Continent as part of the British Expeditionary Force in the late summer of 1914, a few days after war had been declared. The men were experienced soldiers who had seen service before the war. Cummings, a 27-year-old from Belfast, who had a better disciplinary record than his colleague, had joined the Irish Guards in 1904. He spent the next eight years as a signaller before joining the army reserve in 1914. He was highly regarded as an 'exemplary character' and considered by his superiors to be an 'excellent man'.

Smythe, some five years older, had a very different record. He had enlisted in 1909 and a year later was made a lance-corporal. However, the promotion did not last long and he was demoted after a bout of drunkenness. His problems continued when he joined the Dragoon Guards. He eventually had enough of the rigours of army life and deserted but then decided he would give himself up. This action helped to mitigate his punishment and the authorities showed considerable leniency, to the extent that he was later granted a pardon and allowed back into service. In France, however, Smythe returned to his old ways and his superiors were far from impressed with his attitude. One colleague would later remark that 'since he has been on active service he has not done very well.'

During the autumn of 1914 the two men and their battalion would be in continuous action, and by late October the strain was beginning to show.

The men of the 1st Battalion were weary of battle and in November, on the Ypres salient, their resolve would be tested to breaking point in relentless fighting on the fringes of Zillebeke wood. Constant shelling by the German artillery placed the British lines under siege and the casualties mounted. The scale of the fighting was recorded in the battalion's war diary, which for 1 November reads:

> The enemy continued the bombardment of the front trenches with light field guns at very close range and also on the whole line and the wood in rear with heavy guns all the morning.

The diarist would later add:

> It was useless to send up reinforcements as they could never have reached the trenches owing to the very heavy machine gun fire the enemy directed at them.[1]

Matters got worse as the day progressed. The situation had become serious, and there seemed to be a danger of the enemy breaking right through. Cummings and Smythe found themselves at the centre of a vicious and lengthy German assault. Heavy fighting continued for days, and the Irish regiment would eventually lose almost six hundred killed or injured. These losses meant that the battalion was operating at less than half its normal strength.

On 1 November, Smythe volunteered to be a stretcher-bearer to assist his dying and wounded comrades. He took the casualties from his regiment down to a dressing station and then returned to the front lines. It was at this point that he claimed he was separated from his comrades.

> I went forward but got separated from my mate as we were under fire. I lost my way but found a French battalion with whom I stopped six weeks. I first started for Hazebrouck but on the outskirts of that town found that my battalion was at La Bassée so tried to go there and on my way stopped at the farm, where I was apprehended. I was just resting there.[2]

Smythe's disappearance was quickly reported after a roll-call was taken the next day, when he was recorded as missing, presumed dead.

The fighting continued and in the days that followed Smythe's absence his battalion suffered numerous casualties. Cummings stayed in the line and witnessed the onslaught.

On 6 November the Germans launched more attacks and many of the Irish Guards had to withdraw to their support trenches for safety; others who found themselves isolated at the front were killed by the enemy. By now the battalion was in tatters.

When the roll-call was taken the next day the scale of the devastation became clear. The long list of missing men was read out and it included the name of Thomas Cummings. He would later state that during the fighting he became separated from his comrades. Like his fellow-absentee Albert Smythe, Cummings would claim that he spent the next few weeks trying to rejoin his regiment:

> I wandered about for a long time and eventually came upon some French troops. I spent about two days with the French troops and then tried to find my battalion. I have been walking about the country ever since and could not find it. I had been staying at the farm when the military mounted police found me for about three days. The day before the military mounted police found me I had heard that my battalion was at La Bassée and that evening I had intended starting off to rejoin it.[3]

Although they disappeared at different times, Cummings and Smythe would eventually meet and they would be found together on farmland at a place called Choques. There the farmer's wife allowed the Irishmen to stay in a barn close to her farmhouse. Their presence had at first gone undetected, but soon the woman's neighbours started to notice the two strangers. After three weeks word quickly spread about the soldiers' whereabouts and this news reached the ear of the town's first citizen, the Mayor of Choques. By January 1915 the soldiers' sojourn was coming to an end.

The two men were charged with desertion, and their court martial took place at Locon some four days later. In their defence the two men gave a similar account, stating how they had got lost and had then met French troops. The men then claimed their stay in the farmhouse was a temporary one, because they were planning to travel to La Bassée to rejoin their unit.

Their accounts elicited little sympathy from senior officers. The battalion had just witnessed fierce fighting and suffered appalling casualties and the hierarchy had little time for men who they believed had walked away from battle. The men's superiors did not believe that Cummings and Smythe had seriously attempted to return to their unit.

Both men were found guilty of desertion by the court and were sentenced to death by firing squad. The sentence was considered by a succession of officers, and when the papers arrived with the commanding officer of I Corps, Lieutenant-General Charles Monro, he was in no doubt: 'These two cases are particularly heinous ones, and I hope that the extreme penalty which has been awarded by the court will be approved.'[4] His comments were endorsed a day later by Douglas Haig, then the officer commanding the First Army. He wrote on the file that the two prisoners should be shot. The execution was later approved by the Commander-in-Chief, Field-Marshal French.

The men's court martial documents, in the National Archives in London, give few details of the execution. Cummings and Smythe spent their last evening under armed guard on Wednesday 27 January 1915. It was a cold night and in their final hours the two Irishmen would have been visited by the army chaplain, strong drink may have been offered and the traditional last letters would have been written. Thursday morning arrived with an icy hard frost, and at 8:15 a.m. Albert Smythe and Thomas Cummings were placed before a firing squad and then blindfolded. The assembled squad of armed men, most likely members of the Irish Guards, would have stood at a distance of fifteen yards. After a signal from the officer in charge, a volley of shots would have been discharged. The records do not reveal if their deaths were instantaneous, but they do record that these were the first Irishmen to be executed on the Western Front.

In 2004 their case was taken up by the Irish government, which was uneasy about the way the court martial had been handled. The report by the Department of Foreign Affairs concluded:

The courts martial of both Private Smythe and Private Cummings indicate a casual approach by the court and the officers confirming the subsequent sentence—the Brigadier's comment that he did not think they made any effort to rejoin their unit highlights this casualness.[5]

The report's authors also questioned whether the original investigators examined the men's story thoroughly and asked why no weight was given to the long periods of service both men had—particularly the good disciplinary record of Cummings. The Irish government also enquired why no reference was given to the state of discipline in the Irish Guards at the time the men went missing.

It seems that the discipline of Cummings and Smythe's battalion was not a factor. Research carried out by Timothy Bowman shows that the battalion had no serious disciplinary problem at the time—in fact discipline was worse in the summer of 1915, after their deaths, than it was before—which would suggest that the double execution could hardly have acted as a deterrent. It is clear that in 1915 the army hierarchy involved in this case had neither time nor compassion for Cummings and Smythe; after all, the Irish Guards had just lost many men in battle and there were increasing pressures on the regiment.

The two men were treated identically. It also seems evident that Cummings's previous good conduct was of little consequence to the court martial. However, had Cummings been offered legal help his representative would have made much of his previous good behaviour. Interestingly, neither of the accused had support at the trial: the records do not suggest that they used the assistance of a prisoner's friend—a colleague brought in to help defendants. What is patently clear is that senior officers wanted this matter dealt with harshly and quickly. The men were apprehended, sentenced and shot within fourteen days. It was military-style justice, at high speed.

Thomas Cummings and Albert Smythe became the first Irish soldiers to be executed side by side. After the First World War their graves could not be found, but their deaths are commemorated at the memorial at Le Touret.

Their offence was to breach the provisions of the Army Acts as enshrined in the *Manual of Military Law* (1914). The Army (Annual) Act, renewed each year, laid down the regulations for all soldiers in service. It stipulated the punishment that could be handed down if the regulations were broken. It also defined what constituted desertion, cowardice, disobedience and other behaviour considered shameful. Those who deserted, who displayed cowardice or who fell asleep at their post could expect to receive the death penalty if found guilty by a court martial. These were known as capital offences: crimes that carried the ultimate sanction of being tied to a stake in front of a firing squad and executed.

The *Manual of Military Law,* an enormous publication of some nine hundred pages, also described how court martial hearings should be organised. Most of the Great War's military trials, including those of all twenty-six Irish-born soldiers who were executed, were heard by what were termed field general courts martial. As the name implies, these trials took place close to battlefields and were designed to be simple in procedure and easy to administer. At such a court martial three or four officers would sit on the panel, with usually a major or captain acting as president.

Officers who served on military trials were expected to have at least three years' experience. Training was inadequate, which meant that some inexperienced officers had a poor understanding of the regulations governing military trials. As Judge Anthony Babington discovered in his examination of military proceedings, this had understandable results. 'A number of inexperienced and comparatively junior officers were completely out of their depth when sentencing for serious offences.'[6]

This was obvious in the case of Smythe and Cummings, who were executed even though proper procedures were not followed. Similarly, in the same year Patrick Downey was executed because his court martial, staffed by inexperienced officers, erroneously allowed him to plead guilty.

The procedure used during a hearing was designed to be straightforward. Normally the adjutant of the accused soldier's unit would conduct the prosecution and the defendant would be asked if he had a prisoner's friend to defend him, though many soldiers did not use this facility and went through a trial undefended. Others, perhaps overawed by the proceedings, declined to speak at all during the hearing.

Many of those charged with serious offences were ill equipped to deal with a military trial. One of the Irishmen shot for desertion, Benjamin O'Connell from Wexford, could not read or write. Another, Bernard McGeehan from Co. Donegal, described by one officer as a 'worthless soldier', was of low intellect; today he would be regarded as having 'special needs'. Others had limited academic ability and, as the historians Julian Putkowski and Julian Sykes have argued, were often unable to defend themselves properly. 'Little imagination is needed to envisage the scenario of the ill-educated soldier on trial for his life, being led into making unfortunate admissions when questioned by his superiors, in their respective roles as prosecutor and judges.'[7]

After the evidence was presented the soldier or his representative would be given the chance to cross-examine the witnesses, to give evidence himself, or to call other witnesses. The court was then closed while the members discussed the case and considered their finding.

Once the verdict was agreed, the accused was brought back into the hearing and the finding was delivered. If the defendant was found guilty he would then be given an opportunity to make a statement in mitigation.

If a death sentence had been imposed, the court martial file would be sent to a series of senior officers for their opinion. The file would first go to the defendant's commanding officer and then in turn to senior officers from his brigade, division and corps, who would add their opinion about whether the death sentence should be carried out or commuted.

The confirming officers were invited to answer certain questions. They had to give an opinion about the defendant's fighting character and his previous conduct, to outline what the state of discipline was in the unit at the time, and finally in cases of desertion they had to say if they considered that the crime had been deliberately committed. The file was then examined by the Judge Advocate-General's staff to verify that the proceedings were technically correct; and then the ultimate decision of life or death rested with the Commander-in-Chief.

During the Great War there were two Commanders-in-Chief. Sir John French, who held the post until December 1915, was succeeded by Field-Marshal Sir Douglas Haig. Between them these two men were sent more than three thousand cases where the death sentence had been recommended by a court martial. French and Haig recommended that one in ten soldiers should face a firing squad.

The power of these senior commanders' opinion should not be overstated. As the historian Gerard Oram has pointed out, it would be wrong to suggest that they were solely responsible for the executions.

It is highly unlikely that the Commander-in-Chief actually read the courts martial papers of each and every case he confirmed, let alone all those he was required to consider: he had a war to run after all. In the vast majority of cases the role of Commander-in-Chief must, of necessity have been to authorise a decision made elsewhere.[8]

Much influence rested with the office of the Judge Advocate-General, who reviewed each case to see whether the court martial had been run properly.

Once the decision to impose the death penalty was ordered it was usually promulgated within days. This often happened in front of the defendant's unit when they were called to parade. The purpose of this very public statement was obvious: to warn would-be offenders that the consequence of disobedience or desertion could be death. Execution would usually follow within hours; but before the men were shot they would experience a ritual that by the end of the Great War nearly 350 British soldiers would experience.

The night before the shooting the condemned man was usually visited by a chaplain in his cell and he would be given a chance to write a final letter home. Alcohol, often rum, was then offered to the prisoner in an attempt to dull the pain of what lay ahead. If the soldier did not drink he may have been offered medication and some soldiers were given morphine, often secretly mixed in their drinks. Sometimes vast quantities of 'Dutch courage' were offered, as in the case of James Crozier.

Shootings took place at dawn, and the prisoner would be led from his cell and then normally would be blindfolded and tied to a post or to a chair. Requests to be shot without a blindfold or a hood were often denied, though in the case of Harry Farr it is reported that he was allowed to see his killers.

The firing squad, often made up of men from the prisoner's regiment, would usually stand some 15 yards away. To assist the firing squad's accuracy a small piece of scrap paper would be pinned to the prisoner's left breast close to his heart and members of the execution party would be instructed to aim at it.

Invariably, soldiers selected for a firing squad found their task painful and often suffered trauma after the shooting. Sometimes one member of the firing party would secretly be issued with a blank round; this was done in the execution of Patrick Murphy, who became the last Irishman to be executed during the Great War, when he was put before a firing squad in September 1918. The rationale behind the use of a blank round was to try to protect the mental health of the firing party: as no-one would know which executioner got the blank round, technically every member of the firing party could walk away in the hope that he was not responsible for discharging the fatal shot.

In the hours that followed an execution the death would be made public to the ranks, and often the soldiers would be called together for a special parade to be told the news. After the double execution of Smythe and Cummings a fellow-Ulsterman, Leslie Bell, a private with the 10th Battalion of the Royal Inniskilling Fusiliers, remembers having to march five miles to a parade and then being told of his fellow-countrymen's deaths. He recalls how he and his colleagues reacted to the killings:

> There was a feeling that the officer who ordered the shooting should be tried for murder—that was the feeling amongst the men. It was downright murder as the ordinary man thought it was. They reckon that those two lads were shot just for example. People should have been tried for murder instead of being honoured by King or Queen.[9]

However, it is important to place all these events in context and consider how military executions fit in to the wider story of the Great War. It would be foolish to suggest that the total number of those sentenced to death and subsequently shot was large when compared with the war's huge death toll. Three-quarters of a million British servicemen lost their lives in the Great War and twice that number were injured. An estimated thirty-five thousand Irish-born soldiers died during the war, the bulk of them volunteers, as there was no conscription in Ireland. On average, four hundred British soldiers died each day—more than the total number who were executed during the entire length of the war.

The use of military executions was not simply a British phenomenon during the Great War. Other armies also shot soldiers who fell foul of military law. Precise figures for the French army are not known, but it is estimated that several hundred were shot, while the Italians executed around 750. The German use of capital punishment was dramatically less: only 48 of their soldiers faced a firing squad during the Great War. Ten Americans were shot by the US Army, though at least three Americans serving with the British Army met their deaths at the hands of a firing party.

Military commanders who used the death penalty throughout the First World War argued that its use was an attempt to punish offenders and to maintain discipline. Senior officers wanted to punish those who had stepped out of line and to remind their colleagues what would happen if they fled the ranks or refused to take orders. Field-Marshal Sir Douglas Haig believed that men who did not possess 'moral fibre' would give way if there was not the fear of punishment. The writers Cathryn Corns and John Hughes-Wilson, who have examined military executions, have developed this theme and argued that discipline is at the heart of the army's being:

It is the core value that distinguishes the uniformed, regulated fighting force from an armed mob. In order to control an army and order its activities, there has to be an accepted set of rules by which the army can regulate the conduct of its members.[10]

Understandably, all armed services need discipline and a formal set of regulations, and the British Expeditionary Force that landed on French soil in the late summer of 1914 was no different. What is at issue, and has been at the heart of the pardons debate, is how fairly those rules were interpreted and applied, and why certain judgements were made.

In the spring of 1916 the double execution of two privates in the Royal Irish Rifles had echoes of the Cummings and Smythe affair. John McCracken and James Templeton, who both came from Belfast, landed in France in the autumn of 1915 as part of the British Expeditionary Force. In February 1916, as members of the 15th Battalion of the Royal Irish Rifles, the two men were stationed in the Somme region. They were in the trenches close to the heavily fortified German stronghold of Beaumont-Hamel and front-line duty for the riflemen was predictably busy, though casualties were not high.

Twenty-year-old James Templeton, from Enfield Street in Belfast, had been an apprentice in one of the local mills, but when war was declared he, like so many others, joined the army. He enlisted in the 15th Battalion, also known as the North Belfast Volunteers. A month earlier, in September 1914, John McCracken, a year younger than Templeton, had made a similar journey to the recruiting office. The pair would later travel to England, arriving in France a year after joining the ranks.

The two men had similar disciplinary records. Templeton would quickly develop a reputation for going absent. Two days after

Christmas Day in 1915 he disappeared and failed to turn up for a parade. A month later he disobeyed an order from an officer and missed two more parades in one day. In February 1916 he again went missing and once again managed to miss the roll-call at another two parades. By now it seems that officers in the battalion were beginning to lose patience with the Belfast man.

McCracken's army career included a series of misdemeanours, albeit minor ones. He had been absent from a parade, had once been found with dirty ammunition, and had left a working party without permission. According to Julian Putkowski, these petty indiscretions may have been seized upon because McCracken did not get on with one of his superiors:

> These really were minor crimes. The sort of thing a picky officer would cite when wishing to keep his unit on their toes. He may have used McCracken and wanted to make an example of him and as a soldier he may not have liked him or cared about him.[11]

In February 1916 those minor crimes caught up with him, and, like his Belfast colleague, he would find himself fighting for his life.

The first of the men to go absent that month was Templeton. The battalion war diary records that on 20 February the men were in a place called Beaussart, where for two days there had been heavy shelling. The attack continued at night on the trenches at Redan, where a succession of German barrages led to fourteen casualties. That night Templeton went missing. At 5 p.m., when the roll-call was taken, the young Belfast man was warned by his sergeant to remain on duty at the front line, but six hours later Templeton had gone.

After Templeton vanished, McCracken felt ill and was being taken to a field ambulance on a stretcher. He had fallen during operations and claimed to have hurt his back during a march. The medical officer at the dressing station could not find anything wrong with him, and the next day he was ordered to report for duty back at the trenches, some two-and-a-half miles away.

As McCracken was being taken back to the trenches Templeton was going in the opposite direction. The rifleman had walked away from the front line and at 6 p.m. he encountered Lance-Corporal Holdsworth in a village some six miles away. The NCO was in

Templeton's regiment and recognised his comrade, who by now had no rifle.

> I was outside my billet and I saw the accused Rifleman Templeton and another man walking towards me. I asked him what he was here for. He replied I have come from the White City [the trenches beside Hamel cemetery] and I want to give myself up and I want to give myself up as I am sorry for what I have done or words to that effect.[12]

Templeton was arrested and detained overnight. By this stage McCracken was back at the front line and had been placed on sentry duty with his platoon. At 8 p.m. a routine check showed that another member of the battalion was missing and this time McCracken could not be found. He had left his post, but, like Templeton, he would eventually walk back to members of his own regiment.

The next night at 7 p.m. Sergeant Carlisle was relaxing in his billet in a village some five miles from the front line:

> The accused Rifleman McCracken walked into my billet and reported that he was an absentee from the 15th Battalion of the Royal Irish Rifles—This battalion at the time was in the trenches—I placed him in close arrest, the accused was sober and wore his regimental badges but was deficient of his rifle and equipment.[13]

Templeton and McCracken were both charged with desertion. They appeared before a court martial on 27 February. Templeton's hearing appears to have been very short. In his defence all he said was that he was 'sorry for what he had done.' McCracken's defence was similar, and he also spoke about his medical difficulties. 'I had only just come out of hospital and was not feeling fit. I am sorry for what I have done.'[14]

The soldiers' contrition did little to sway the minds of the court martial. Both men were found guilty of desertion and sentenced to death by firing squad. As was normal practice, the court martial files were referred up through the chain of command and it was then that it became clear that proper legal procedures had not been followed. Witnesses had not been sworn in before giving their evidence, and, as McCracken had implied, there may have been medical reasons for his behaviour and therefore a medical witness should have been called to give evidence. Instructions attached to the court martial papers show that the officers were urged to remedy the omissions and attach the additional reports to the original notes of the proceedings. These instructions were seized upon by the Department of Foreign Affairs in 2004 when officials in Dublin investigated the Templeton and McCracken case.

> There is evidence in the file that members of the courts martial may not have been well versed in legal proceedings. There is a request for them to alter the trial notes after the fact to include that the men were sworn in and to include reference to the men's fighting character. Although neither request seem to be in any way untoward they do highlight the fact that these court martials were at times carried out by officers with little or no legal experience.[15]

McCracken was medically examined and comments about his character were sought from his superior officers and added to his trial dossier. Major W. B. Ewart, who commanded the 15th Battalion, wrote of McCracken that although his character was 'poor' this may have been due to the fact that shortly after he arrived in France his mother had died. The major added that the soldier's misdemeanours up to that time had been minor ones and though there is little doubt that he left the front line he added: 'I think the man did not know the seriousness of his action.'[16]

Ewart wrote in similar terms about James Templeton. He was also described as having a 'poor' character, being 'naturally' of stubborn disposition and being guilty of offences of a minor nature. Ewart stated that he believed the accused had deliberately left the front line but, like McCracken, did not realise how serious the offence was. The major adds that 'no case of this nature had previously occurred in the battalion.' Major Ewart may have been technically right, but it is not true to say the battalion did not experience desertions. Other soldiers from the 15th Battalion had gone absent—misbehaviour seized upon by the divisional commander that would ultimately seal the fate of Templeton and McCracken.

However, if Major Ewart felt his views would save his men from death he was mistaken. Brigadier-General Withycombe, who commanded the

107th Brigade, declared that discipline in the battalion was fair—implying that it could be improved upon—and he therefore recommended that the executions be carried out.

The officer commanding the 36th (Ulster) Division, Major-General Oliver Nugent, agreed with Withycombe. He also wanted an example to be made of the two rifleman. On 3 March, Nugent maintained that the executions would serve as a deterrent, as there had been three previous cases of desertion in the battalion, but on those occasions the death sentence had been commuted.

One of the cases Nugent was referring to was heard on the same day as McCracken and Templeton's court martial. Rifleman Beattie from North Belfast had deserted from his duties and was sentenced to death. However, his life was spared and he was sent to prison for five years. A month earlier Rifleman Waterworth, another member of the battalion, had also been found guilty of desertion and was sentenced to five years' penal servitude. McCracken and Templeton would not be so fortunate.

On 19 March, as daylight broke across the Somme, the two men were placed before a firing squad and were shot side by side. The two Ulstermen would later be buried at Mailly-Maillet.

Did their deaths have the desired effect and improve discipline? Timothy Bowman, who has studied the behaviour of the Irish regiments in the First World War, argues that the double execution stopped the flow of deserters from the ranks and improved discipline. His figures show that the number of courts martial in the battalion halved in the five months following the deaths of Templeton and McCracken and there is evidence of how the double execution affected the soldiers.

In the hours after the double execution soldiers from other Irish battalions were called together and informed of the deaths of Templeton and McCracken. One of those who was told of the shooting was Leslie Bell, a private with the 10th Battalion, Royal Inniskilling Fusiliers. He marched five miles that morning and was then told the news. In the autumn of 1992, in an interview for a BBC Radio Ulster documentary, he remembered vividly how he and his comrades were informed that March morning in 1916.

The adjutant drew out a sheet of paper, read out that two men of the Royal Irish Rifles had been shot at dawn that morning for desertion. There was great murmurs in the ranks at this statement. The colonel gave a yell out of him: 'Order in the ranks, or I will have every sixth man shot!' Of course that kept everybody silent, but it left a sadness over the battalion. Some of the lads thought it was awful to volunteer for your country and find out that you were going to be shot by your own men. Everybody didn't feel a liking for the trenches. It is a very nerve-wracking business after seven days in the trenches; maybe shelling and a lot of wounded and dead. Everybody's nerves didn't stick it.

After that day Leslie Bell and his comrades looked at their officers very differently:

We were vexed by these people and there were a lot of remarks passed. I remember one remark especially. Some lad said, 'Some poor mother, tomorrow morning she will receive a telegraph from the War Office stating that her son has died in action; little does she know that he was put up against a wall and shot by his own men.' It went down very badly with the people, the regiment. They thought that these two lads had been sacrificed to set an example to the rest of us. We never had the same respect for the officers when we found out anyone could meet the same fate.[17]

Ten years after the radio interview with Leslie Bell was broadcast a copy of it landed in London on the doormat of Eileen Hinken, great-niece of James Templeton. When researching her family history she had become aware of James's death, and she had contacted the Shot at Dawn campaign, which sent her the tape of Leslie Bell's interview.

I started to cry when I heard Leslie Bell talk about James. It was one of the most emotional things I have ever heard. This was living history, the words of a man who was there. It was very upsetting, and it brought the horror of James's death home. This was not just history: this was family history, and Leslie Bell brought the story of James to life. It was very moving.[18]

Upset at what she had heard, Eileen Hinken and her mother, Sadie, began writing letters and helped organise a petition calling for pardons for the executed men.

Initially when I had discovered how James died I just assumed that there must have been a reason for his death. I thought maybe he was the black sheep of the family and probably deserved it. However, the more I looked at it and got information and discovered the truth the angrier I got. I was really annoyed that this was allowed to happen all those years ago and when you think James and all the other Irishmen were volunteers, it simply adds to the injustice.[19]

James Templeton and John McCracken were the last Irish soldiers to be shot side by side. Their double execution in March 1916 came during the bloodiest year for British military executions—a death toll that included ten Irish soldiers. And it was a year of bloodshed not only in the killing fields of France and Flanders but back home on the streets of Dublin.

| DYING FOR IRELAND

Poor Ireland is always in Trouble.
—FRANCIS LEDWIDGE, SOLDIER AND POET,
ROYAL INNISKILLING FUSILIERS

In the early hours of a May morning an Irishman was taken into a
stonebreaker's yard by armed captors. Ever since he had challenged
authority and then faced a court martial he knew this moment
would arrive. He seemed stoical in the face of death, proudly resigned
to his fate. Yet this would be no routine execution. In one of his last
letters, written from his cell, he had told his mother that he did not
wish to live and was ready to die. In his final moments, as he waited in
the darkness, a line of soldiers stood in front of him, readied themselves, held their rifles in position, and on a command took aim. He
was killed at once. The firing squad's target was the son of an Irish
mother and an English father. Like his killers, he saw himself as a
committed and patriotic soldier. His name was Patrick Pearse.

The killing in Dublin on that May day in 1916 brought the policy of
military executions to the heart of the British Empire and created a
martyr and a hero for Irish republicans. Here, for the first time since
the war began, British soldiers found themselves on home ground,
using their guns to execute their own citizens.

Pearse's crime and that of his co-accused was to have taken part in
an 'armed rebellion and in waging war against His Majesty the King'—
an offence considered by the military hierarchy and the state to be as
serious as desertion and cowardice and one that automatically carried
the penalty of death.

The Easter Rising some days earlier had taken many people by
surprise. Though nationalist feeling had been building in Ireland in the
early part of the year there was little suggestion on Good Friday of what

lay ahead over the next seven days. The rebellion had been planned in earnest from the summer of 1915 and its timing rested much with events on the Western Front. Republicans seized on the British government's difficulty and preoccupation with the war effort, and Pearse had great hopes that by Easter 1916 some ten thousand Irish men and women would support an uprising. His optimistic estimate was wide of the mark, and only 1,800 men and women would eventually take to the streets of Dublin.

The plans had first been discussed in 1914, when members of the Irish Republican Brotherhood had agreed that the war in Europe would provide the perfect backdrop for a rebellion. When the nationalist MP John Redmond called on Irishmen to support the war effort and join up, republicans took a different path and the die was cast. The Irish Volunteers split, with the bulk following Redmond and supporting his call for Irishmen to join the British Army. This split made a rebellion inevitable and republicans in the Volunteers began planning for a military uprising and increasingly looked to Germany.

Germany was an obvious choice for republicans, not only because of the war but because the Germans had supplied guns in the past to both the UVF and the Irish Volunteers. The liaison with Germany was set up with the help of Sir Roger Casement, who had been brought up in the Glens of Antrim and had attended Ballymena Academy. Born to a Protestant father and a Catholic mother, he became a distinguished British diplomat and served in Africa, notably in the Congo and in Brazil. His efforts with native workers on the Amazon and the Congo had earned him a knighthood in 1911. On his retirement from the diplomatic service he settled in Dublin and became a member of the Irish Volunteers.

Casement began discussions with German officials with the aim of securing weaponry for an assault in Dublin. He believed that arms and men would arrive in Ireland at the same time that the German army would begin a new offensive on the Western Front. Through his contacts with the German establishment Casement also tried to set up an Irish Brigade in the German Army—where Irishmen would serve under Irish officers and would be paid handsomely for their efforts— but there were few volunteers. His poor luck continued at Easter 1916 when the original help that was offered by officials in Berlin did not materialise, through a combination of poor planning and misfortune.

A ship laden with German arms was intercepted off the Irish coast by the British authorities only days before the rising began.

Casement had more misfortune when he returned to Ireland in a German submarine and went ashore in Co. Kerry only to be arrested immediately afterwards. He was on his way to try to persuade the leaders to call off the planned rebellion. However, he never got to offer his words of caution and was taken into custody and later hanged in London for treason.

In the end, Pearse and his comrades got no help from outside Ireland and the rebels had to act alone. When the rebellion finally arrived on the streets of Dublin it was short-lived, poorly organised, and not immediately popular. Some Dubliners watched the initial events with bemusement; others, loyal to Britain and supporters of Irish efforts on the Western Front, saw the attack as a German-inspired rebellion.

Pearse and his co-accused seized the General Post Office, a factory, a hospital and other central buildings on Easter Monday and issued a Proclamation of an Irish Republic. Government forces quickly surrounded them and over the next few days overpowered the rebels. In the opening days Irishmen in British uniform, including men from the Royal Irish Rifles, the Dublin Fusiliers and the Leinster Regiment, helped quell the revolt.

After a week of gunfire and shelling, clearly outgunned and outmanoeuvred, Pearse and his fellow-rebels surrendered amidst the smoke and the rubble. The rising was over and within ten days many of its leaders would be executed.

The seven signatories of the Proclamation of the Irish Republic—Thomas J. Clarke, Seán Mac Diarmada, P. H. Pearse, James Connolly, Thomas MacDonagh, Éamonn Ceannt, and Joseph Plunkett—all faced a firing squad, as did others who took part in the rebellion, including Pearse's brother William.

The events of those dramatic days in Dublin understandably made an impact on the Western Front. When the news of the Rising reached the ranks of the Royal Dublin Fusiliers, Noel Drury would write in his diary in April 1916:

Isn't it awful. Goodness knows what they think they are going to gain by it. It's a regular stab in the back for our fellows out here, who don't know how their people at home are.[1]

For the Irish soldiers in France and Flanders it was a confusing time, as they relied on letters from home and the occasional newspaper to keep them informed of the news. Although there was no widespread support for the rising there was a change of mood among some soldiers when news of the executions became known, as John Lucy, a sergeant in the Royal Irish Rifles, would recall:

My fellow soldiers had no great sympathy with the rebels, but they got fed up when they heard of the executions of the leaders. I experienced a cold fury, because I would see the whole British Empire damned sooner than hear of an Irishman being killed in his own country by any intruding stranger.[2]

In his memoirs Lucy would also recall how he was later introduced to a fellow-soldier who had been involved in the fighting against the rebels in Dublin.

I cocked my ears and the smart little sergeant spoke: 'Yes I was there. As a matter of fact I had the job of seeing them off.' My heart pounded. Sickeningly I looked at the Irish harp of his cap-badge, and I stared bitterly at his beady brown eyes. He was restless, and wanted to talk. Knowing my sympathies by hearsay, he had come to me somehow like a man coming back to the scene of some doubtful act to attempt reconciliation. He was the first of a number of unhappy Englishmen who tried, and tried vainly, to square their acts against Ireland with me.[3]

For some Irishmen serving the Crown the events of Easter 1916 caused a huge personal dilemma. It awakened issues of loyalty, identity and patriotism. Tom Kettle, a lieutenant with the Royal Dublin Fusiliers, was on leave in Ireland when the rebellion began. Though he was not a supporter of the rising, as a nationalist writer and former MP for East Tyrone he had been friends with a number of those who were executed. He would poignantly remark about the 1916 leaders: 'These men will go down in history as heroes and martyrs; and I will go down—if I go down at all—as a bloody British officer.'[4]

Tom Kettle's soul-searching was not unique. Francis Ledwidge was another Irishman in a British uniform who was affected by the events of Easter 1916. Ledwidge had been friends with Patrick Pearse and

Thomas MacDonagh. From Co. Meath, a former farm labourer and trade union organiser, he was a member of the Royal Inniskilling Fusiliers and saw action in Gallipoli and later at Ypres. Ledwidge had been an original member of the Irish Volunteers and when the movement split over involvement in the war he at first supported the breakaway Volunteers and then changed his mind and heeded John Redmond's call. 'I joined the British Army because she stood between Ireland and an enemy common to our civilisation and I would not have her say that she defended us while we did nothing at home but pass resolutions.'[5]

Ledwidge had enlisted at Richmond Barracks in Dublin—the same place where one of the architects of the rising, Thomas MacDonagh, would be sentenced to death. MacDonagh, like Ledwidge, was a poet, and the two knew each other. On the day the first executions took place Ledwidge wrote to Bob Christie, a Protestant friend from Ulster:

Yes, Poor Ireland is always in Trouble. Though I am not a Sinn Feiner and you are a Carsonite, do our sympathies not go to Cathleen ni Houlihan? Poor MacDonagh and Pearse were two of my best friends. Now they are dead, shot by England.[6]

Although he was not a supporter of the republicans, Ledwidge was so moved by the death of his friend that he wrote a poem simply entitled 'Thomas MacDonagh'. The opening lines read:

He shall not hear the bittern cry
In the wild sky, where he is lain
Nor voices of the sweeter birds
Above the wailing of the rain.[7]

If there was sympathy with men such as Thomas MacDonagh among Irish soldiers in British uniforms it did not manifest itself in acts of indiscipline on the Western Front. However, that did not stop the Germans trying to exploit 'England's difficulty'. In May 1916, as the executions began in Dublin, men from the Royal Munster Fusiliers at the front line found themselves being taunted by German soldiers, who had written placards in English. One read:

Irishmen. Heavy Uproar in Ireland. English guns are firing at your wives and children.

Another notice displayed by the Germans to the 7th Battalion of the Leinster Regiment read:

Sir Roger Casement persecuted. Throw your arms away. We will give you a hearty welcome.[8]

These unsophisticated attempts to spread discomfort in the Irish ranks failed. As the executions of the rebels continued, the deaths in Dublin did little to change the daily lives of the thousands of Irishmen embattled on the Western Front.

As Irishmen were dying in Dublin at the hands of the British Army, many other Irishmen in British uniforms were preparing for their first experience of warfare. Along the Western Front important battles were either taking place or in the final stages of preparation. By the early summer of 1916 plans for what would become known as the Battle of the Somme were well advanced.

———

In Flanders, at Ypres, members of the Canadian Expeditionary Force were dug in near Mount Sorrell as part of an operation aimed at recapturing a point known as Hill 62 from the Germans. Among their number was 37-year-old James Wilson, an Irishman in the uniform of the Commonwealth. Standing nearly six feet tall, with a fair complexion, brown hair and blue eyes, Wilson was a Presbyterian from Limerick. An unmarried labourer, he had previously seen service for nine years with the Connaught Rangers. After his army service, like many of his generation, Wilson had sought a new life abroad and when war broke out he was in Canada. In September 1914 he enlisted with the 4th Battalion of the Canadian Infantry at Valcartier camp in Québec. This camp, the largest on Canadian soil, would play host to thousands of members of the Canadian Expeditionary Force.

Within weeks of enlisting, Wilson was back across the Atlantic and found himself billeted at Salisbury Plain in southern England. Here his behaviour began to develop a pattern that would ultimately end his war and his life. The Irishman became a serial absentee. In November he disappeared for a month, only to be recaptured and taken into custody. Within days he broke free from the guardroom, only to be arrested by military police who discovered him in the nearby city of Salisbury.

By now Wilson's battalion was due to set sail for France, but the Limerick man would not be joining them. His superiors decided that they did not want to retain the runaway soldier, whom they described as undesirable, and he was discharged.

However, Wilson's affinity for the Canadians did not take long to be rekindled. Three weeks later he managed to get himself back into uniform and re-enlisted, this time with the 9th Battalion of the Canadian Infantry, which promptly sent him to Shorncliffe training depot in Kent. Here Wilson fell back into his old ways and began to disappear regularly from duty. His record sheet began to fill up with a series of indiscretions, including being absent without leave on five occasions.

Before he and his battalion were due to sail for France, Wilson was again absent from duty and on this occasion he was also charged with being drunk, kicking an NCO and using abusive language. Wilson was becoming a serious problem for his superior officers; but, unlike the hierarchy of the 4th Battalion, the officers of his new unit decided to keep the troublesome Munster man in uniform.

Wilson's superiors may have hoped that when they arrived at the Western Front his behaviour would improve. When his latest detention ended, Wilson and his comrades set sail for France in July 1915; but the change of scenery and the prospect of battle did little to change his behaviour. Within days he was drunk again and, not surprisingly, went absent without leave. He was once again detained, but he found the punishment too hard to bear, and, just as he had done in England, he escaped from custody. His freedom was inevitably short-lived and he was caught, put before a court martial, and given seventy days' field punishment no. 1. This punishment involved being tethered to a wheel for a few hours each day. The prisoner's hands and legs were tied, with his body spreadeagled in the form of an X, which led to the punishment getting the nickname of the 'crucifixion'. It was very painful, and sometimes the victim was tied so tightly that the rope left lasting marks on his body.

Many soldiers found the sight of a comrade tied up in such a way disturbing. John Lucy, a sergeant with the Royal Irish Rifles, witnessed the punishment many times.

> Confinement of any kind is abhorred to an indescribable degree by Irishmen. No words can describe the stigma of being tied to a tree or a wheel, and of being handcuffed as well as being imprisoned. The punishment also included pack drill under the provost sergeant. These men bore it with hard set faces which showed no more emotion than the faces of the dead. We are all sorry for them, and the passing troops averted their looks in shame and compassion when passing the bound prisoners.[9]

The punishment was used some sixty thousand times during the Great War. It would be suspended when the offender's unit went into battle but would be resumed when the men returned from the front line.

By the beginning of 1916 James Wilson again found himself facing a court martial. This time he was found guilty of disobeying a lawful command and was sentenced to eighteen months' hard labour, which was commuted to ninety days' field punishment no. 1. By now the offences were getting more serious, and in return the punishments were becoming longer. It appears that Wilson's poor disciplinary record meant that he was continually being watched by his superior officers, and the slightest infringement of regulations was seized upon. That may be the reasoning behind an incident involving a camera. Possessing such an item was in contravention of routine orders, yet Wilson had managed to get hold of one. He was disciplined for having it and again given ninety days' field punishment—which by now he was well used to.

By May the Canadians were preparing for battle close to Mount Sorrell on the Ypres salient, and right on cue Wilson again disappeared from the trenches. He was later arrested and, to make matters worse, later swore at a warrant officer and urinated in his billet. It seems likely that he committed these acts when he was drunk.

With the final assault at Mount Sorrell about to take place it appears that the Limerick soldier was given one last chance—an opportunity that could have kept him alive. Julian Putkowski has studied his case.

He was temporarily released from custody on 12 June in order to take part with the rest of the battalion in the final successful assault that ended the battle of Mount Sorrell. However instead of dutifully marching off to play his part in the offensive, Wilson deserted, yet again surrendering himself after four days absence.[10]

This would turn out to be Wilson's final indiscretion; he would go before a court martial for one last time.

The details of his fourth and final trial have been lost. The file went missing in the 1920s, so we do not know what was said during the proceedings. However, a post-war summary unearthed by Julian Putkowski, written by Wilson's commanding officer, reports that the Irishman was viewed as a very bad character. He was regarded as the leader of a gang of seven or eight characters, men whose behaviour was seen as sullying the unit's good disciplinary record. What is clear is that Wilson's officers had simply run out of patience. In their eyes he was of little use as a soldier; he was misleading others, he had become a liability, and he did not show any signs of improving his behaviour.

It is apparent that much of Wilson's trouble stemmed from alcohol, as Putkowski has concluded:

He would consequently have been viewed as a nuisance by his platoon and company commanders and aside from personal animus, with a measure of justification the latter would have maintained that an erratic, ill-tempered drunk was not a military asset.[11]

On 9 July 1916, at 4:20 a.m., James Wilson was placed before a firing squad and shot.

Given his record, involving numerous absences, it is easy to establish that he had been given countless opportunities to change his behaviour.

Despite his poor record, Wilson, like the other Irishmen shot at dawn, remains a victim of an execution policy that was deeply flawed. This was recognised when the Canadian government studied his death in 2001. Twenty-three Canadian soldiers, including Wilson, were shot during the Great War; and though the Canadian government stopped short of granting a pardon to the men, the Minister of Veterans' Affairs, Ronald Duhamel, offered these words:

To give these 23 soldiers a dignity that is their due, and to provide closure to the families, as the Minister of Veterans' Affairs, and on behalf of the Government of Canada, I wish to express my deep sorrow at their loss of life, not because of what they did or didn't do, but because they too lie in foreign fields where 'poppies blow amid the crosses, row and row.' While they came from different regions of Canada, they all volunteered to serve their country in its citizen army, and the hardships they endured prior to their offences will be unrecorded and unremembered no more.[12]

Although the Canadian government's decision was supported by the country's main political parties, it was not universally accepted, and the debate that followed in the letters pages of national newspapers and on the Canadian air waves mirrored the arguments witnessed in Britain in the 1990s. Those against the official apology argued that the Canadian government was simply rewriting history; others suggested that by formally honouring those who had been executed the government was tarnishing the memory of those confirming officers who had ordered them shot.

In 1916, after the bloodshed of a rebellion in Dublin and during the slaughter of the Somme, Wilson's death was simply another statistic in a long list of casualties. His execution understandably merited little attention. Yet nine decades later the circumstances of his demise would engage the collective thoughts of three governments: the British, the Irish and the Canadian, governments that would all come to consider if he deserved a pardon.

Wilson's death, unlike that of Patrick Pearse, did little to change history. Pearse's execution would aid the rise of Sinn Féin and ultimately lead to the establishment of an independent republic. Pearse would be viewed as the brave hero who died a martyr, one of the founding fathers of the Irish state whose death paved the way for freedom. Wilson's record shows he was a troubled, ill-disciplined soldier, haunted by a bad temper and a strong liking for drink. Ninety years later his execution seems utterly pointless. Ironically, like Pearse, he has received more attention dead than he ever did alive.

At first glance the killings of these two very different Irishmen seem to have little in common. After all, Wilson was a working-class Protestant from Limerick, and Pearse was a middle-class Catholic from Dublin. Yet the two men share some common ground. They were of a similar age: Pearse was thirty-six, Wilson a year older. They were both born into a divided country caught up in troubled times of choices and conflict, a confusing moment in history when questions over loyalty, identity and nationhood took centre stage. In 1916 they were both engaged in a personal struggle against authority and died, in their own way, as soldiers of Ireland.

Chapter 6 ⌒

| DEATH ON THE SOMME

It seemed that out of battle I escaped.
—WILFRED OWEN, SOLDIER AND WAR POET

The bugles sounded, the whistles blew, and the morning stillness was broken. In the hours that followed, an entire generation walked to its death. In the bright sunshine of a fine summer's day, wave after wave of men fell and lay together. Brothers, friends and workmates were the dead and the dying.

Nothing had prepared anyone for this bloodletting and as night fell, one of the survivors could take no more. The Battle of the Somme had only begun when Albert Rickman decided that he simply couldn't carry on. A private in the Royal Dublin Fusiliers, he deserted after he witnessed the carnage and mayhem of a July day that would become a defining moment of the war.

On 1 July 1916 men from fourteen British divisions had begun the advance towards enemy lines across an eighteen-mile front and they had been expected to make quick and steady progress. Instead many were mowed down within minutes by a mixture of artillery and machine guns. By sunset 57,000 men were injured and 19,000 were killed. Ninety years later, the Somme remains a byword for slaughter. The devastation and awfulness of that time still touch the national consciousness and the opening attack remains the blackest day in British military history.

Many hundreds of Irishmen died that bright morning as they advanced across no-man's-land at walking pace towards enemy lines. When the day ended, the 36th (Ulster) Division's blood sacrifice would be huge, with some five thousand casualties. The Ulstermen's bravery on that opening day did not go unnoticed and later four Victoria Crosses would be awarded. Men from the 36th Division temporarily succeeded in capturing the impressive German stronghold of Schwaben Redoubt but had to surrender the ground later in the day. Despite the personal acts of heroism, the opening hours of the attack are remembered more with sadness than with pride. The Irish contribution to the battle was huge and the sacrifice would be felt in towns and villages in every county of Ireland.

Herbert Beattie, a Belfast man who saw action with the Royal Inniskilling Fusiliers, would write to his mother after he witnessed the slaughter in the sunshine:

> Tell them there is not another Grosvenor Road fellow left but myself. Mother, we were tramping over the dead; I think there is only about four hundred left out of 13 hundred . . . Mother, If God spares me to get home safely, I will have something awful to tell you. If hell is any worse I would not like to go to it.[1]

In the neighbouring sector close to the Ulstermen, soldiers from the Royal Dublin Fusiliers fought and across the Somme they were joined by many thousands of Irishmen, including men from the Irish Guards and the Tyneside Irish.

The events of those first bloody hours took the men by surprise and did not resemble the battle plans that had been outlined to soldiers such as Albert Rickman in the weeks before the advance.

The Somme initiative had at first been a French idea, conceived at a series of Anglo-French summit meetings and then accepted by the British. Originally the British divisions were to be the minority partner in the operation, but with the French heavily engaged in fighting at Verdun the British forces would eventually take the leading role.

For seven days leading up to 'zero hour' on 1 July, one-and-a-half million shells had pounded the German lines. Such was the scale, noise and sheer ferocity of the British bombardment that the shelling was heard across the Channel in England.

The plan of attack, involving French and British troops, was meant to be straightforward: after the artillery had worn down the defences the infantry would then move forward and capture German positions. As the men advanced, further artillery assaults were also envisaged, so the advancing troops could be protected by a curtain of fire as they marched towards enemy lines. The orders were also that the men must advance even if it was not clear whether the wire that lined no-man's-land had been destroyed.

Private Albert Rickman and his comrades in the 1st Battalion of the Royal Dublin Fusiliers had their own particular orders. The battalion's objective was outlined in a note written in June by their commanding officer, Lieutenant-Colonel Nelson. He described how the German trenches would be bombarded for 96 hours and then the Dublins would move out of the trenches with the aim of securing ground from the Germans in a series of stages.

Nelson also wanted his men to capture a German communication trench. The aim was to leave their own trenches quickly and then advance towards the German positions close to Beaumont-Hamel. The plan was to advance across no-man's-land, making headway through gaps in the barbed wire, and take control of the first German position; then, once it had been secured, to move forward and take another German position on the second line.

Nelson's operational orders were clear regarding what was expected of his men once they reached enemy lines. On 5 June he wrote, 'The captured line is to be held at all costs, and every effort made to render it impregnable.'[2]

The objective set for them and the subsequent events of that July morning could not have been more different. Daybreak brought with it a gentle breeze and as Rickman stood in line to go over the top in the morning sunshine, the battle plan began to fall apart.

The battalion was divided into four companies. Two would take up positions at the front, with the remaining two in reserve. The Dubliners would be supported by soldiers of the 16th Battalion of the Middlesex Regiment. The men had great difficulty advancing from their trenches and as they struggled to move forward quickly the German machine-gunners were able to strike with ease and the battalion took many casualties.

Having only joined the unit in April, it was Rickman's first experience of warfare on the Western Front. Originally from Milford-on-Sea, Hampshire, the 27-year-old had previously been at the Suvla landings in Gallipoli with the 7th Battalion of the Royal Dublin Fusiliers. He was invalided home and in the spring of 1916 had volunteered again for active service, this time with the 1st Battalion. Though he was a veteran and had witnessed the horrors of battle in another theatre of war, like his comrades he was not prepared for the bloodshed of the Somme. The battalion war diary of 1 July records the painful difficulties Rickman and his comrades faced:

It was very difficult for companies to move up to the Front Line owing to the trenches being blocked by a number of men of the battalion in front. Consequently it was 0800 before we were able to begin moving up to the parapet. Our own barbed wire was cut only at intervals of about 40 yards and by this time the Germans had machine gunners trained on these gaps. The result being our casualties were very heavy and only a few of our men got through our own wire and still fewer of those succeeded in advancing more than 50 or 60 yards before being shot down.

The diary adds:

At noon the attack here was abandoned and we were ordered to hold and consolidate our own front line.[3]

Rickman and his comrades withdrew to their own trenches close to Auchonvillers. Bloodied and depleted, the 1st Battalion was at last able to gauge its losses; and the news was catastrophic. By the end of the first day there were 311 casualties. At 6 p.m. Acting-Sergeant Kirkham called a roll-call of his section. He had seen Private Rickman an hour earlier in the trenches, but now the Gallipoli veteran was missing. Rickman would later claim that he left the trenches at nightfall with the help of other soldiers:

Some time during the night of July 1st/2nd. I felt ill probably owing to a shell having burst very near me during the day. I was lying in the trench when two men led me away down the communication trench. I think these men belonged to the Middlesex Regiment, but I am not prepared to swear to that. These men put me in an ambulance motor which took me to a hospital tent where I remained one or two days.[4]

Back at the front line the Dublins spent their time repairing trenches, collecting the bodies of their dead comrades and helping the wounded.

The battalion war diary records that there were no casualties on 2 July. For the time being the slaughter was over; and for Rickman so too was his war. As his comrades remained on duty, Rickman says he was receiving medical help behind the lines.

From there [the hospital tent] I was taken to a hospital where I remained about a week. I am unable to say where the above mentioned tent or hospital were. At the hospital I was only given milk. After about a week I was given some papers which I have lost and told to rejoin my regiment.[5]

From hospital Rickman claims he was given a lift in a lorry to the outskirts of Abbeville, a town 80 miles to the north-west of Albert. The town was full of British soldiers; many were based there, and Rickman claimed it was at this point that he became worried about being away from his unit.

I was frightened about being absent from my regiment and therefore stayed at Abbeville. I must have been there for at least a week and got my food at the YMCA. I slept anywhere. One night the ground was wet so I crawled under a hut to sleep.[6]

Rickman's choice of hiding-place led to his discovery. The hut was used by soldiers of the Royal Engineers, including Sapper Chapman of the Signal Company. On the morning of 20 July, nearly three weeks after Rickman's desertion, Chapman noticed a bad smell around the hut. He thought it was coming from under the floor. He went outside to investigate and discovered what he thought was a sack wedged under the hut. Unable to move it, Chapman called for help from a staff-sergeant, and the pair of them tried to pull the 'sack' from under the hut. It would not budge, so the men removed the floorboards, only to discover Rickman lying underneath. He was wearing a coat and trousers but had no boots or socks. There was no sign of any army equipment by his side and Rickman was then arrested and taken to the guardroom. A lance-corporal began questioning him, and he was asked for his name and regiment. He told his questioner that his name was Andrews and that he came from No. 11 Platoon of the Hampshire Regiment. He would later admit to the lie. 'I gave a wrong name and regiment as I was frightened for I knew I ought to have been with my regiment.'7

Taken into custody by the military police, Rickman was charged with desertion. He was considered fit to be tried for the offence, and, nearly seven weeks after his arrest, his court martial was heard on 7 September before a major, a captain and another officer.

Rickman pleaded not guilty. His trial papers do not contain any details of any previous convictions but do include positive references to his past behaviour as a soldier. A lance-corporal who served with him wrote that he had known Rickman for eleven months and that in that time he had found him to be of good character, willing, hard-working and sober.

Rickman's commanding officer, Lieutenant-Colonel Nelson, who had sent him into battle on 1 July, had similar words of praise:

> From enquiries I have made from Senior NCOs who know him, I find that he has a good reputation as a fighting soldier. I feel convinced that he would never have committed the offence he has been convicted of, unless he had been temporarily bereft of his wits after the action of July 1st.[8]

Rickman made a plea for leniency after he was found guilty.

> I was wounded whilst serving with my 7th Battalion in Gallipoli. I was invalided home and joined the 1st Battalion home on active service in April 1916. I am willing to volunteer for any risky work.[9]

As a Gallipoli veteran, Rickman had experienced the disastrous landings at Suvla Bay, where many dozens of his comrades were gunned down as they tried to come ashore. He would have witnessed the horror of seeing bodies lie for days as they decomposed under the heat of the Mediterranean sun. He would also have had to avoid dysentery in the summer months and later frostbite in the winter; yet despite such hardship he volunteered again for active service after he was invalided home.

Rickman's war record and the kind words offered by some of his comrades did little to impress those in higher authority. After the court martial had found him guilty and sentenced him to death, the commanding officer of the 86th Infantry Brigade, Brigadier-General Williams, wrote:

> I recommend that the sentence be carried out. My reasons are that there is nothing to convince me that the crime was not deliberately carried out. I am of the opinion that with this battalion a strong and relentless discipline is necessary to maintain its fighting value.[10]

Four days after the brigadier-general's letter the death sentence was confirmed by Douglas Haig.

By September, Rickman's battalion had left the Somme and his former comrades were in action at the Ypres salient close to a place called Canal Bank. It was there, on 15 September, that the battalion's war diary records that as daybreak arrived Private Rickman was shot for desertion.

Albert Rickman's execution raises a number of fundamental issues. The sentence appears harsh when one considers that he had no record of previous convictions for desertion. His colleagues also spoke highly of his soldiering abilities and one officer wrote of the difficulties Rickman had faced after he lost many comrades in the first day at the Somme.

Was Rickman so traumatised and confused by the events of that bloody July day that he left his unit to seek help? Could his explanation that a shell landed near him during the day be the simple reason for his later absence from the trenches? Was he suffering from shell-shock, and was his condition missed, or ignored? It is difficult to assess Rickman's medical condition, but from the trial papers there is no evidence that his health was thoroughly investigated, except a brief report that says he was fit enough to face a court martial.

What is clear in this case is that senior officers believed that an example had to be made of Rickman; and that is exactly what happened.

However, an analysis of Rickman's unit shows that his comrades had a proud record of discipline, and desertion was not a problem. Records show that in 1916 Rickman was the only member of his battalion to be brought before a court martial. The battalion's war experience and the very difficult conditions at the Somme and at Ypres make that statistic all the more important.

However, what goes against Rickman is his verbal and written account of his absence and his attempt to deceive investigating officers when he was arrested. His story that he had medical treatment during his absence is hard to confirm, as he could provide neither places nor dates for when he received treatment. Similarly, his attempt to conceal his identity would have done little to win the hearts and minds of the court martial panel. On 15 September 1916, as day began on the Ypres salient, Albert Rickman's life ended.

———

Five days later, on 20 September, a Donegal man would become the latest absentee. Bernard McGeehan, a private with the 1st/8th (Irish) Battalion of the King's Liverpool Regiment, went missing as his battalion was preparing to go into action. The men of the Liverpool Regiment had experienced a bloody and devastating few weeks at the hands of their German opponents. In August half the battalion had become casualties in the attack on Guillemont. On high ground, the German-held village was a strategic point in their second line of defence and it could be approached only across uncovered land, known as 'Death Valley'. Since the start of the Somme offensive in July the area had remained in enemy hands and despite numerous attempts none of the British units had managed to capture it. Men from the Irish Battalion had briefly taken control of the village but, outnumbered and out-gunned, had been forced to surrender.

Bernard McGeehan was not a natural soldier. The 28-year-old's expertise lay not with guns or shells but with horses. Born in Raphoe, Co. Donegal, he moved to Derry as a young boy with his older brother Neil and sister Nellie. He first got a job with the Post Office as a messenger boy but then joined his father, who had established a successful business buying and selling horses.

Bernard's father bought and sold horses throughout Ireland and before the outbreak of the war shipped them to England, where many ended up being used by the army. Young Bernard was a great help to his father, often assisting him in transporting the animals from Dublin to Liverpool and then on to Chelsea Barracks and Wellington Barracks in London. By now the father-and-son team were a regular sight at the dockside in Dublin and Liverpool as they shipped their stock across the Irish Sea.

The pair were spending much of their time in Dublin, so the family decided to leave their home in the north and move south to a house on North Strand Road, Dublin. After the outbreak of war in the late summer of 1914, Bernard enlisted, joining the Irish Battalion of the King's Liverpool Regiment.

After training in Kent and Bedfordshire he arrived in France in May the following year. With his past experience of handling horses he was posted to the Transport Section and during his first few weeks in France his disciplinary record was unblemished. However, in July he went absent from duty, for which he was punished. Seven months later he fell foul of his superiors again when he failed to obey an order and lost some saddlery. This time he was fined to the value of the lost equipment and was also given field punishment no. 1.

By the late summer McGeehan's battalion was locked in the army's continuing struggle to gain ground at the Somme. The battle was already two months old and the much-talked-about breakthrough had failed to arrive. The regiment was still depleted from the heavy losses it had suffered earlier at Guillemont, but there was no time to dwell on the setback. After staying at Mametz, four miles east of Albert, the men were ordered back to the trenches; but Private McGeehan would not be with them this time. By daybreak on 20 September he had vanished.

Even nine decades later, McGeehan's precise movements at this time remain a mystery and the court martial papers give only scant information about his whereabouts. What is known is that before he disappeared he was in the guardroom on 17 September. No reason is given for his being there, but the papers state that he was released and handed back to his company. On the evening of 19 September Corporal Cooke showed McGeehan where to sleep. The next day, when his battalion marched off, he was reported missing.

Five days later he turned up at Montreuil, a town close to the coast and some hundred miles from Albert. In the town he approached Sergeant Law of the Royal Engineers:

> The accused came to me and asked for something to eat and drink as he had nothing for three days. I asked him where he came from and he said the Somme. I asked where he was going to. He said to join his regiment in Boulogne. I said I had nothing there, but I could

show him a place for both. I took him to the Assistant Provost-Marshal's office at Montreuil and handed him over.[11]

McGeehan was then questioned by a sergeant in the APM's office, who wanted to know where the Donegal man had travelled from.

I asked him how he came here. He said I have been walking for a week. I asked him where from. He said Ginchy. I asked him how he got past the posts. He said I dodged them.[12]

McGeehan is then reported to have told his questioner:

I got lost coming out of the trenches.[13]

Three days later Private McGeehan was escorted back to his regiment, but it was not a happy reunion. By now his colleagues were in Brandhoek and he was taken to the guardroom and locked up. He was charged with desertion, and on 21 October, just over a month after he went absent, he was brought before a court martial. The court papers are very brief and suggest that the hearing was not a lengthy one. McGeehan pleaded not guilty to desertion and in mitigation said:

Ever since I joined all the men have made fun of me, and I didn't know what I was doing when I went away. Every time I go to the trenches they throw stones at me and pretend it is shrapnel, and they call me all sorts of names. I have been out here 18 months and had no leave. I was in transport first. I had been with the battalion about two months when this happened.[14]

A character witness was then called to make a statement about McGeehan's behaviour and manner as a soldier. Second-Lieutenant McCabe, who was a contemporary of his from his days in Ireland, told the court martial:

I knew the accused before he joined the battalion. He used to be in the Londonderry Post Office as telegraph messenger about 15 years ago. He moved to Dublin with his father. I next saw him when he enlisted. He was with me when we came out to France. He was with transport. There was nothing against him at any time, except that he was inclined to be rather stupid.[15]

A damning report written by McGeehan's commanding officer, Lieutenant-Colonel Leech, is also contained with the court martial papers:

This man was employed in Transport section for some time; afterwards being returned to his company as useless. In the trenches he was afraid and appeared incapable of understanding orders.

The officer then added:

My opinion of this soldier is that he committed the crime deliberately with intent to avoid the particular service involved.

Then, in a brutal critique of McGeehan's ability, the lieutenant-colonel concluded his report with a line destined to seal the private's fate.

He seems of weak intellect and is worthless as a soldier.[16]

Bernard McGeehan was found guilty of desertion by a four-man court martial presided over by a major and staffed by three captains. The record of his military trial is in the National Archives in London. The eleven-page document, which was confidential for seventy-five years, lacks detail and may well have been edited. The papers do not give any indication whether McGeehan was given any legal representation or offered the services of another soldier or 'prisoner's friend' who could speak on his behalf.

After finding him guilty, the panel recommended that he be shot for the crime. Writing the next day, Brigadier-General Clifton Stockwell, who commanded the 164th Infantry Brigade, stated:

The character of the accused from a fighting point of view is indifferent. His general behaviour is however good. The state of discipline of his battalion is good except with regard to crimes of desertion in which respect it is bad. The opinion of the commanding officer is attached (Lt Col. Leech) I concur in his opinion that the crime was deliberately committed with intent to avoid going into battle. I recommend that the sentence be carried out in view of the above reasons.[17]

That view was endorsed by the Commander-in-Chief, Douglas Haig, who confirmed the sentence a week later. On 2 November 1916 at sixteen minutes past six in the morning, at Poperinge, near Ypres, Bernard McGeehan was shot by firing squad.

At the core of this case are essentially three issues: McGeehan's behaviour, his suitability as a soldier and the way he was treated. Though he had disciplinary problems in the past, they were quite minor compared with his final offence. Officers did accept that McGeehan's soldiering abilities were limited. What they did not comment on—assuming McGeehan's claims were correct—was the issue of bullying and his mental state.

Julian Putkowski argues that the officers dismissed McGeehan's story too easily:

The officers who sentenced him to death gave no thought to the evidence that McGeehan's nervousness might have been made worse by the bullying. Nor did it ever occur to the officers who purported to claim great familiarity with McGeehan's purportedly innate weakness in combat, that the soldier could have been a military asset if he had been drafted to serve in a non-fighting capacity.[18]

McGeehan's military trial and the subsequent execution were investigated by the Irish government in 2004. The report of their investigation into his death was compiled by officials of the Department of Foreign Affairs, and it concluded:

All the evidence in this case points directly to Private McGeehan being of the disposition as to either not comprehend orders in time of battle, or simply being unable mentally to cope with life as a soldier. His state of mind was further adversely affected by his treatment at the hands of the other men, but the question remains to be answered as to the intellect of a man who is so unnerved by being in the trenches that he can actually be convinced he is under attack when the other men are throwing stones at him.[19]

The report also stated that it was a 'damning indictment' that senior officers did not see the connection between the character references and McGeehan's subsequent action. The investigation also emphasised the lack of a prisoner's friend, particularly as it was 'well known that he was intellectually incapable of even the most basic tasks.'

More than ninety years after his death, the case of Bernard McGeehan has been championed by someone who had an understandable reason to see the Donegal man pardoned. John McGeehan is a second cousin of Bernard's, and not only has he investigated his relative's death but he now runs the Welsh office of the pressure group Shot at Dawn, which campaigned for pardons. He believes Bernard was subjected to treatment that would now be classed as bullying:

I do believe he was picked on because he was Irish. He was clearly seen by some officers as a thick 'Paddy'. Today Bernard would probably have been classed as 'special needs'. He was not very bright. He was used to being in the background looking after the horses, then suddenly he is pushed into the front line and he cracked. We all crack some time, and Bernard was susceptible to machine-gun fire and shelling.[20]

Bernard McGeehan was the last Irishman to be executed while the Battle of the Somme still raged. His death in November 1916 came during the conflict's final throes. The weather finally brought the fighting to an end, after snow and then a thaw had turned the battlefield into a waterlogged quagmire. The twenty-week campaign had seen the British line advance some seven miles at a cost of one million casualties on both sides—a hundred men for every yard.

Chapter 7 ~

THE SHOCK OF BATTLE

I lose my head in the trenches. At times I do not know what I am doing at all.
—PRIVATE JOSEPH CAREY, 7TH BATTALION, ROYAL IRISH
FUSILIERS

It was a momentous objective to try to force the German army to retreat and then seize the high ground—an ambitious plan that would ultimately take eighteen months to achieve. For Samuel McBride this was his last big chance to make a name for himself.

A member of the 2nd Battalion of the Royal Irish Rifles, the 26-year-old was dug in at the strategic escarpment of Vimy Ridge, 25 miles north of the Somme. The area had become a crucial battleground, the scene of a series of long-running assaults and counter-attacks by the Germans. The Allied forces knew that if they could secure the ridge they would have a commanding view of what was going on behind the German front line. First the French had tried to control it, but the Germans had dug in and built a series of tunnels under it. Now, in the middle of 1916, it was the turn of the British to try to succeed where the French had failed.

The fighting in May 1916, two months before the Battle of the Somme would begin, was particularly fierce. The shelling was intense and heavy and the daily toll of casualties was high. For Rifleman McBride it was an opportunity to prove his worth as a soldier. Though he had joined the battalion in January 1915 he had seen little military action, because within days of joining the British Expeditionary Force he had fallen foul of his superiors.

He had deserted the ranks in the early days of 1915. He was apprehended quickly and on 25 January was sentenced to two years' imprisonment. In May he escaped from prison, was rearrested the next day and once again found himself back in jail. This time McBride remained behind bars for eight months, until January 1916, when he was freed and then rejoined his old comrades in the Royal Irish Rifles.

With his jail sentence suspended it seemed that he was a reformed character. In May, as he and members of his battalion launched an assault against the Germans, the rifleman began to win praise for his soldiering. One colleague would remark:

I always found him a good and willing worker, both in and out of the trenches. I saw Rifleman McBride in action on Vimy Ridge about 8 May 1916 . . . He was carrying bombs to the front line. On this occasion he was working very hard.[1]

During May, McBride and his fellow-Ulstermen were at the heart of the assaults on Vimy Ridge and by the middle of the month their daily lives had developed a certain routine. Two of the battalion's companies would be put in the front line and the two others would be placed in reserve. Then the companies would swap places and those soldiers who had been resting would go into battle later in the day.

By 17 May McBride's company had been withdrawn for some rest, but it seems they got little chance of a respite. The Germans began shelling the ground where the Irish troops were positioned, and there were numerous casualties.

McBride's platoon was expected to return to the front line later that day, but when the men assembled it became clear that something was wrong, as Sergeant Kelly would recall:

On the day in question the accused's platoon were back [from the front line] and the ordinary custom was followed . . . They fell in at 'stand to' to carry material to the front line at 4.30 p.m.

Immediately after 4.30 p.m. I received a report from the accused's platoon Sergeant, who is now away wounded about the accused. In consequence I made a report to the company officer and the follow-ing morning I searched for the accused and found that he was absent. I went round all the brigade dressing stations to look for him but could not find him, nor could I find any trace of him passing through any dressing station.[2]

McBride had disappeared. He would later explain how he came to be separated from his colleagues.

> While we were on the Vimy Ridge, I was very tired and very sore on my feet. I had a headache and I felt bad all over. I went into a dugout and lay down and went to sleep. When I woke up I saw some KRR [King's Royal Rifle Corps] men and asked them if they had seen the Irish Rifles. They told me they had gone out, so I tried to find out where the regiment was but there was no one who could tell me where they were. I had been in the dugout about a day and a half.[3]

The rifleman explained how he had spent his time away from his battalion:

> I left my rifle and equipment at St Eloi where I slept the night after I left. I left them because they were taken away from me during the night. My health was pretty good while I was wandering about. I managed to get something to eat here and there from soldiers whom I saw. I was trying all the time to find the Irish Rifles. I told a lot of NCOs and men I had lost my rifle. I did not know I ought to report to an officer or to anyone who could tell me what I ought to do. I had no intention whatever of leaving the regiment. I walked along roads and by day made no attempt to conceal my movements.[4]

Rifleman McBride would remain at large for the rest of the summer of 1916. His four-month unofficial leave of absence would come to an end in the middle of September. It is not clear where and how he spent his time away from his comrades, but it seems likely that he spent long periods of it sleeping rough, away from the prying eyes of military patrols. By 17 September he had travelled north towards the coast and had reached a military hospital at Outreau, near the port of Boulogne. A lance-corporal in the military police discovered the runaway soldier in a tent and three days later, under armed escort, the Ulsterman was handed back to his original battalion in the Royal Irish Rifles.

Normally a court martial would have been hastily convened within days, but on this occasion McBride was to wait for two months to know his fate. An administrative bungle over the number and availability of witnesses meant that proceedings did not begin until late November.

When the trial took place, two sergeants in McBride's battalion gave him good references. Sergeant Kelly, his platoon sergeant, wrote: 'I have always found him a willing worker an all round good soldier and willing at all times to volunteer for any dangerous work to be carried out.'[5]

An officer stated that although there had been five previous cases of desertion in the battalion the discipline in the battalion was good. It seems clear that McBride's imprisonment for a previous case of desertion sealed his fate and on 28 November one of his senior officers wrote, 'I can give no reason why the extreme penalty should not be inflicted in this case.'[6]

McBride was given no legal representation during the hearing and he spoke in his own defence. The four-man panel, which included a Captain Ferguson from McBride's own battalion, found him guilty of desertion and sentenced him to death. Although Haig commuted the overwhelming majority of cases that crossed his desk, he was not inclined to give the Ulsterman another chance. McBride's previous desertion and his escape from prison did little to engender sympathy. The recommendation of senior officers also carried much weight.

On Monday 4 December, Haig confirmed the death penalty. He was to have a busy week sanctioning executions. Two days later he would be presented with another case of desertion, this time concerning an officer who had left the ranks. Haig would write in his diary that day:

This is the first sentence of death on an officer to be put into execution since I became Commander-in-Chief. Such a crime is more serious in the case of an officer than of a man, and also it is highly important that all ranks should realise that the law is the same for an officer as a private.[7]

The next day Rifleman Samuel McBride was taken to Hope Farm near Ploegsteert Wood, south of the village of Messines. Shortly after seven o'clock in the blackness of a December morning he was placed before a firing squad made up of men from his own battalion. These were men he knew: comrades he had trained with, joked with and fought alongside. At ten minutes past seven he was dead, killed by his own countrymen. Today his grave, marked with the traditional white headstone, can be found at the Hyde Park Corner of the Commonwealth war graves on the Ypres salient.

Ninety years later, what assessment can we make of Samuel McBride's treatment? Clearly, senior officers felt his soldiering worth was minimal, as he had absconded in effect three times—twice from his colleagues and once from prison. His imprisonment had not reformed him and commanders had to deal with a soldier who, it seemed, wanted to fight only when it suited him.

Senior officers also wanted to send a message to other soldiers regarding desertion and so McBride's death was used to keep other soldiers in line—particularly as five others had deserted from the battalion.

There is one area of McBride's story, however, that has received little examination. The military hearing did not consider that his experience on Vimy Ridge had left him shell-shocked and contributed to his desertion and later behaviour. McBride's medical claims do not appear to have been thoroughly investigated.

It is this issue of health that officials of the Department of Foreign Affairs examined in 2004. As part of their submission to the British government, the Irish officials concluded in their report that McBride's treatment raised a number of important questions:

> The symptoms described by the accused in his defence would seem to be consistent with what we know of shell shock, in that tiredness and general non specific pain were very much evident. This, the fatigue experienced as a result of enduring a prolonged bombardment and the effect of so many colleagues being lost, were not taken into account by the courts-martial, or the confirmation process.[8]

The term 'shell-shock', used in the Irish government report, is now firmly part of our language, but at the start of the Great War it had never been heard. It is thought to have been first used in 1915 in an article written by a University of Cambridge psychologist, Charles Myers, which appeared in the *Lancet,* a leading medical journal. When war broke out he began working at the Duchess of Westminster Hospital in Le Touquet in France. Here he encountered soldiers who had seen action in the front line and had been subjected to shelling at close range.

Myers began to notice that a number of men appeared to have suffered some form of mental breakdown or nervous collapse. Some were exhibiting erratic behaviour, becoming uncontrollable and suffering mental relapses. Myers began to investigate this condition and after examining numerous soldiers and investigating their backgrounds eventually named it 'shell-shock'. The term quickly became part of military parlance, and by 1916 it is estimated that Charles Myers had seen two thousand patients with shell-shock and similar disorders.

The army hierarchy was naturally wary of this research, and some senior officers believed the 'condition' would be used by some soldiers as a way of avoiding duty. When soldiers who were charged with desertion used the 'shell-shock' defence it was routinely challenged during their court martial.

There was also a belief among many officers that the lower ranks were using this new 'condition' to explain away cowardice or fear. Lieutenant-Colonel Frank Maxwell, who would win a Victoria Cross for his bravery, had little time for the term.

Shell shock is a complaint, which to my mind, is too prevalent everywhere; and I have told my people that my name for it is fright, or something worse, and I am not going to have it.[9]

Other officers higher up the chain of command had similar thoughts. When Douglas Haig was asked to spare the life of Private Arthur Earp, a soldier with the Royal Warwickshire Regiment who had claimed to have been shell-shocked during the Battle of the Somme, he wrote: 'How can we ever win if this plea is allowed.'[10]

———

The day after Arthur Earp was executed another soldier faced a firing squad in similar circumstances. Like Earp, the Irishman James Cassidy would claim that his nerves had been affected by the battle conditions, and, like the Warwickshire soldier, his appeals for clemency would be given short shrift by senior officers, including Haig.

Cassidy, a 38-year-old private with the Royal Inniskilling Fusiliers, was one of the oldest Irishmen to be executed during the Great War. An experienced solder, he had enlisted in August 1914 when war broke out, joining the Inniskillings in 1915. The same year he took part in the landings at Gallipoli, where he was wounded twice and then hospitalised for five months. By June 1916 he and his comrades in the 1st Battalion were on the Western Front, close to Louvencourt.

Cassidy had a record of misdemeanours. He had been rude to a senior officer and had been drunk on duty and most recently had left his post for a number of hours without permission. His last offence had resulted in a field punishment for ten days. On 23 June, when his punishment ended, Cassidy was handed back to his company by Sergeant Lyons, who was responsible for keeping watch on the prisoners.

> The accused and the other prisoners were daily handed over to their companies who were practising for the attack—on the day the battalion left Louvencourt on the 23rd of June the accused was handed over to his company to go up to the firing line. It was common knowledge that the battalion was going to attack in a short time, after a bombardment of five days.[11]

The next day Cassidy was on watch in the early morning from 8 to 9 a.m. Private Connolly, who was in the same platoon, had the same job as his comrade, but his stint was a little later, between 10 and 11. When Connolly finished his shift he went for some food at one of the dugouts, and discovered that someone had not eaten his rations. He then realised that his platoon colleague was missing. Connolly, who by now was the only surviving member of his platoon, reported the matter to his superiors, and Cassidy was officially listed as missing.

Within days the mystery was solved. On 30 June, Cassidy was discovered walking along the canal at the nearby town of Flexicourt. He was approached by a private in the French army, who asked the Irishman for his papers. He failed to produce his army identification and he was arrested and then handed over to the British military police.

Three weeks later Cassidy appeared before a court martial charged with desertion. He claimed that his disappearance was a result of shellshock.

> On the morning I was charged with leaving my dugout, I went to the latrine and while there a shell came along and exploded beside me. I was covered with clay by the explosion. I got nerve shock and proceeded down the trenches. I wandered from the trenches and did not know where I was going. I was two days and two nights wan-

dering about the country. When I came to the canal I was arrested by the French. I was wounded in the Dardanelles on 16 August 1915 and have ever since been nervous of shell fire.[12]

Cassidy pleaded not guilty to the charge of desertion. He had no legal assistance and represented himself during the proceedings.

During the trial an unsigned confidential note was produced that had clearly been written by one of his superior officers. It contained a number of comments that may have given Cassidy some hope that the court would show some leniency towards him. The note read:

His general character was bad but from a fighting point of view his conduct was fair. He has never shown cowardice in the firing line to my knowledge, he did his sentry duty and other duties satisfactorily in the trenches. My opinion is that Cassidy did not leave the trenches with the sole object of avoiding duty there. He was of an insubordinate and morose disposition and I question whether he is entirely responsible for what he does. He was without a sense of discipline and would not in my opinion be capable of considering the consequences of his actions. I do not think he was at all the kind of man to consider his own safety at that time or any other.[13]

This note, with the vital line 'My opinion is that Cassidy did not leave the trenches with the sole object of avoiding duty there,' failed to convince the court martial. He was found guilty of desertion and sentenced to death.

There was to be no leniency either from senior officers, who endorsed the finding and agreed that the fusilier should be executed. The major-general commanding the 29th Division supported the decision, even though he acknowledged that the discipline in the battalion was excellent. His view was also endorsed by Haig, who sanctioned the execution on 20 July. Three days later, on 23 July 1916, James Cassidy was placed before a firing squad and shot.

The irony of Cassidy's death is obvious. Here was a veteran who had survived the horrors of Gallipoli and dodged Turkish fire, who had experienced the slaughter of the Western Front and escaped German shelling, and yet it was a British bullet that would ultimately kill him.

The Irish government, which investigated Cassidy's case in 2004, believed his death was needless and could have been avoided.

Presented with the most convincing of evidence that Private Cassidy was suffering some form of mental illness, and taking into account the excellent discipline in the battalion, how the confirming officers could see no extenuating circumstances in which to recommend leniency or to commute the sentence is very difficult to understand. This case personifies the blatant ignorance of the military at the time to the debilitating medical conditions experienced by men who carried out prolonged periods of service in the front line.[14]

In 1916 other soldiers in Irish regiments were also feeling the strain of life in the mud and mayhem of the Western Front, including Private Joseph Carey, a Dubliner with the 8th Battalion of the Royal Irish Fusiliers. The 35-year-old, from the North Wall area of Dublin, had enlisted in April 1915, arriving at the Western Front in February 1916 after sailing from Southampton.

It was in Hampshire, before the battalion travelled to France, that Carey's first disciplinary problems began. He ignored orders and went absent without leave. The following month his punishment was considered and he was given fourteen days' detention.

In France, Carey and his comrades, as part of the 16th (Irish) Division, found themselves at the front line within weeks. The battalion was placed close to Hulluch on the Loos salient. In late April, along with other Irish battalions, they were attacked by Germans of the 4th Bavarian Division. The raid came in the early morning of 27 April, when the British front line was threatened with a mixture of artillery fire and gas. Later, hand-to-hand fighting took place, and over a period of three days the 16th Division suffered heavy losses. By nightfall on 29 April there were nearly two thousand casualties.

Much of the devastation in the Irish ranks had been caused by the gas the Germans had released. One Inniskilling fusilier would later recall the horrors of this type of warfare. 'It is I can assure you, worse than being wounded or even killed, as the agony is terrible.'[15]

On 4 May, five days after the German day attack, Joseph Carey left the British line without permission. His disappearance was quickly discovered and he was found guilty of being absent without leave. On

16 May he was given field punishment no. 1 and for ninety days was tethered to a cartwheel or a stake in the field for two hours each day. For Carey's superiors the advantage of this punishment over detention was that he was still available for active service throughout this time.

The punishment and public embarrassment did little to persuade Carey to stay in the ranks. During the weeks of May and June the Irish Division continued to serve in the front line. Men were under constant attack from shell, machine gun and gas. As the summer took hold the casualties grew. In the middle of June, Carey walked away from his duties on two occasions. On 14 June his battalion colleague Sergeant Featherston warned him for duty, and later in the day, when he called the roll, Carey was absent. The next day he was discovered in a billet while his battalion was in the trenches. He told officers that he was suffering from loss of memory and did not remember leaving his unit, which he said was in the trenches.

Five days later Sergeant Featherston spoke to Carey again. Mindful of what had happened only days earlier, and being acutely aware of his poor disciplinary record, he told Carey what was expected of him:

I warned the accused that his platoon were to move support trenches to front line trenches at 8 p.m. that evening. On falling in the platoon and calling the roll I found the accused absent.[16]

The following afternoon the absentee was found by an off-duty lance-corporal. He knew where Carey's battalion was, so he questioned him about why he was not with them. Carey replied that he was lost. He was then charged with two counts of desertion, one on 15 June, the other five days later.

His military trial was scheduled for August, but before it took place a medical board met to consider Carey's mental health. The three-man panel concluded that he was of sound mind and that there was no evidence that he was insane when he had left his post on 15 June.

On 21 August his court martial was convened, and Private Carey pleaded not guilty to the charges. He asked no questions of the witnesses that were produced by the prosecution, but he did speak:

I lose my head in the trenches. I do not know what I am doing at all. My family is afflicted the same way. My father committed suicide over it. My brother's death in Phoenix Park Five years ago on the 17th March 1916 was due to the same thing.[17]

The court martial found Carey guilty of both charges of desertion. Though death was recommended, the finding was that mercy should be shown, on the grounds of Carey's 'defective intellect'. After he was made aware of the findings Carey stated in mitigation:

Though I am affected the way I am by heavy shelling. I try to do my best. I came up voluntarily to serve my King and Country.[18]

What followed Carey's military hearing was a bureaucratic paper chase that would take three weeks to conclude. Within days of the verdict a letter written by the brigadier-general began the process. He suggested that Carey's crimes were deliberately committed and that, because discipline in the battalion was not good, the sentence should be carried out. The next day Major-General William Hickie of the 16th Division put pen to paper and entered the Carey debate, but he came to a very different conclusion. He wanted to show compassion to the accused. 'I recommend that the sentence be commuted and the prisoner be given a chance to redeem his character in the near future.'[19]

Hickie's was to be a lone voice. A popular officer, Major-General Hickie was a thoughtful, tactful man who cared deeply about his men. Barely was the ink dry on his report when another opinion was proffered, this time from the pen of the lieutenant-general commanding the First Army. He recommended that the sentence be carried out, as it was 'apparently committed deliberately.' The next day Carey was sent to hospital in Boulogne with an abscess in his groin.

By the end of August 1916 the 16th Division had moved from Loos down to the Somme in readiness for battle. The change meant that the division was no longer under the control of the First Army and was now part of the Fourth Army, commanded by General Henry Rawlinson. The change of command meant also that Joseph Carey had new guardians. As he received hospital treatment, more questions were being raised about his case. A captain in the Fourth Army wrote to the Deputy Judge Advocate-General requesting advice.

Will you please advise as to the validity of the convictions in this case. The medical evidence contained some hearsay, but I doubt if it need be taken as invalidating the case.[20]

By now questions were also being raised about why Carey's execution had not been carried out. On 8 September the commander of the Fourth Army, General Rawlinson, wrote:

I am unable to account for the unusual delay in trying this man as the offence occurred in 1 Army—Had it not been for this delay I should have recommended that the sentence be put into execution.[21]

Four days later the paper trail came to an end when Carey's file landed on Haig's desk. He took the majority view and ignored any suggestion of clemency promoted by Hickie, and on 12 September he sanctioned Joseph Carey's execution. Three days later, as daylight began to filter across the Somme valley, Joseph Carey was shot by a firing squad.

Like the executions of other Irishmen, Carey's death raises a range of important questions. What is intriguing, though not uncommon, is that a senior officer's plea for leniency was ignored by the Commander-in-Chief, and the recommendation for leniency made at the original trial was also ignored.

In 2004, officials of the Irish government concluded:

This is a particularly shocking case. Presented with evidence of a family history of mental problems the court martial verdict recommended clemency on the grounds of a defective intellect. That this recommendation was ignored in the confirmation process, taking into consideration the fact that the medical evidence contained some form of hearsay, is very difficult to comprehend. There is no mention on file that Private Carey was evaluated at one of the British 'shell shock' centres which evaluated mental illness.[22]

The report's authors added:

It can only be assumed [that] his medical and mental problems were ignored as the discipline in the battalion was not good at the time, and an example was thought necessary in spite of the recognition by the court of his aforementioned difficulties.[23]

What conclusions can be reached about the execution of Joseph Carey? The court martial files make it clear that the military authorities considered him to be a fit and able soldier who was simply shirking his responsibilities and his record of deserting did little to engender sympathy at higher levels. It is also apparent that any personal difficulties he may have encountered were not entertained by the senior command and that a decision was reached early on in the proceedings that an execution was needed to keep discipline in order. That would support Douglas Haig's blunt decision to ignore both the court martial ruling and Major-General Hickie's call for clemency.

Hickie's comments were crucial but were not acted upon. A respected figure, Hickie could not be viewed as a 'soft touch'. On other occasions he had recommended death by firing squad, and in this case he was well placed to judge what punishment was necessary.

Why were Hickie's comments ignored? What is clear is that Carey's battalion did have a discipline problem. Figures compiled by Timothy Bowman show that between December 1915 and September 1916 the battalion conducted seventy-three courts martial, a figure much higher than those for Irish battalions in other brigades. The figure seems particularly high when one considers that Carey's battalion arrived in France only in February 1916. Significantly, in September, the month of Carey's death, as his former comrades fought at the Somme, the number of courts martial in the battalion fell to three—the lowest figure in six months. Was this a coincidence?

Joseph Carey's death may well have been the catalyst that kept his comrades out of trouble and in the trenches. However, it did not stop other Irish soldiers in other regiments falling foul of the authorities.

Chapter 8 ∿

LOOKING FOR HOPE

I had no intention of going absent when I left the trenches.
It was a sudden impulse.

—PRIVATE THOMAS HOPE, 2ND BATTALION, LEINSTER
REGIMENT, 1915

1916 would not only herald the Easter Rising and the Battle of the Somme—two pivotal moments in the history of Ireland—but it was also the year in which the secret world of British military executions would begin to be exposed. Two Irish parliamentarians would help to bring the story into the open and their pointed questions in the House of Commons would spark a national debate.

During the first year of the Great War the treatment of those executed for desertion and cowardice had largely remained a mystery. The detail of the 'shootings at dawn' were not for public consumption. To the army's top brass these were military matters, private affairs about the discipline of soldiers, which in their view were of no consequence to the outside world. And there was another fundamental reason why the government and the army hierarchy wanted to keep the executions secret. The military authorities knew that recruitment levels at home could be seriously affected if the full details of the battlefield executions were made public.

As the establishment tried to cover up how those charged with desertion were being treated, it was inevitable that some information would leak out. At home, most of the families of the executed men knew some of the details about their loved one's deaths. Their accounts were sketchy, often based on limited official correspondence, combined with the stories of eye witnesses and friends who had served with the deceased. Despite what was known, however, the families preferred to keep their stories private, and so unwittingly the relatives added to a culture of secrecy. Many families were embarrassed and felt stigmatised at having a so-called coward in the family, and understandably they had little reason to make public the details of their case. This meant that in the early months of the war this was one story that no-one wanted to talk about and it remained well away from the public gaze.

In 1916, however, the first glimpses of this hidden world began to emerge. In January, Philip Snowden, MP for Blackburn, asked the Under-Secretary of State for War, Harold John Tennant, if he could state how many soldiers had been shot for desertion and other offences since the war began in August 1914. Tennant was evasive, arguing that it was not in the public interest to give details. He added: 'But I will ask my honourable friend if he will be good enough not to believe that the number has been considerable.'[1]

If Tennant had hoped this reply would stifle debate and end the matter he made a grave mistake. Snowden's question prompted many more enquiries from MPs, including the Irish Party MP for East Limerick, Thomas Lundon. In March he stood up in the House of Commons and questioned Tennant. Lundon was interested in the way the relatives of those shot for desertion were being informed. He asked whether it was true that post-cards were used to notify the parents of executed soldiers of the death of their son. Lundon thought it was better if the details of the courts martial and executions were left off the card. Tennant was taken aback by the question and answered accordingly:

I am not aware that deaths taking place in the circumstances being mentioned have been notified by means of an open post card. Record offices are provided with forms on which to notify deaths. As regards the last part of the question, it has been decided that as, in these cases, the relatives were bound to know sooner or later, the circumstances of death, it was better that they should be informed at once.[2]

By now a growing number of MPs had seized on the issue. Tennant found himself being questioned relentlessly about the subject, and then MPs began to become interested in the precise nature of certain cases. By mid-summer, campaigners were becoming fascinated by the specifics as well as the general arguments.

In May, J. P. Farrell, MP for North Longford and owner of the *Longford Leader*, raised the case of a young Irishman, Thomas Hope, a private with the 2nd Battalion of the Leinster Regiment. Twenty-year-old Hope from Mullingar, Co. Westmeath, had been executed a year earlier in the spring of 1915. Farrell wanted to know when Hope had been told that he faced execution. He also wanted to know if Hope's good record had been examined during the court martial, and whether or not he had been defended. Tennant responded to Farrell's questions by stating that Thomas Hope had been told of his sentence well in advance of it being carried out. He added that the Irishman had called no evidence regarding his previous conduct, and that counsel could not be employed in the field.

Private Thomas Hope's tragic story began two days before Christmas 1914 when he and his colleagues were based in the front-line trenches at L'Épinette. The battalion war diary records that it was a 'quiet day' and that snow fell in the morning.

That night Hope was part of a ration party with three other men. The party left the trenches at 6:30 p.m. As he walked back, Hope decided he had had enough of life at the front line. He left the trenches after he claims he became upset on hearing that his two brothers, also serving in the army, had died. He would later tell his court martial:

I had no intention of going absent when I left the trenches. It was a sudden impulse. The first night I was away I got by mistake into the German trenches. The enemy kept me for three days and took me to their headquarters at Lille. I escaped from the Germans during an attack and got into the French trenches and stayed there two days. Then I met some British troops and stayed there some 3 or 4 days. I have been walking around since and tried to find my own regiment.[3]

Hope would be absent from his unit as it celebrated its first Christmas of the war. Like others stationed near Armentières, a town south of Ypres, men from the Leinster Regiment witnessed the unofficial Christmas Day truce.

The ceasefire and the gatherings that took place between British and German soldiers would become part of First World War folklore. For a few short hours the horror of war was suspended as men who had spent weeks trying to kill each other smoked and drank together, swapped souvenirs, and even played football. To some it marked the true spirit of Christmas, a story of peace and human kindness that brought to an end a bloody and dramatic year, a year that would be seen as a watershed in world history. As soldiers on both sides celebrated the festive season as best they could under the most difficult circumstances, a senior officer with the Leinster Regiment recorded the day's events in his battalion war diary.

> Christmas Day. Without previous arrangement, but apparently by mutual consent, this has become a day of peace. No shots have been fired on our right or centre, but on the left there has been a little hostile sniping. Our men have been digging outside in front of their trenches whilst the Germans have buried some dead that lay between the two lines. Later, some consultations between the two sides took place in the open, both officers and men of both sides being concerned.[4]

The officer added:

> Christmas Cards from H.M. the King and H.M. the Queen and Presents from H.R.H. Princess Mary received and issued to the troops today.[5]

The Christmas truce was frowned upon by the army's hierarchy. The officer in command of the Second Army, General Sir Horace Smith-Dorrien, who would later have a role in Thomas Hope's case, was very unhappy about British troops fraternising with the enemy. A veteran commander, Smith-Dorrien visited the front line on St Stephen's Day and issued a stern warning to those who were tempted to lay down their arms and walk into no-man's-land to share the Christmas spirit with German soldiers.

> To finish this war quickly, we must keep up the fighting spirit and do all we can to discourage friendly intercourse. I am calling for particulars as to names of officers and units who took part in the Christmas gathering, with a view to disciplinary action.[6]

No-one knows exactly where or how Thomas Hope spent his first Christmas in France, but it certainly was not with his comrades. His absence would last throughout the festive period and stretch well into the new year. In total he would be missing for nearly seven weeks, and he would eventually turn up in the nearby town of Armentières. On 9 February he was found dressed in a greatcoat with a lance-corporal's stripe and a police badge. According to the arresting officer he was drunk and when he was challenged gave the false name of Lance-Corporal Stout.

Hope was charged with desertion, drunkenness and conduct prejudicial to good order and military discipline. He insisted that he was not a deserter and was attempting to find his regiment when he was arrested. However, when the court martial met to consider his behaviour it is clear that his story was not believed. His previous record went against him: he had three previous convictions for going absent without leave and was described by his commanding officer as a bad example to other soldiers. The officer stated:

Private Hope had made up his mind not to serve creditably.

And he concluded:

I am of the opinion that the act of desertion for which he is now under sentence was part of his normal way of conduct, to avoid all military duty as far as possible.[7]

Hope's court martial met on 14 February. He was not defended at his trial, and after hearing the evidence the three-man panel found him guilty and sentenced him to death. Senior officers would later endorse the panel's findings.

General Sir Horace Smith-Dorrien, who had sought to discipline the soldiers involved in the Christmas Day truce, was equally angry at the behaviour of Thomas Hope. Nine days after Hope's sentence was handed down the veteran commander put pen to paper.

The Brigade discipline is 2nd worst and the battalion discipline also the 2nd worst in the Army. The case is a very bad one indeed and I recommend that the extreme penalty be carried out.[8]

By now the Irishman's destiny was sealed and within days of Smith-Dorrien's comments the death sentence was confirmed by the Commander-in-Chief, Sir John French.

The evening of 1 March 1915 was Thomas Hope's last night. He was kept under guard, and the next morning at 7 a.m. he was taken from custody and placed before a firing squad and shot. Little is known of his last moments. His military file offers little detail, except to record that the execution was carried out by a captain.

Thomas Hope has no known grave, but his name is commemorated on the memorial at Ploegsteert, about ten miles south of Ypres, where much of the fraternisation between the Germans and the British took place at Christmas 1914.

His case illustrates the old adage that history has a habit of repeating itself. In 2003, nearly ninety years after an Irish politician first brought up the matter with the British government, another Irish voice was raised within earshot of a British Minister. Brian Cowen, then Minister for Foreign Affairs, may not have been aware of the remarks of J. P. Farrell in the House of Commons in 1916 but his sentiments were the same. Just as Farrell had tackled the British government over the treatment of Thomas Hope, Brian Cowen would follow suit in his discussions with British Ministers. He would later ask his officials in the Department of Foreign Affairs to investigate Hope's case and that of the twenty-five other Irish-born soldiers who were executed.

The report by the Department of Foreign Affairs would conclude that in Thomas Hope's case a number of important questions remained unanswered—questions that go to the heart of his story.

> The file and the confirmation process particularly, indicate that Private Hope's story including the death of two brothers, was not verified by the court even though it would be easy to do so in the latter instance given that the names of Private Hope's brothers were known. However improbable his story may seem, it is the purpose of the court to ascertain the truth—was there an attack on German positions in Lille toward the end of 1914? The discipline in Private Hope's unit proved to be the fatal factor in the deliberations of the court and those who subsequently confirmed his death sentence.[9]

Thomas Hope's court martial file makes reference to his claims that his two brothers had been killed in action. The file states, however, that his claim was not verified and that the brothers could have been Private Hope in the Royal Munster Fusiliers and Driver J. Hope in the Royal

Field Artillery. There is no evidence on the file that Hope's other claims regarding his capture by the Germans were investigated.

What clearly swayed the trial was Hope's history of disappearing, his length of absence and suggestions that there was a problem of discipline in the battalion. It is clear that senior officers wanted to use Hope's execution as an example to bring wayward soldiers back into line and improve discipline. Only one other soldier from Hope's regiment had been sentenced to death since the outbreak of the war. In November 1914 a soldier from the 2nd Battalion of the Leinster Regiment was found guilty of cowardice, but his death sentence was commuted to two years' imprisonment. Was Hope shot because senior officers believed it would be wrong to let a second offender escape the firing squad?

———

Hope became the first soldier from his regiment to be executed, but he was not the only Irish soldier to disappear from the ranks in the early months of the war. 1915 was only a few weeks old when a private in the Royal Munster Fusiliers left the trenches and, amazingly, would not be discovered for most of the year.

The story of Private James Graham and his disappearance has become one of the most intriguing 'shot at dawn' cases. The 21-year-old was the son of Jane Graham, who lived in the Old Market Place, Cork. Graham was joined in his battalion by natives of his home city and men from Tralee and Fermoy, towns with a strong attachment to the regiment.

In the summer of 1914 the battalion had been stationed in Aldershot, Hampshire, and in August as part of the British Expeditionary Force the men from Munster had landed at Le Havre days after war had been declared. In the opening weeks of 1915 Private Graham and his colleagues in the 2nd Battalion of the Royal Munster Fusiliers were stationed in trenches close to the front line at Cuinchy. Some thirty miles south of Ypres, the village of Cuinchy was home to hundreds of British soldiers and in the early hours of 25 January the men came under heavy attack from German shelling.

In his diary for that day Douglas Haig, then commanding the First Army, would write about how the attack affected nearby towns and villages.

It was difficult to know exactly what was going on because the tele-
phone wires had been broken by artillery fire. As usual in such chaos
the first reports were very alarming indeed . . .[10]

James Graham was not around to see how the attack had affected
the front line. The next day, after a roll-call was taken, he could not be
found. The Cork man would tell his court martial that a corporal
had asked him to leave his equipment in the trenches and report to
battalion headquarters. Graham would later state that when he got
back to headquarters the corporal did not arrive. There is no official
account of what Graham did next, but it is clear that he did not return
to the trenches and there is no record of his attempting to rejoin his
comrades.

Graham's disappearance must have puzzled his superiors and for
nine months he evaded capture. What now seems apparent is that he
left the trenches and sought shelter close to the nearby city of Béthune.
He was probably regarded as 'missing in action', presumed dead, and as
his comrades continued to fight during the spring and summer months
it appears that he was lying low nearby.

Private Graham's reappearance in the winter of 1915 would
undoubtedly have startled his colleagues. Not only the fact that he was
alive but the nature of his arrest must have surprised many. For some
time the military police in Béthune had been aware of a British soldier
who was posing as an officer and had been conning local inhabitants
out of money. The soldier was known to local people as 'George' and
often claimed that he was on official army business. No-one had been
able to link these incidents with Graham's disappearance some nine
months earlier.

In October, Josephine Baillon was at home in Verquin when there
was a knock at the door. She answered it and was greeted by a British
soldier who asked her to exchange an English money order for francs.
The officer claimed the money order was worth 100 francs and that he
would be willing to exchange it for 50 francs. He said he would go to
the post office later that morning to get her the money. She handed
over 50 francs, and the officer promised to return later; but he never
did. The order was in fact worth just over 1 franc; it was a classic scam.

The next month the bogus officer tried the same trick again, and
again his victim was a local woman. On 13 November Martina Hyacinth

was at home when what appeared to be a British soldier came to her door. He told her he was an officer's servant with the King's Regiment and that he had to get dinner ready for three captains. He wanted to borrow 40 francs for immediate purchases and told the woman that his colleague had gone to change a 100-franc note and that as soon as he returned the money would be refunded. The 40 francs were duly handed over, and, just as he had done a few weeks earlier, the soldier thanked his host, left, and did not return. For the doorstep fraudster it was another easy hit; but the next day time eventually ran out for 'George'.

At a quarter to nine on the evening of 14 November two military policemen, Lance-Corporal Gibson and Lance-Corporal Preece, were on duty in the Grande Place in Béthune. The NCOs were approached by a man from the nearby brothel, known as the 'Red Lamp'. They were told that a man had gained admission by claiming to be a military policeman on duty.

When the two lance-corporals arrived at the brothel a dispute was under way. They found the bogus officer pinned up against a wall. He was surrounded by local people and was bleeding from the mouth. Preece and Gibson questioned the injured man about his bona fides and then concluded that he was an impostor. They also discovered clothing that matched descriptions given by those who had been conned out of money by the mysterious British soldier known as George. When asked for his identity disc the man produced one that stated he was a Private Bird of the 2nd Battalion of the Worcestershire Regiment.

Preece and Gibson arrested the brothel's unwanted guest and took him into custody. It was only then that his identity became clear. He was not Private Bird of the Worcesters, nor was he called George, but in fact was the missing Cork soldier James Graham. Graham was identified by his former comrades, who were brought to see him and were able to confirm to the military police who their prisoner was. The captive was also identified by the two local women who claimed he was the mystery man who had called at their houses and then conned them out of money.

The Corkman was now in serious trouble and was charged with three offences. The first and most important was the charge of desertion, which carried with it the death penalty. He also faced two charges of obtaining money under false pretences, which would normally have resulted in a period in prison or other field punishment.

On 9 December in Béthune his court martial began in front of a four-man panel. Graham said little in his defence except that he had been asked to leave the trenches by a Corporal Green. He did not explain how he had spent the nine months when he was away from his comrades, nor did he offer any explanation of the money incidents or the altercation in the brothel. He did not cross-examine any of the witnesses, nor is there any evidence on his court martial file of the prosecution cross-examining him. Graham pleaded not guilty to all the charges. The court martial found him guilty of desertion and therefore decided not to proceed with the two deception charges.

Graham's military file, which, like those of the other executed men, is now in the National Archives in London, is a slim volume of papers and contains little information. This lack of documentary evidence was seized upon by officials of the Department of Foreign Affairs in their report of 2004 when they investigated Graham's trial and subsequent execution.

> The absence of a conduct sheet or of a submission as to Private Graham's fighting character is notable in that in other files where this is the case they are requested as part of the confirmation process. They were not requested in this case.[11]

Nothing was said at Graham's trial about his fighting character and no witnesses were called to support him. It was a very one-sided trial, and there is no information in his file that suggests he was given the support of a prisoner's friend or any other legal assistance. The court martial notes suggest that the trial was a short affair, and it seems likely that the proceedings lasted minutes rather than hours.

Graham was sentenced to death for desertion. His punishment was considered by the then commander of the First Army, Douglas Haig. Less than a week after the sentencing Haig endorsed the court martial's findings and recommended that the sentence be carried out. Haig's views were supported by the Commander-in-Chief, Sir John French, whose endorsement of Graham's execution would be one of his last battlefield acts as commander of the army on the Western Front, as he was succeeded on 19 December by Haig.

Two days later, as dawn was breaking, James Graham was taken to the abattoir in the village of Mazingarbe. This drab brick municipal building would be used for more than the slaughter of cattle: during the Great War it would play host to eleven military executions. At twenty-two minutes past seven on the morning of 21 December 1915 gunfire echoed around its walls as James Graham's name was added to the bloody roll-call.

Chapter 9 ∾

HEADING FOR HOME

Take me back to dear old Blighty,
Put me on a train for London town.
Take me over there, drop me anywhere:
Liverpool, Leeds, or Birmingham—well, I don't care!
—FIRST WORLD WAR SONG

In his uniform, Peter Sands looked at ease, back in the familiar narrow streets close to his home in West Belfast. To the casual observer the lance-corporal looked like any other serviceman enjoying a few days' leave with his family away from the horrors of battle. However, the 26-year-old harboured a secret: he should have been with his battalion in France and was now officially listed as a deserter.

For weeks the stay-at-home soldier lived openly with his wife in their terrace house in Abyssinia Street, near the Falls Road. However, his respite in the calm and ordered world of domesticity would be short-lived. No-one knows who informed the authorities in Belfast—it could have been a neighbour or an acquaintance—but when Constable Clarke of the local Royal Irish Constabulary was told about the behaviour of Peter Sands, the lance-corporal's unsanctioned home leave came to an abrupt end.

Though the Belfast man was the only Irish soldier executed after overstaying his home leave, there were many others who failed to return to the front after a break at home.

The issue of home leave during the war was contentious and the source of much unhappiness in the ranks. Much to the annoyance of ordinary soldiers, officers were granted leave more often than the lower ranks. Privates would sometimes serve for as long as eighteen months before leave was granted, whereas most officers would be allowed home

Frank Percy Crozier of the Royal Irish Rifles, who would have a role in the execution of his namesake James Crozier.

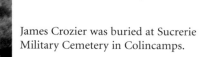

James Crozier was buried at Sucrerie Military Cemetery in Colincamps.

SCHEDULE.

Date 14th February 1916. No. 93.

Name of Alleged Offender (a)	Offence charged	Plea	Finding, and if Convicted, Sentence (b)	How dealt with by Confirming Officer
Not more than six names to be entered on one form. N° 9/14218 Rifleman James Crozier 9th R. I. Rifles.	When on active service deserting His Majesty's service.	not guilty	Guilty. ——— DEATH	Reserved [illegible]

C.M. 2533. III Army.

✗

Confirmed

D. Haig. Gen

23 Feb 16

Certified that above proceedings have been promulgated and that the sentence was was duly executed at 7.5. a m on 27th February 1916 —

O. S. Nugent.

Major General

28th Feb 1916 Comdg. 36th Division.

(a) If the name of the person charged is unknown, he may be described as unknown, with such addition as will identify him.

(b) Recommendation to mercy to be inserted in this column.

[signature] Convening Officer.
Comdg 107th Inf Bde.

[signature] Major
R. I. Rif Regt.
President.

James Crozier's court martial papers. The death sentence was confirmed by Douglas Haig on 23 February 1916. Crozier was executed four days later. (*National Archives, London, wo71-450*)

JUDGE ADVOCATE-GENERAL'S OFFICE,

29th March, 191_6._

PROCEEDINGS OF COURTS MARTIAL SUBMITTED FOR THE INSPECTION OF
THE ADJUTANT-GENERAL.

Rank	Name	Regiment	Offence	Sentence	Remarks
Second Lieutenant	Arthur J Annandale	9th Bn: Royal Irish Rifles:	Conduct to the prejudice of good order and military discipline	Dismissal: not confirmed	To see.

Arthur Annandale deserted the ranks, just like his colleague James Crozier. However, he was not executed and was allowed to leave the army on medical grounds. (*National Archives, London, WO339-1416*)

James Templeton, 15th Battalion, Royal Irish Rifles, who was executed in March 1916. (*Eileen Hinken*)

Four months after his execution, James Templeton's relatives were informed of his death. (*Eileen Hinken*)

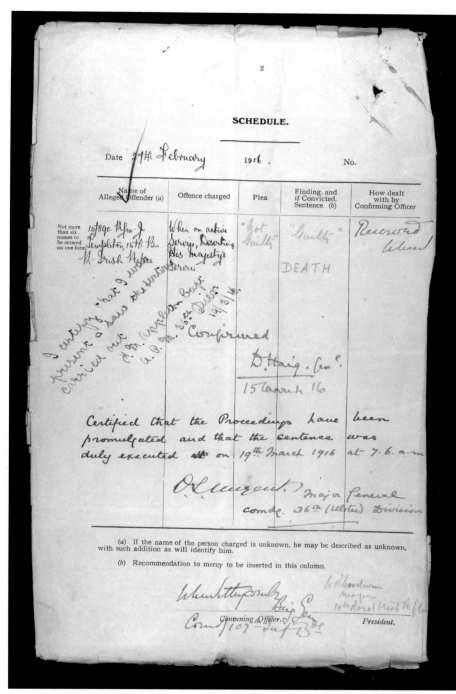

James Templeton's death sentence was confirmed by Douglas Haig. The court martial file also records that the execution was witnessed by a captain of the 36th (Ulster) Division. (*National Archives, London, WO71/454*)

Any further communication on this
subject should be addressed to—

> The Secretary,
> War Office,
> London, S.W.,

and the following number quoted.

105/Gen. No./2331. (A.G. 3.)

WAR OFFICE,

LONDON, S.W.

12th January, 1917.

Sir,

I am commanded by the Army Council to inform you that they have had under consideration the question of the method of carrying out Field Punishment No. 1, with special reference to paragraphs 2 (*b*) and 2 (*c*) of the Rules for Field Punishment (Manual of Military Law, page 721), and they have decided that, with a view to standardizing the method in accordance with which a soldier may be attached to a fixed object, the following instructions will, in future, be strictly adhered to :—

With reference to paragraph 2 (*b*), the soldier must be attached so as to be standing firmly on his feet, which if tied, must not be more than twelve inches apart, and it must be possible for him to move each foot at least three inches. If he is tied round the body there must be no restriction of his breathing. If his arms or wrists are tied, there must be six inches of play between them and the fixed object. His arms must hang either by the side of his body or behind his back.

With reference to paragraph 2 (*c*), irons should be used when available, but straps or ropes may be used in lieu of them when necessary. Any straps or ropes used for this purpose must be of sufficient width that they inflict no bodily harm, and leave no permanent mark on the offender.

An illustration of a method of attachment which complies with these regulations is given overleaf.

> I have the honour to be,
>
> Sir,
>
> Your obedient Servant,

R. Brade

To all *General Officers Commanding-in-Chief, Abroad.*

(B17/762) 20000 1/17 H&S 4033wo

A previously unpublished War Office memo from 1917, detailing exactly how soldiers should be treated when they were given field punishment no. 1.

Method of
tying feet

Thousands of soldiers were subjected to this punishment during the Great War, including a
number from Irish regiments who would later face a firing squad.

A mock execution involving members of the Royal Irish Fusiliers. This photograph, taken at billets in Ploegsteert Wood between November 1914 and March 1915, was used for propaganda purposes: to dissuade Belgians from spying for the Germans. (*Courtesy of the Trustees of the Royal Irish Fusiliers Museum*)

Thousands of Irishmen from all parts of the country volunteered to fight during the Great War. Although conscription was considered, it was never introduced in Ireland. (*Topfoto*)

The Cabaret-Rouge British Cemetery at Souchez in France. Peter Sands from Belfast and John James Wishart from Omagh are commemorated here. Sands was shot in 1915 after he returned home to Belfast on leave and failed to go back to the Western Front. Wishart was executed for desertion in 1917. (*Alamy*)

Samuel McBride is buried in Hyde Park Corner Cemetery in Belgium. He was executed after he deserted during fighting on Vimy Ridge. (*Lize Chielens*)

McBride's medal card, stored in the National Archives in London, records his war service. On the right-hand side, you can read the words 'Shot for desertion'. (*National Archives, London, wo372/12*)

3

1ˢᵗ army A.

I see no reason why the extreme penalty
should not be carried out.

Adjutant General's Branch
of the Staff
No. CM. 2487
Date 6.9.15.
Headquarters, 1st Army.

W. P. Pulteney

6/9/15

Lieutenant General.
Commanding 3rd Corps.

A.G.
G.H.Q.
This is a bad case and I recommend
that the extreme penalty be carried out —

D. Haig. Genˡ.
Comˡ. 1ˢᵗ Army.

7 Sept. 15

Peter Sands' court martial papers. The comment from Douglas Haig, then commanding the
1st Army reads: 'This is a bad case and I recommend that the extreme penalty be carried out.'
(*National Archives, London, wo71-432*)

Poperinghe was the scene of a number of executions during the Great War. (*Courtesy of Flanders Fields Museum, Ypres*)

Bernard McGeehan from Co. Donegal, who served in the King's Liverpool Regiment, was executed in Poperinghe. He is buried in the town. (*Lize Chielens*)

The abattoir at Mazingarbe, where eleven British soldiers were executed during the Great War, including Private James Graham of the Royal Munster Fusiliers. (*Gérard Delporte*)

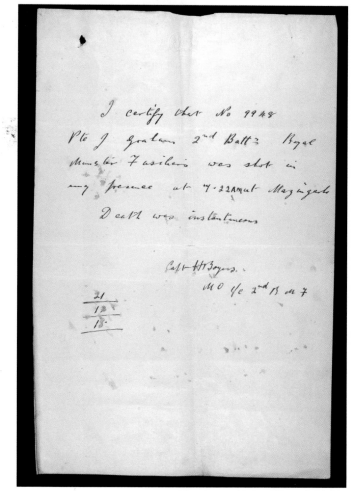

I certify that No 9948 Pte J Graham 2nd Batt: Royal Munster Fusiliers was shot in my presence at 7.22AM at Mazingarbe Death was instantaneous

Capt HH Boyers.
MO i/c 2nd B M 7

The court martial papers of James Graham show that his death at 7:22 a.m. on 21 December 1915 was recorded as 'instantaneous'. (*National Archives, London, WO71-438*)

Private Harry Farr was executed for cowardice in October 1916 while serving with the West Yorkshire Regiment. His family were at the forefront of the pardons campaign. (*PA Photos*)

Gertie Harris, Harry Farr's daughter, at the Cenotaph in London with Andrew Mackinlay MP. (*Jim Booth*)

The National Memorial Arboretum in Staffordshire. 306 stakes, representing those shot at dawn, are arranged in the form of a Greek theatre around the statue of Herbert Burden, executed at Ypres in 1915. (*Getty Images*)

A post commemorating the death of Thomas Cummings, a Belfast soldier who served with the Irish Guards. He was shot in Locon, France, in January 1915 in a double execution alongside his fellow-Ulsterman Albert Smythe. (*Getty Images*)

John Hipkin, who founded the Shot at Dawn campaign. (*Newcastle Journal*)

(*Left to right*) Irish Shot at Dawn campaigner Peter Mulvany, Dermot Ahern, Minister for Foreign Affairs, Christy Walsh and Senator Paschal Mooney, outside Government Buildings in Dublin. (*Department of Foreign Affairs/Maxwells*)

for a break after only six or seven months' service. Some officers recognised that this inequality needed to be addressed. One captain in the Royal Army Medical Corps wrote about the subject of leave in 1917:

> This is a perfectly inexcusable state of affairs and should not be allowed to continue for a minute. In the British Army the officer, on campaign, is supposed to share the hardships of his men. Here there is a gross disparity between the treatment of the two.[1]

Such leave was so controversial and beginning to cause so much disquiet that it became the subject of parliamentary questions in the House of Commons.

The lack of leave prompted some soldiers to try to return home unofficially, and many headed for the coastal cities of Boulogne and Calais, the very places where their wartime experience had begun. However, very few managed to cross the English Channel and make it back onto home turf. Inevitably, naïve and poorly thought-out bids for freedom by would-be deserters ended in failure and the fugitives were routinely apprehended within a matter of hours.

In France, escapers often stood out. Without equipment, identity discs or military passes and sometimes looking dishevelled after sleeping rough, they quickly attracted attention. Days later the absentees would usually be on their way back to their unit, with a court martial to follow and the likely prospect of a death sentence.

Peter Sands, a lance-corporal in the 1st Battalion of the Royal Irish Rifles, travelled legitimately back to Belfast with a comrade after being given temporary leave to return home. It was a chance for him to spend some time with his wife, Eliza-Lillie, and his daughter Mary. The travel warrant was for four days' leave, and Sands and Sergeant Whelan were expected to return to France on 1 March. On that day both men were due to board a train and begin the journey back to the front. However, when Sergeant Whelan turned up at the railway platform he was on his own and Sands was not to be seen.

It was most unusual for the lance-corporal to be missing. A regular soldier, he had some nine years' army service and was well versed in the regulations governing home leave. Whelan returned on his own to the battalion's base at Estaires, some ten miles west of Armentières, while Sands remained at the family home in Belfast.

To the officers of the battalion Sands's failure to return to France must have been puzzling. As well as being very experienced he was well regarded and was viewed as a good soldier; but the absentee would later claim there was an understandable reason why he had failed to appear back at base. During his stay at home Sands claimed he lost his military travel papers, which would have secured his passage back to France. He said that on the day he was expected back for duty he went to a barracks in Belfast to obtain a fresh travel warrant. There he allegedly spoke to a Corporal Wright, who told him he knew nothing about him. Sands would later tell his court martial that he left the depot empty-handed and that while he continued to stay in Belfast he wore his uniform at all times.

Over the next few months, as Sands readjusted to civilian life in Ireland, he and his former comrades lived in two very different worlds. At the Western Front the men he had left behind took part in the battle of Neuve-Chapelle in March and two months later saw action at Aubers Ridge, where the British casualties would number eleven thousand.

At home in Belfast life was more comfortable for Peter Sands, though there were constant reminders of the war he had walked away from. Recruiting offices around the city were attracting hundreds of young men as the war effort became intensive. Belfast's hospitals continued to take in the injured from France, and in May the centre of the city came to a standstill as men of the 36th (Ulster) Division paraded in front of thousands of well-wishers as they set off for the front.

We do not know how all this affected Peter Sands, but the local war effort clearly inspired one public-spirited individual to turn Peter Sands in. In July, as a result of a tip-off, the police arrested him for desertion. Documents attached to the trial papers report that when he was charged by Constable Clarke at Roden Street Barracks in Belfast, Sands admitted the offence. A military escort was then organised to travel with him, and, as was customary, he was brought back to France for the court martial. Proceedings began on 30 August and the papers suggest that the trial was not a lengthy one.

In his defence Sands recounted the story of going to the depot for a new warrant and added in mitigation: 'Had I intended to desert I would have worn plain clothes, but up to that time I was arrested I always wore uniform.'[2]

Sands was found guilty of desertion and sentenced to death. His character references were good ones. The brigadier-general commanding the 25th Infantry Brigade wrote: 'His commanding officer gives him a very good character, both in ordinary behaviour and as a fighting man.' But such kind assurances were only part of the story. The same officer wrote: 'I consider this a bad case of desertion and I recommend that the sentence be carried out.'3

A series of senior officers endorsed this position, notably Douglas Haig, then commanding the First Army. He said the desertion was a bad case and recommended that the extreme penalty be carried out.

Little is known of Peter Sands's final hours. It is most likely that he was visited by a chaplain, was given a chance to write a final letter home, and possibly was offered alcohol. His military papers simply record that at dawn on 15 September 1915 he went before a firing squad at Fleurbaix, near Armentières. He was buried in the nearby churchyard, but after the war his grave could not be found, so his name was later commemorated in Cabaret-Rouge Military Cemetery at Souchez.

What clearly hindered the Belfast man's case was the length of time he had been absent from France, amounting to some four months. This prolonged period of unofficial absence, and the fact that Sands does not appear to have made sustained attempts to rejoin his unit, sealed his fate. As an experienced soldier he would have known that such behaviour would be seen as desertion and would warrant the death penalty. In mitigation Sands claimed that he remained in uniform during his time in Belfast and argued that that was hardly the behaviour of a genuine deserter.

However, an examination of the court martial file leaves many questions unanswered. The papers do not give a detailed explanation of why the death penalty was necessary, nor does it appear that Sands's story about his lost travel warrant was thoroughly investigated. Was Corporal Wright, to whom Sands claims he spoke also at the Belfast barracks, ever interviewed to confirm his account? If so, did he confirm Sands's story? On the issue of Sands's previous good behaviour, was this not considered worthy enough to have led to the sentence being commuted?

Peter Sands's case was one of those championed by the Irish government, which asked the British government to pardon the executed soldiers. Officials in Dublin investigated the Sands trial and execution and concluded that there had been a casual approach to his case. The Irish officials wanted to know why the hearing had taken place in France and not Belfast; and there was concern that Peter Sands's story concerning the lost travel warrant had not been fully examined. The report concluded: 'There doesn't seem to be any substantial evidence to support this sentence being handed out, nor why it was subsequently confirmed.'[4]

_____

Peter Sands's treatment seems particularly severe when one considers what happened in later months to another Ulsterman who went missing in similar circumstances. The story of Private John McMurdie has never been told before, and I unearthed his details during research at the National Archives in London.

The story bears an uncanny similarity to the Sands case. McMurdie was a private in the Royal Inniskilling Fusiliers, and in May 1916 he was issued with a travel warrant that allowed him home leave for ten days. Like Peter Sands, McMurdie travelled back to Belfast to see family and friends and on 25 May he was expected at Waterloo Station in London to begin the journey back to France. The fusilier did not turn up for the return trip and was later reported as absent. Like Sands, McMurdie claimed he lost his travel papers and ticket and then wrote to his commanding officer asking how he could return to the front. He claimed he never got a reply to his letters, and a month after he was due back in France, as he waited in Belfast, he was arrested for desertion.

McMurdie, again like Sands, was then taken back to his battalion in France and brought before a court martial and tried for desertion. Just as Sands had done, he explained his difficulties over the travel warrant. He would also say that on the day of his arrest he had been planning to give himself up.

Like Lance-Corporal Peter Sands, Private John McMurdie had a good service record. He was a veteran of the campaign in Gallipoli and was clearly viewed by his superiors as a valuable soldier.

McMurdie was found guilty of desertion and was sentenced to death. However, his service record proved invaluable; it saved his life, and his sentence was commuted to three years' penal servitude, a decision that had the blessing of the Commander-in-Chief, Douglas Haig.

McMurdie was spared the firing squad because senior officers took into account his past behaviour; and yet in the Sands case little weight was given to his good character or record.

The two soldiers had similar stories to tell. They were highly regarded as fighting men, faced identical charges, and yet bizarrely there were two very different outcomes. Their cases reinforce the view that the court martial system used in the Great War was often a lottery: the lucky winners survived and the unfortunate losers paid with their lives.

––––

Statistically, the stories of soldiers like Sands and McMurdie are rare, though the desire to go home was ever present, particularly among soldiers in the front line. Most who tried to escape home only got as far as the French coastal towns and never managed to cross the Channel. The busy cities of Calais and Boulogne, the most obvious ports with a link to England, became a favourite destination for absentees, in the hope that they could somehow scramble aboard a ship and disappear back home. But it would often prove impossible to reach the coast undetected. British and French intelligence monitored the ports, and military police patrolled the roads and railway stations. Soldiers travelling on their own or in small groups who did not have proper documents faced arrest as deserters or spies.

One Irishman who headed for the French coast was John Bell, a Dubliner who was a driver with the Royal Field Artillery. He made for Boulogne after he was separated from his unit as he took part in a march in the Ypres area. From Finglas in Dublin, Bell had been with his regimental comrades as they made their way towards the Belgian town of Poperinghe. The travelling party stopped short of their destination, and Bell would later claim that he and a comrade, Driver Wilkinson, asked an officer for permission to get some food, as they were both hungry.

The party stopped, and Bell would allege that when he and Wilkinson returned, the rest of the unit had moved off without them.

Bell and Wilkinson spent the night in a French billet, and the next day the pair say they went to the headquarters of the 1st Division to seek help. They claim that an orderly informed them that the officers were too busy to see them. Eventually the two men reported to the Belgian headquarters and managed to get on a train, which they soon realised was taking them away from Boulogne and towards Paris. They got out at the next stop and began walking in the right direction for the coast. They would remain at large for eight weeks, as Bell would later recall.

> We took a long time not knowing the way. When we arrived at La Cappelle we asked the way to Boulogne. I found it was only seven kilometres. A woman asked us to come into her house. We did not remain long as we wanted to report ourselves before dark at the base and we were just starting when a Gendarme came up and asked us where we were going and we explained to him as well as we could that we had lost our unit and we were going to the base at Boulogne.[5]

Bell and his comrade were arrested by the French authorities on 18 December 1914, nearly two months after they left the Ypres area.

John Bell's statement to his trial differs from the official version given by a number of gendarmes. The French authorities say they went to the house where Bell and Wilkinson were staying after they received reports that the two men had been calling at houses where the husband was absent. They would ask to have a sleep and request something to eat. The gendarmes say that when Bell and Wilkinson were detained they resisted arrest on three occasions—but this account is different from that given by the men, who say they behaved in a calm way after they were detained.

John Bell's account of his time away from his regiment is vague and raises a series of questions about dates, times and places. He gives little information about his whereabouts from the time he left Poperinghe to his arrival in Boulogne. It is a long journey, and it is odd that Bell and Wilkinson did not divulge more information about their absence, as they had been missing for two months.

By Christmas 1914, the first festive season of the Great War, the two men had little to celebrate. They were now prisoners rather than soldiers and they knew that the new year would bring a court martial and a possible death sentence.

As the troops in Boulogne marked the holiday season as best they could under the circumstances, Bell lay in his billet and hatched a plan.

On St Stephen's Day his desire for freedom got the better of him. He had been placed under close arrest and was told not to leave the barracks, but when a roll-call was taken on the night of 26 December he had disappeared. Bell claimed he left the camp with a soldier from the North Lancashire Regiment. He said they got lost, and as it was too late to return they began to walk towards the town of Saint-Omer, which is to the east of Boulogne.

For a little over three weeks Bell walked and slept along the roads and the fields of northern France, but on 20 January his luck ran out and he was again arrested as a suspected deserter. He was taken to the Assistant Provost-Marshal at Saint-Omer and was there put into the same room as a German spy. It was this choice of cellmate that Bell claimed led him to escape again. He claimed he was unhappy at being placed close to a German prisoner and that he complained to a superior officer and asked to be returned to his unit.

Six days after he arrived in Saint-Omer, Bell was on the move again; but his shortest escape would be his last. He was caught the next day by a military policeman as he walked along a road on the outskirts of Saint-Omer. He would tell the NCO that he was on his way to Belgium to join officers who had sent for him. His story was not believed, the NCO recognised Bell as a deserter, and the Irishman was taken into custody for the third time in two months. Bell would later say that he ran away because when he was put in custody he was placed close to German prisoners.

The military trial of Bell and Wilkinson took place in April 1915. Bell faced three charges of desertion and had one charge dismissed. He was found guilty and sentenced to death. Wilkinson fared much better: though he was found guilty of desertion the charge was commuted by Haig, who accepted that Wilkinson had been influenced by Bell.

Wilkinson's life was probably saved after officers made statements praising him. He had helped put out a fire and had shown bravery, actions that impressed his superiors and resulted in his avoiding the firing squad. His comrade had no such luck. Clearly, Driver Bell's behaviour as a serial absentee did little to impress the army's hierarchy.

The officer commanding the First Army—unaware that Bell was Irish—wrote: 'Driver Bell is a determined shirker during a time of war and unworthy of being a soldier or Englishman.'[6]

Shortly after 7 a.m. on 25 April, John Bell's life came to an end when he was taken from custody and put before a firing squad and shot.

Nearly ninety years after his death, Bell's case was examined by officials of the Irish government, who claimed that his court martial and execution raised a series of questions. They felt there was a great disparity between the treatment Bell received and that of his comrade, and also argued that there was no evidence that the soldiers' version of events was properly investigated.

Bell's name is commemorated at the Le Touret memorial—the same place where one will find the names of the Irish Guardsmen Thomas Cummings and Albert Smythe.

Bell's death in April brought the number of Irish executions to four in the first eight months of the war; but he would not be the last to be arrested for desertion on the French coast.

———

Arthur Hamilton, a private with the 14th Battalion of the Durham Light Infantry who was originally from Belfast, made a beeline for Calais after he left his regiment in February 1917. Military policemen in the area were well accustomed to spotting deserters, and by mid-afternoon on 15 February Lance-Corporal Webb believed he had discovered another absentee. In the Rue de Dunkerque the NCO approached Hamilton and asked him a series of questions. He wanted to know his name, what he was doing in the city, and whether he had a military pass. Hamilton replied that he had come to Calais to visit a friend and said he had arrived from Étaples. He had no army book but said his name was Private Blanchard of the Durham Light Infantry.

The answers did little to convince Lance-Corporal Webb and he arrested Hamilton and took him to a nearby army camp. This was the end of a week on the run for the private, who had slipped away from the trenches on the morning of 8 February. His escape from the front line had not gone according to plan, and as he walked into a nearby village he was spotted by one of his superiors. Acting Sergeant-Major Jeffreys would later tell the hearing how surprised he was to see Hamilton.

I saw the accused coming down the road. I asked him what he was doing. He informed me that he had permission from Sergeant Hope to come to the village to purchase something. I ordered him back to the trenches. About 2.30 p.m. the same date I got back to the trenches and made enquiries about the accused. I was informed by Sergeant Hope that he had given the accused no permission to leave the trenches and he had not returned.[7]

Hamilton was returned to his unit under escort and a month later appeared before a court martial. Charged with desertion, he decided to defend himself and questioned the witnesses brought forward by the prosecution. The trial notes give the impression that he was not over-awed by the occasion, and in a series of direct questions he queried much of the prosecution case.

In response to the charge of desertion Hamilton made a stout defence of his behaviour. He claimed he had left the trenches with the intention of going to the canteen in the village. He said he had been suffering from bronchitis and trench foot and when he met Acting Sergeant-Major Jeffreys in Annequin the NCO spoke to him in what he felt was a 'bullying manner', which upset him. He said that when he got to Calais he had not intended giving a wrong name—his full name, he claimed, was Arthur Hamilton Blanchard—and he said he had not deliberately misled the military police.

In mitigation he then listed a range of medical conditions that he claimed he had suffered from, including bronchitis and vascular disease of the heart. He stated that he had been discharged from the Royal Irish Fusiliers in 1912 because of his health. He also explained that his experience of warfare had been limited and he considered himself use-less in the trenches. He was also fed up, claiming he had received no pay since early November.

Hamilton's plea and long list of complaints did little to sway senior officers. He was found guilty of desertion and sentenced to death. His superiors all recommended that the sentence be carried out. On St Patrick's Day there was little cheer for the Irishman as the major-general commanding the 6th Division wrote:

I am of the opinion that this man deliberately absented himself with a view to avoiding duty in the trenches. I can see no extenuating cir-cumstances and recommend that the extreme penalty be inflicted.[8]

This view was endorsed by Haig, who sanctioned Hamilton's execution. At 7 a.m. on 27 March, at Nœux-les-Mines, Arthur Hamilton was shot by firing squad.

Ninety years later Hamilton's case, like that of John Bell, was re-examined by the Irish government. Officials sympathetic to Hamilton's plight believe that in 1917 his medical problems were discounted too easily by the army's hierarchy:

> With ailments such as trench foot, bronchitis and vascular disease of the heart, and considering Private Hamilton was an experienced soldier having served in the army prior to the war, it is not un-reasonable to expect that some weight would have been given to his assertion that he was unfit for duty in the trenches.[9]

What is clear from the trial papers is that Arthur Hamilton's allegations of poor health made little impact on the prosecution. The fact that he was arrested far away from his unit, and that he had repeatedly told lies, clearly influenced the court martial and ultimately led to his death.

———

As Arthur Hamilton was brought before a firing squad in the dying days of March 1917, another Irish soldier was preparing to make a break for the French coast.

After duties in the trenches, men of the Royal Inniskilling Fusiliers were at a rest camp at Hazebrouck in northern France. Eighteen miles from Ypres, the area was used to accommodate troops before and after their tour of the front line. Among their number was 24-year-old John James Wishart, a married man with one child whose family came from Omagh, Co. Tyrone. The son of a soldier, he had joined his father's old regiment when the war broke out in 1914.

After resting, Wishart and his comrades from the 7th Battalion gathered at Hazebrouck railway station on the evening of 31 March, ready to return to action. When the roll-call was taken, all were present, and the men climbed on board their wagons bound for Bailleul, eight miles to the west.

But Wishart had no intention of making the trip with his comrades and as the journey began he left his battalion. His disappearance was noticed only when the men arrived at Bailleul and the roll-call was taken again; but by this time the absentee was on his way north, towards the coast and the port of Boulogne. The city offered him the best chance of getting out of the country. Wishart was keen to return to Ireland, as he had been told in a letter from his wife, Margaret, that his daughter Susan was sick. At his court martial he would claim that he simply wanted to be with his family.

At Boulogne, Wishart may have hoped that he might be able to secure a pass home from one of the army camps, or find his way onto a troopship bound for England. For the best part of the next three weeks he was a fugitive and remained at large, away from the eyes and ears of military patrols. He made it to the coast and to Boulogne, only to be discovered at the very place that he hoped would lead him home.

On the evening of 20 April, Lance-Corporal Slowgrove of the military police in Boulogne was doing his rounds. He and a colleague had come across Wishart and began chatting to him. The fusilier raised their suspicions. He was asked a series of questions, but his answers did little to convince the two NCOs and he was detained as a suspected deserter. He was then taken to the guardroom and detained for eight days in Boulogne before being handed back to his regiment and then under escort was taken back to Hazebrouck, where his escape had begun.

The very public return to the rest camp and the seriousness of being caught as a suspected deserter did little to dampen Wishart's desire to go home. Two days later he made another attempt to cross the Channel. On 29 April he had been billeted with his comrades in Hazebrouck; the next morning, when roll-call was taken, the deserter had gone again.

Lance-Corporal Hughes, who had been sleeping close to Wishart, was the first to notice his absence. When Hughes woke not only had his neighbour vanished but the lance-corporal's revolver was missing as well.

In the darkness of an April morning Wishart retraced his steps and travelled again to the coast and the port of Boulogne. For eleven days he went undetected and by now he was perhaps becoming confident that this second bid for freedom would be successful.

On 11 May in Boulogne his latest desertion came to an end, and again it was a military policeman who discovered him. Lance-Corporal Knee came across Wishart at 10 a.m:

I saw the accused who was in civilian clothes, being suspicious of him, I ordered him to produce his pass. Being unable to do so and also not being able to give a satisfactory reply to my questions, suspecting him of being a deserter. I handed him over to the Dock M.P.[10]

Wishart was returned to his unit for a second time and charged with desertion on two occasions. He insisted that there were good reasons for his disappearance, and he later told his court martial:

About December 1916 was the last time I heard from home. I received a telegram during December from my wife saying my child was ill. I tried to get a pass for home but could not do so. I was down at Etaples [the camp near Boulogne] for a week but did not get home. I was very worried.

In mitigation he added:

It was only worrying about my child that made me absent myself. It was not through cowardice.[11]

The fusilier's story did little to impress the court martial of three officers—two of whom were from Wishart's own battalion. Such familiarity did the fusilier no favours, and he was found guilty of two charges of desertion and sentenced to death. Ironically, the hearing was held on his daughter's first birthday.

Wishart's trial papers, which were kept secret until 1993, are brief and, unusually, do not include any remarks from senior officers endorsing the conviction. Before his first disappearance Wishart had a good disciplinary record and appears to have been regarded as a competent soldier. Second-Lieutenant Wilson praised his abilities when in a character reference he wrote:

I have known the accused for four months in the trenches. He has always been a good character and willing and has always done well in the trenches.[12]

After the obligatory confirmation from the Commander-in-Chief, Douglas Haig, Wishart's execution went ahead at Merris, near Hazebrouck, on 15 June 1917.

Irish government officials who investigated the case believe that not enough was done by the army hierarchy to ease Wishart's worries over his sick child. Their report in 2004 concluded:

If his request [for leave] had been granted, or if an alternative method of ascertaining the situation at home had been proposed, there would have been no need for his absence, and therefore no need for his subsequent execution.[13]

Some observers may question this observation. In the middle of 1917 the army was being stretched in France, and casualties were high. Inevitably it meant that even though compassionate leave was granted to soldiers, these personal problems were hardly a priority for commanders. In April the Nivelle offensive was launched, without success, and in July the British Expeditionary Force would once again see action in a new advance at Ypres—crucial stages in the prosecution of the war. In short, John Wishart's death may have been due to some simple truisms. He had clearly tried the patience of his superiors; in the heat of battle, compassion was in short supply; and in the opinion of others he was dispensable—and the Inniskilling Fusilier paid the ultimate penalty.

Julian Putkowski finds the case puzzling.

The absence in the dossier of any remarks by confirming officers is unusual, even allowing for his conviction on more than one charge especially because Wishart had a clean disciplinary record and appears to have been an asset in combat.

Putkowski also questions the rationale of executing Wishart.

Wishart's execution appears gratuitous—wasting the life of a useful soldier at a time when British Expeditionary Force casualties were high.[14]

John James Wishart was buried at the Merris churchyard near Hazebrouck, and he is commemorated at a memorial at Cabaret Rouge, where the name of Lance-Corporal Peter Sands is also recorded— Ulstermen who found the call of home so strong that they paid with their lives.

Chapter 10 ～

| NOT IN MY NAME

I don't think they gave him a chance. Mr Haig saw to that.
—PADDY BYRNE, NEPHEW OF AN EXECUTED IRISH SOLDIER

War, by its very nature, involves deception, from the boy-soldiers who gave recruiting sergeants a false age to the battle-hardened generals who lied to their men to keep morale high.

There are often important reasons for a half-truth or a falsehood. Behind each public lie there is always a private story—a personal justification for why it seems necessary to be economical with the truth. Those who were executed for desertion told their fair share of lies. Sometimes they lied to protect themselves or to hide past misdemeanours; occasionally they misled their superiors to protect others.

Three such men—Thomas Hogan, Robert Hope and Stephen Byrne—shared a common lie. The three Irishmen told the army they were somebody else, and each of them had enlisted under an assumed name. The three would all be executed for desertion, but it was only after their deaths that their real identities became known.

Their use of aliases was not uncommon and among young soldiers the reasons for giving a false name were varied. Some recruits had a criminal record and were keen to start afresh with a new identity; others had deserted from another regiment and wanted a chance to start again. Some volunteers who were under age or too old used a false name, as did some young men who enlisted against the wishes of their parents. Irishmen caught up in the political atmosphere of Dublin in 1916 may have decided that it was better to hide their background when taking the King's shilling.

Hogan, Hope and Byrne would separately face firing squads in 1917—a year of enormous tumult on the Western Front, best remembered for the Battles of Arras, Messines, Cambrai and Passchendaele. For Haig, the year would prove to be his toughest. With a change in government at home the new Prime Minister, David Lloyd George, wanted 1917 to be the year of victory, and the pressure was firmly placed on the army's hierarchy.

Haig would begin the year considering fresh military options but also found himself having to deal with a continuing problem: the discipline of his own men. His diary for early January records how he had to consider the fate of men from the Durham Light Infantry:

> Of the 11 cases sent to me I confirmed the proceedings on three, namely 1 sergeant and 2 corporals. The sentences on the remaining 8 I commuted to 15 years' penal servitude and suspended the sentences.[1]

Throughout 1917, as he had done continuously since becoming Commander-in-Chief in December 1915, Haig would regularly have to consider what punishment was appropriate for soldiers who had a death sentence imposed on them. Like the previous incumbent, Sir John French, Haig commuted most of the death sentences to time in prison.

The first Irish case that landed on Haig's desk in 1917 was that of Thomas Hogan. The son of John and Jane Hogan of Tralee, Co. Kerry, he joined the 2nd Battalion of the Royal Inniskilling Fusiliers in 1915, enlisting under the name Thomas Murphy. The reason he used an alias is not known, but a study of his behaviour and character may offer some indications.

Hogan's disciplinary record with the Inniskillings was a poor one. He often went missing and had a history of committing misdemeanours. This might suggest that he had used a false name to cover up a previous military background. His age of thirty-one also suggests that he may have seen service before the war. While it was not unusual to have a Kerryman in the ranks of the Inniskillings, Hogan's choice of regiment is interesting. The Inniskillings normally recruited in Counties Tyrone, Fermanagh, Donegal and Derry. Whatever his precise reasons for joining a northern regiment and under an assumed name, it is clear that he wanted to start his army career pretending he was somebody else.

Hogan's record shows that he arrived in France in June 1915. He was hospitalised once that year and on another occasion in 1916. However, it was not his health that would prove to be his downfall. Ironically for an Irishman, it was on St Patrick's Day in 1917 that matters took a serious turn. At 5 p.m. that day, as he sat in a dug-out, Hogan was ordered with his platoon to get ready to move towards the trenches. A few minutes later he was spotted by an officer outside the dug-out. When the platoon assembled to move off Hogan was missing. He would later insist that he had not intended to desert or leave his comrades but had simply gone to prepare some tea.

> I went to look for some wood to make some tea with. I thought the platoon would be staying the night in the dugout.[2]

He would later claim:

> It was getting dark and I lost my way in the trenches and found myself in a village. My feet were very bad as I had been standing guard . . . I rested them for a few days and I eventually found my way to Le Quesnel.[3]

When the absentee arrived in the village some sixteen days after he disappeared he was spotted by Sergeant-Major Phillips.

> I saw the accused walking about Le Quesnel in a filthy condition. I questioned him as to what regiment he belonged to and he told me he belonged to the Royal Inniskilling Fusiliers. I asked him why he was absent from his unit and the accused said he had lost his battalion in the trenches some days previously.[4]

The missing Irishman was arrested and returned to his unit and on 26 April he went before a court martial charged with desertion. The records of the hearing are brief and give no indication that he had legal representation. Hogan said little in mitigation and he was found guilty of desertion and sentenced to death.

A record of the proceedings was then circulated to senior officers. The major-general commanding the 32nd Division gave his views a week later:

> I recommend that the sentence be carried out as an example on account of the prevalence of this crime in the battalion and also on account of the man's bad character.[5]

Hogan's chequered past in the Royal Inniskilling Fusiliers was put under the spotlight, and as officers examined his fate the soldier's long disciplinary record was taken out for close inspection. They saw a series of offences centred on absence, the abuse of alcohol, and being insolent. In 1915, the year he joined the regiment, Hogan was disciplined for hesitating to obey an order and shortly after Christmas he was found drunk in his billet. The following year he found himself being disciplined a further five times. He had gone absent three times, had broken out of his billet on one occasion, disobeyed an order and told a lie to an officer. By 1917 Hogan's disciplinary record was flowing into several pages and he was showing no signs of mending his ways. In February he again went absent, this time from a parade, and in early March insolence towards an officer brought further punishment.

Days after his final court martial, senior officers examined Hogan's record and came to a damning conclusion. The brigadier-general of the 96th Brigade wrote:

Private Murphy's [Hogan's] conduct as a fighting man is reported by his commanding officer to be indifferent. His general conduct is bad. He is addicted to absence without leave and insubordination to N.C.O.S.

He added:

The state of discipline in the battalion is at present bad. There have been six convictions for desertion since 1st April last.[6]

The brigadier-general was not exaggerating: the 2nd Battalion had a reputation for being troublesome. Figures compiled by the academic Timothy Bowman show that between October 1915 and September 1916, 117 men went before a court martial. His figures show that the average number of courts martial for an Irish infantry battalion was 58, putting the Royal Inniskillings at nearly twice the average. While there are factors that need to be considered, such as the area of service, battle conditions and the history of the battalion, there is no question that the 2nd Battalion had a disciplinary problem. In May 1917, as the brigadier-general considered Hogan's fate, that subject was uppermost in his mind.

I strongly recommend [that] the sentence of the court be put into execution. At the time Private Murphy deserted it appeared probable that the Brigade would shortly be engaged. This combined with the prevalence of this particular offence in the battalion during the period the brigade was engaged in arduous operations under the most inclement weather conditions makes it essential, if discipline is to be upheld, to make an example of this man.[7]

As Thomas Hogan waited, he knew he was running out of time, and his only chance of survival rested with Haig. On the day that Haig would finally confirm Hogan's future he had other important business to consider. His diary records that he met General Herbert Plumer, who was in charge of the Second Army. They met to discuss the next big military operation, which would become known as the Battle of Messines—an attack that would begin in June.

Not surprisingly, Haig did not record anything in his diary about Thomas Hogan—after all, he had come across this kind of case many times before—but he did make a decision about the Irishman that May day, and it was to sanction his execution.

Haig clearly believed that the Inniskillings' discipline problem needed to be addressed and it seems he accepted the logic of other officers that Hogan's execution would keep the men of the 2nd Battalion in line.

Little is known of Hogan's last moments. Four days after Haig's confirmation he was awoken in the early hours of a summer morning and placed before a firing squad at a place called Voyennes. His comrades would have formed the firing party, and within seconds they killed him. His death certificate records that the shooting took place just before 5 a.m. and that death was instantaneous.

———

As Thomas Hogan was being buried, another soldier from the Royal Inniskilling Fusiliers was getting ready to face a court martial. Robert Hope had much in common with Hogan. He too was Irish, had joined the same regiment, was facing desertion charges and, like his fellow-countryman, had enlisted using an alias. Hope had used the name

Robert Hepple when he joined the 1st Battalion of the Royal Inniskilling Fusiliers in June 1915. His battalion would see service at the Battle of the Somme and, according to Julian Putkowski, Hope was a Gallipoli veteran. The reasons for his new identity are not clear, but it seems that, like his regimental colleague Thomas Hogan, he wanted part of his past kept private.

At the beginning of 1917 Hope was stationed in the Somme region at Carnoy camp, near the town of Albert. Carnoy was used as the battalion headquarters and was the base for units before they went up to the front line. Throughout the war hundreds of soldiers would pass through this part of France as they rested before going to front-line duty. One of those was the war poet Siegfried Sassoon, who wrote the poem 'At Carnoy'.

Down in the hollow there's the whole Brigade
Camped in four groups: through twilight falling slow
I hear a sound of mouth-organs, ill-played,
And murmur of voices, gruff, confused, and low.
Crouched among thistle-tufts I've watched the glow
Of a blurred orange sunset flare and fade;
And I'm content. To-morrow we must go
To take some cursèd Wood . . . O world God made![8]

Like Sassoon, Robert Hope would spend some time resting at Carnoy and then inevitably the call would come to go back on duty at the front line. On 21 January 1917 Hope's company was told to get ready to go back into the trenches. Hope, as instructed, assembled with his comrades, but by the time the company arrived at the front line he had disappeared.

Hope had gone missing en route and his absence would puzzle his colleagues. No-one knew exactly where he had gone and his disappearance lasted three-and-a-half months, an absence all the more remarkable because the Irishman would eventually turn up only five miles away in the town of Albert.

Hope was discovered late at night inside a derelict house by two British military policemen who were on a routine patrol. It is not known whether they were acting on information or whether it was a chance discovery, but inside the building they found the missing Irishman fast asleep.

One of the men who came across the absentee was Lance-Corporal Bolas.

I was on duty and on entering an unoccupied house found the accused asleep—I woke him up and asked him where his battalion was. He replied 'at Bapaume' further saying 'I have come down to do some shopping for my captain.' I asked him to produce his pay book and not being satisfied with his answer I arrested him.[9]

Hope was detained and brought back to his unit. He would later claim that despite his fourteen-week break he was on his way back to his unit. 'When police arrested me I told them that I was on my way to join my battalion—I thought they were somewhere in the Bapaume district.'[10]

As final preparations were being made for Hope's court martial, hundreds of his fellow-countrymen were taking part in a battle that would help change the history of the war. Soldiers from the 16th (Irish) and 36th (Ulster) Divisions went into battle together in a well-planned attack at the Flemish village of Wytschaete. It would become known as the Battle of Messines, and fighting here would eventually see British fortunes improve on the Western Front and provide a much-needed morale-boosting victory.

On the first day of the battle, 7 June, some of the largest mines ever used in the war exploded. A series of nineteen mines containing a million pounds of high explosive had been dug under the German lines south-east of Ypres; the explosions were so loud that they were heard in Paris and London. The British infantry advance would catch the Germans by surprise, and among the successes would be the capture of Wytschaete by the Ulstermen and units of the Irish Division. That day Douglas Haig would joyfully record in his diary: 'The operations today are probably the most successful I have yet undertaken.'[11]

Understandably, the German General Erich Ludendorff would see the opening attack at Messines much differently. In his memoirs he wrote:

The moral effect of the explosions was simply staggering . . . 7th of June cost us dear, and owing to the success of the enemy attack, the price we paid was very heavy.[12]

In his diary for that day Haig would also record that he met his French counterpart, Marshal Henri-Philippe Pétain, Commander-in-Chief of the French army. Coincidentally, the issue of military executions would be raised in their conversation.

Pétain had not long been promoted and the two commanders compared notes on the day's events at Messines and the conduct of their armies. A discussion arose about morale and discipline, and Pétain told Haig that recently a number of French soldiers had refused to go into the front line, claiming they had not been given leave. There had been a mutiny in May, and it had spread among some units. Some of the men were tried and were shot. Haig would record that Pétain was worried about the discipline of his men. In the summer of 1917, as the two armies fought a common enemy, it is clear that they shared many difficulties.

As men from all parts of Ireland fought on the Messines ridge, Robert Hope was fighting for his life in a very different arena. On 9 June he appeared before a court martial made up of three officers. The 23-year-old pleaded not guilty to the charge of 'deserting His Majesty's service' and in mitigation claimed that despite his three-and-a-half months' absence he was planning to return to his unit.

His court martial records give only scant details about the hearing. They do not contain any character references or give any information about his history with the battalion. It is not clear which officers were involved in the consultation process after Hope was sentenced.

This lack of detail was emphasised in 2004 by officials of the Department of Foreign Affairs when they investigated Hope's case:

The material in this file is very threadbare—with no real defence put up by Private Hepple [Hope] or any evidence as to his previous character as a fighting man the court were left with little option but to find him guilty.[13]

What is clear from the case notes is that after he was found guilty and sentenced Robert Hope's file was sent as usual to Douglas Haig. Just as he had done with Hope's regimental comrade Thomas Hogan, the Commander-in-Chief would look closely at Hope's offence and background and consider whether the death sentence should be commuted.

Hope would have to wait nearly three weeks to find out. Haig travelled to London in the middle of June for a series of meetings involving the Prime Minister, David Lloyd George, and the War Cabinet. On his return to France he considered the young fusilier's fate. There is no account of what Haig thought of the accused, but there is a record of his final consideration. Today if one examines Hope's court martial file one will find Douglas Haig's neat signature inside. It is dated *29th of June 17,* and under the column that refers to the death sentence Haig has clearly written the word *Confirmed.*

On 5 July, Robert Hope followed in the footsteps of his fellow-countryman Thomas Hogan, and as daylight was breaking he was shot. The 23-year-old was buried at the Ferme-Olivier cemetery near Ypres in Belgium.

———

In August, as a new offensive took hold at Ypres and a month after the execution of Robert Hope, another Irishman left the ranks.

Like Hope and Hogan before him, Stephen Byrne had given an alias when he enlisted. From Dublin, he joined the 1st Battalion of the Royal Dublin Fusiliers in the spring of 1917. He had lived in a three-storey house in Usher's Quay with his two brothers and sister, and in 1916 he enrolled in the British Army, using the surname Monaghan. He was a serial enlister, and his home regiment would prove to be his last. Before he signed up with the 'Dubs' he claimed to have been a member of the West Lancashire Regiment—a unit he says he joined in January 1916. Byrne stated that he remained with the English regiment until he joined the Leinster Regiment while still in England. His battalion came to France, and Byrne claims he saw front-line action with them before deciding to join the Royal Dublin Fusiliers.

Byrne's short history with the West Lancashires and the Leinsters is puzzling. It seems odd that he made such regular transfers between regiments, though this was not unusual; his family do not know why he moved so quickly between units. If he was often changing regiments it seems strange that he would not have been the subject of rigorous questioning from officers, questioning that should have led to his identity and background being uncovered. It raises the suggestion that Byrne enlisted in England with the Lancashires under the alias of

Monaghan and then joined the other regiments because of some personal difficulties.

Stephen's nephew Paddy Byrne, who is nearly eighty and lives in London, cannot understand why his uncle used an alias.

It is hard to fathom really, hard to understand. I just don't know the reasons. It is possible that he may have enrolled twice—once using a false name to get extra money; maybe just to get another king's shilling. No-one really knows. It's all a bit of a puzzle.[14]

His great-nephew Derek Dunne is also mystified by Byrne's behaviour. He accepts that the alias may have been used to cover up a past indiscretion or may even have been used for political reasons.

It is possible he had deserted before. It is possible he was covering something up. He might just have decided to use a different name because in 1916 in Ireland some people would have said joining the British Army was not the cleverest thing to do.[15]

By 1917 Stephen Byrne had managed, through a series of moves, to become a member of his home regiment. As the summer began he was wearing the insignia of the Dublin Fusiliers and was now stationed with his battalion close to Ypres. His disciplinary record shows that he was guilty of a small number of petty crimes and had particular difficulty adhering to regimental guidelines regarding cleanliness. Twice during May he was admonished for being dirty while on parade. He also failed to turn up for an entire parade, another offence for which he was punished.

For two months Byrne's record was clear, but in August he made a decision that would have dramatic consequences. On the morning of 5 August the platoon sergeant went around to inform his men that they would be moving towards the front line that night. Byrne was informed of the move as he lay in his bivouac. When the sergeant returned later that day and called the roll, Stephen Byrne was missing. His absence was reported to the officers, who began a search of the camp, but the absentee could not be found and his platoon moved off towards the front line without him.

Private Byrne had moved away from the camp and had gone in a completely different direction from his comrades. He would later claim that he had not been well and needed some sustenance.

Feeling cold and ill I thought I would get some coffee, but finding the shop closed and feeling ill I stayed in the hedge for the night. I then thought I would go back but found the battalion had gone. I then wandered about and should have reported at Poperinghe but I was too afraid of what might happen to me. So I wandered about until I felt better.[16]

Byrne would remain at large for more than a month, until he was apprehended by the French authorities on 9 September. The French handed him back to their British counterparts, and Byrne was returned to his base camp and placed in custody. At this point Stephen Byrne knew he would face a trial within days and most probably a death sentence. For the next twelve days, as he considered his fate, he was locked up and kept under guard with other prisoners in Eton Camp at Elverdinghe, near Ypres.

On 22 September, Byrne and six other prisoners left the guard hut and went to the latrine, supervised by a private. The six returned, but Byrne disappeared and made another bid for freedom. He would later recall:

I walked out of the camp, and went to the YMCA hut. I reported myself the following day after having my feet dressed at a field ambulance.[17]

Byrne was again placed in custody and was charged with two offences. The first charge, of desertion, related to his initial disappearance in August; the second related to his escape from custody in September. He appeared before a court martial and pleaded not guilty to both offences.

After Byrne gave his version of events, in mitigation he raised the issue of his health.

About March 1917 I joined the battalion my sight was very bad and in the afternoons I sometimes could not see at all. I was examined for my eyes in 1916 and in January 1917 I got some glasses but they were no good.[18]

The prosecution called a witness from the Royal Army Medical Corps to give evidence about Byrne's health. Captain Kelly said that he may have treated Byrne before 5 August (the day of his first disappearance) and that if he had been unfit for duty at that time he would have been sent to hospital. Captain Kelly was then cross-examined by Byrne and admitted that he may have treated him for pains in his head but did not recollect anything about it.

When officials of the Department of Foreign Affairs examined Stephen Byrne's case in 2004 it was the issue of his health that they concentrated on. They concluded that Byrne's medical history was not properly investigated:

> This evidence was not taken into account and was effectively dismissed by the testimony of a medical officer who may or may not have treated Private Monaghan [Byrne]. No connection was made between the two symptoms described by Monaghan, even though it would seem obvious that one may have been causing the other. No medical report is on file, and no thorough evaluation was carried out prior to his execution.[19]

Byrne was found guilty by the court martial, and the death sentence was later confirmed by Douglas Haig. The Commander-in-Chief clearly believed that a prison sentence would have little effect on Byrne and agreed that the Irishman's crimes deserved the ultimate penalty.

On 28 October, at Basseux, Stephen Byrne was placed before a firing squad. At 6:25 a.m. he was shot dead. His death, according to a report written by one of his superior officers some hours later, was instantaneous. Byrne's place of burial is not known, though his name is commemorated on the memorial to the missing at Arras.

Nine decades after Stephen Byrne was executed his memory is being kept alive by family members. Paddy Byrne recalls being shown the telegram that was originally sent to the family home in Dublin in 1917 after Stephen was executed.

> I was shown it many years afterwards. It had been kept and was a bit tattered and torn. It was from the War Office and was addressed to Thomas, Stephen's brother, and it simply said Stephen had been

shot. It is hard to fathom what happened out there, hard to understand. I don't think they gave him a chance. Mr Haig saw to that.[20]

Derek Dunne, Stephen Byrne's great-nephew, was active in the Shot at Dawn campaign and was thrilled when the British government finally agreed to pardon those who were executed:

It meant everything, especially to the elderly relatives. They were not ashamed of him, and everybody was proud that he volunteered and did fight. It just means so much to have Stephen's name cleared and exonerated.[21]

It was only in death that the identity of Irishmen such as Stephen Byrne, Thomas Hogan and Robert Hope became known, volunteer soldiers who deliberately shielded their background and took their secrets to their graves. Now, nine decades later, their names have been restored and, perhaps most importantly, so too have their reputations.

Chapter 11 ⌣

A CLASS OF THEIR OWN

I consider him an insubordinate man of low class.
—OFFICER'S OPINION OF AN IRISHMAN FACING A
COURT MARTIAL

In the heat and dust of an August day, soldiers from the Royal Dublin Fusiliers and the Royal Warwickshire Regiment lay sprawled on the dusty cobbled streets of Saint-Quentin's main square. Wounded, hungry and exhausted, the two depleted battalions were in retreat after the Battle of Mons, the first major battle of the Great War. The men, members of the British Expeditionary Force, had landed in France some weeks earlier and were simply too tired to carry on.

It was 1914, the war was in its infancy, and what was about to happen would go down in military history. As the soldiers rested in the warmth of a summer's afternoon their commanding officers sought out the town's mayor. The officers wanted to secure some food and a train that could transport the injured and the weary towards the safety of the British lines. As the officers talked to Saint-Quentin's first citizen a note arrived and was passed to the mayor, who instantly became excited and agitated. According to the note the town was surrounded by the Germans and all exits were blocked.

The mayor said he was prepared to surrender the town and its people and then turned to his British guests and insisted that their troops leave at once. He argued that the presence of British soldiers in the town would provoke a German bombardment and that the shelling would kill civilians.

The two officers, Lieutenant-Colonel Arthur Mainwaring of the Royal Dublin Fusiliers and Lieutenant-Colonel John Elkington of the Royal Warwickshire Regiment, listened sympathetically to the plea. When it was explained that the soldiers needed to stay and rest, the mayor became agitated. Undaunted by the soldiers' reluctance to move, he persisted with his demand that the troops should leave the town. He was clearly very persuasive. The two officers, by now as tired as their men, pledged that they would not fight in the town and would move from the area before the advancing German forces arrived.

Elkington and Mainwaring then addressed their battalions and ordered the men to leave, but not one soldier was prepared to move. Mainwaring, who, like his men, had not slept properly for three days, would later recall:

> The fact is the men could do no more for the time being. Their limit of endurance was reached. I considered it my duty to protect these men, who had nobly done theirs.[1]

The two colonels agreed that, as their men were unable to march, they would make an undertaking that was to have enormous repercussions: they would surrender unconditionally. They drafted a hastily written surrender document, which stated that they would not fight the Germans if they entered Saint-Quentin, and the document was handed to the mayor. Mainwaring would later claim he had been left with little option.

> Even as I wrote the words I paused; but the state of my brain was such that I felt if I argued to the conditions it might leave an opening for the Germans to shell the town and kill the civilian population, and then I felt my duty was to make no attempt at terms.[2]

To complete the surrender, the men of the Royal Dublins and the Royal Warwicks gathered their rifles and ammunition, which were placed in a railway shed. However, within hours everything would change.

On 27 August, Major Tom Bridges of the Royal Irish Dragoons, part of the 2nd Cavalry Brigade, arrived on the scene. The Dragoons had taken part in the fighting at Mons, and Bridges' force was a reinforcement drafted in to protect the Saint-Quentin stragglers from the Germans. When he arrived in the town he could not believe his eyes. He found the Dubliners and the Warwicks resting on the pavements and in the gutters. Some were fully stretched out on the ground and already asleep; others had made their way to nearby houses, where they were in bed. Many of the Irishmen and their English counterparts were in a dishevelled state and had discarded their packs, belts and water bottles. A few were drunk, and there was little sign of order.

Bridges was then greeted by the mayor, who informed him of the surrender plan. Stunned at what he had heard, Bridges asserted control and quickly turned the situation around. The bedraggled soldiers were given half an hour to parade in full kit with their weapons, and were told that not one British soldier would be left stranded in the town. Then the major had an inspiration:

There was a toy shop handy which provided my trumpeter and myself with a tin whistle and a drum and we marched round and round the fountain where the men were lying like dead playing the British Grenadiers and Tipperary and beating the drum like mad. They sat up and began to laugh and even cheer.[3]

Bridges got the men to their feet, put the wounded in wooden carts and, with the aid of his makeshift band, rallied the troops.

The Irishmen and Englishmen may have been on their feet and on the march again, but their commanding officers' careers were over. Elkington and Mainwaring would later face a court martial. Their surrender plan was in direct breach of the disciplinary code that all soldiers were required to abide by.

The episode became known as the Colonels' Surrender, and in September 1914 Mainwaring and Elkington were found guilty of 'behaving in a scandalous manner unbecoming the character of an officer and a gentleman.' Both were cashiered for their behaviour.

Thereafter their fortunes diverged. Fifty-year-old Mainwaring returned to civilian life in England and never engaged in military service again. Elkington went to Paris and joined the French Foreign Legion. He distinguished himself in battle and was later honoured for his bravery with the legion, and for his efforts he was awarded the Distinguished Service Order. In 1916 his rehabilitation was complete when he was reinstated as lieutenant-colonel of the Royal Warwickshire Regiment and granted a royal pardon for his role in the Saint-Quentin surrender.

Elkington and Mainwaring's crime in the opening days of the war came before any soldier had faced a firing squad. However, it sent shock waves through the military hierarchy and prompted the Commander-in-Chief, Sir John French, to write:

> The Commander-in-Chief takes this opportunity of again impressing on all ranks the absolute necessity for the maintenance of the strictest discipline, without which success cannot be maintained. Failure to maintain the highest standard of discipline will result in the infliction of the most severe punishment.[4]

Mainwaring and Elkington, as commissioned officers, were cashiered from the army. Though this was a humiliating punishment, it was not an option that was on offer to the rank and file. Even after the passing of ninety years the different punishment officers received compared with the treatment meted out to ordinary soldiers remains a controversial issue.

The Colonels' Surrender was highlighted by the Irish government in 2004. The Irish government maintained that its research showed that there were two types of justice during the Great War: one for officers and the other for ordinary soldiers.

More than three thousand soldiers were sentenced to death during the Great War, and one in ten of these were actually put to death. Yet out of that number only forty-six officers ever faced courts martial for leaving the ranks, and only two were executed.

Only two Irish officers were tried for desertion. Lieutenant Murray of the Connaught Rangers was sentenced to death, but this was reduced to penal servitude. Second-Lieutenant Davidson of the Royal Irish Fusiliers was tried for desertion in 1918 but acquitted.

Many officers found guilty of breaking regulations were simply dismissed from the army. Altogether a thousand were thrown out of the service, and four hundred were cashiered. Two-and-a-half thousand officers simply escaped with a reprimand. Even when officers were found guilty of breaching regulations they escaped some penalties that were routinely inflicted on other ranks. No officers were ever subjected to the humiliating and degrading field punishments, unlike the eighty thousand rank-and-file soldiers who were given field punishments during the Great War.

All the rank-and-file men who were shot were working-class soldiers, who were tried not by their peers but by men of a different social standing. The officers who sat on the courts martial were well educated and articulate, often the product of public schools. In contrast, the condemned men were sometimes illiterate, with poor social and communication skills, who very rarely had any legal representation at the hearing. Class undoubtedly had a hand in the court martial process, sometimes openly and on other occasions covertly.

The issue of class is perfectly illustrated by the case of Second-Lieutenant Arthur Annandale of the 9th Battalion of the Royal Irish Rifles. Annandale, aged twenty-three was a member of the same battalion as James Crozier, the young Belfast rifleman shot for desertion in February 1916. Days before James Crozier was executed, Annandale faced a court martial, charged with leaving the trenches without permission and not returning to duty.

Annandale, from Polton, Midlothian, appeared to have all the appropriate officer credentials. He was educated at Merchiston Castle School, a prestigious establishment in Edinburgh, and had been in the Officer Training Corps. He had also served in the Royal Scots Regiment and after recommendations from a lieutenant-colonel and his headmaster was transferred to the Royal Irish Rifles, where he was commissioned as a second-lieutenant.

This officer was well known to the battalion's second in command, Frank Percy Crozier. Annandale first attracted Crozier's attention when the battalion's medical officer informed him that the junior officer had contracted gonorrhoea. Crozier wrote about the incident in his memoirs. Perhaps to spare the blushes of Annandale's family, he refers to him as 'Rochdale'. He recalled how the medical officer explained his predicament:

'Young Rochdale has venereal, gonorrhoea, in fact he is in an awful stew. He is engaged to be married. If I send him down to the venereal hospital it is sure to get out at home where he is.' The medic continued, 'If he goes to Amiens to one of those French doctors for three or four days and gets a cure—at a price—he may be all right.'[5]

For a man who had often lectured his troops on the dangers of sexual encounters with local women, Frank Percy Crozier showed remarkable compassion towards Annandale. He allowed the officer to leave headquarters and spend ten days in Amiens in the hands of French doctors. The officer then returned to duty, apparently cured.

It would not be the last time that Annandale's behaviour was called into question. In January 1916 throughout the Somme region the German artillery continued to pound British lines. In the small hours of the morning Annandale was on duty in his dug-out as the shelling began. The noise was deafening, the trenches were rocked, and the soldiers' nerves were stretched. Annandale decided he had had enough; he ran down the trench past his men and disappeared from view. The next day he was found sleeping in a French dug-out behind the lines. It appeared to be a classic case of desertion.

Annandale was found guilty of leaving his post without permission—though surprisingly the word 'desertion' was never used in the proceedings. Crozier believed that Annandale's absence and his evasion of duty constituted a serious breach of discipline, and he would later remark, 'He has shown apparent cowardice in front of his men.' He was found guilty of leaving his post, and the court martial recommended that he be dismissed from the service. However, the penalty was suspended until a medical board had been convened to enquire into the state of Annandale's health.

In his memoirs Crozier claimed that a letter was sent stating that Annandale must be 'released from arrest and all consequences.' No record of any such correspondence exists in Annandale's file, which is now in the National Archives in London, though the files were edited before they were made public. Crozier clearly believed Annandale was given preferential treatment and says the letter was the work of the young officer's 'influential friends'.

Annandale was placed on sick leave and never served again with the 9th Battalion. He was sent to a hospital in Scotland, and in August 1916 he was examined in Edinburgh. A medical board later concluded that he spoke with hesitation, was sleeping badly, had myopia and had been suffering from shell-shock. The board concluded: 'It is most improbable that this officer will ever be fit for service.'[6] In August 1916 he resigned his commission and returned to civilian life.

The decision to allow Annandale to leave the army was not well received by the men of the 9th Battalion. David Starrett, who was Frank Percy Crozier's batman at the time, wrote about the way Annandale and James Crozier were treated differently.

The Colonel [Crozier] was off the deep end for days about both and few could get near him. Both were tried by field general court martial and the man was shot and the officer got off. That gave me a bit of thought about King's Regulations, but not very clear thought. If the officer did not know what he was doing, did the man. We did not think so.[7]

To be fair, Frank Percy Crozier also openly conceded the different treatment meted out to Annandale compared with James Crozier. 'The least said about this the better, except to remark that had justice been done according to our code regrets would have been fewer in the case of Rifleman Crozier.'[8]

Annandale's case reeks of class prejudice, and the difference in the fortunes of the men involved in this affair could not be more stark. James Crozier, the working-class boy from Belfast, was shot and buried within eighteen months of enlisting. Arthur Annandale, the public-school boy, avoided the death penalty and returned to civilian life, maimed and scarred by his wartime experience but nonetheless fortunate to have escaped a firing squad.

The career of the man at the centre of this affair, Frank Percy Crozier, blossomed. He was awarded the Distinguished Service Order, and he eventually rose to the rank of brigadier-general.

———

The issue of class arose again in 1916 in the case of James Mullany, a driver with the Royal Field Artillery. The Irishman did not desert or go absent but it was a fist fight that would ultimately end his life. His crime, a relatively unusual offence, was that he hit a superior officer. The incident had occurred because Mullany claimed all he wanted was a cup of tea. The victim of Mullany's rage was Battery Sergeant-Major Hughes, who would tell the court martial that he had ordered the Irishman to harness some horses.

I then heard Driver Mullany shout out what about some fucking tea. I placed the accused in open arrest. The accused then came up to me and asked if he could be placed in close arrest. I told him to go and get harnessed up. The accused then turned away and said It is always the bastard same in this battery or words to that effect.[9]

Hughes then ordered him to the guardroom, at which point Mullany reacted violently. He knocked Hughes to the ground and continued to punch him while he was on the ground. A bombardier managed to pull Mullany away from Hughes, but when Hughes got to his feet he was then knocked down again by Mullany.

Mullany was restrained and then taken to the guardroom while investigations began into the incident. The legal process was quick. Two days later Mullany found himself before a court martial with another driver, Thomas Hamilton, who some six days earlier had committed a similar offence. Hamilton had also struck an NCO, this time in a dispute involving smoking.

Mullany pleaded not guilty, and while he did not dispute that there had been contact with Battery Sergeant-Major Hughes he claimed he did not hit him. Mullany claimed he went up to the NCO and raised his hand, and the sergeant-major took a defensive position. He then alleged that they both ran into each other and 'fell to the ground.'

Questioned about his reasons for demanding to be placed under close arrest, Mullany told the hearing: 'Simply because I was fed up with the unit I was in and also because it was absolute torture to serve in the battery.'[10]

Mullany's disciplinary record in the battery was good. He had one previous minor offence of making an improper reply to a superior officer some three months previously. However, his attitude and background were drawn upon in a series of character reports written at the time. Second-Lieutenant Taylor stated that Mullany had been an acting-bombardier but had resigned from this rank after failing to be promoted. He added that Mullany had a habit of being insolent when his requests were refused, though Taylor added that he was never openly insolent. Major Barnwell, commanding officer of the 38th Brigade, Royal Field Artillery, insisted that Mullany had been insolent on two occasions. Barnwell also reported that Mullany had previously faced a court martial for hitting a civilian, but the case had been dropped. A further report into Mullany was particularly unfavourable.

Driver Mullany was not appointed acting bombardier while under my command but joined with a stripe on his arm—he is quite unfitted for such an appointment—I consider him an insubordinate man of low class.[11]

The prejudicial remarks about Mullany's background may have been irrelevant to the charge under investigation but were designed to paint a picture of an individual who was insubordinate, who did not know how to behave and who should be punished.

Both Mullany and Hamilton were sentenced to death, a finding endorsed by Lord Cavan, the corps commander. Three days after the court martial he wrote: 'I recommend that the death sentence be carried out as discipline in this battery is bad.'[12] On 3 October 1916 the two drivers, Hamilton and Mullany, were executed together. They would later be buried side by side in Ribemont Communal cemetery at the Somme, south west of the town of Albert.

In 2001 Cathryn Corns and her colleague John Hughes-Wilson, a former army officer, examined the deaths of Hamilton and Mullany. They concluded:

> In both cases, had the men simply groused in the usual way of soldiers they would probably, at worst, have been given FP [field punishment] No. 1, but an army can not function if the 'rank and file' physically attack their NCOs and officers. Hamilton and Mullany died to remind other soldiers of that stark and simple fact.[13]

So were their deaths really necessary to keep their comrades in line? What is clear is that even in 1916, in the middle of the war, their deaths caused unease in the upper echelons of the military establishment. In the history of military executions, the case would become a landmark.

In a letter written before the men were shot the brigadier-general of XIV Corps had enquired if the punishment was not unduly severe. He was informed that discipline had become lax, and the commander of the 38th Infantry Brigade was a sound and good disciplinarian. Despite this response the unease within the army's hierarchy did not disappear, and thereafter no other soldiers were executed after being convicted of striking a superior.

Ninety years later the disquiet over James Mullany's court martial and execution was publicly voiced by the Irish government. His court martial and execution were examined by the Department of Foreign Affairs. In Mullany's case the report's authors seized on what they regarded as inadequacies in the legal process, and the report's conclusions were damning.

This case bears all the hallmarks of a miscarriage of justice. There is contradictory evidence on what actually happened . . . there are discriminatory comments against Mullany which describe him of being low class.

The report concludes by stating:

What chance did Mullany or others like him, have of proving their innocence in the face of this type of treatment by superior officers?[14]

If Mullany had been an officer would he have suffered the same fate? Most probably he would have escaped execution, as officers found guilty of capital crimes had their sentences commuted. The issue of different treatment for officers and rank-and-file soldiers was investigated by the Irish government. Its report cites the cases of eight officers who were court-martialled and found guilty of military offences but who were later reinstated and often pardoned. The point made was a simple one: in the Great War there appeared to be two tiers of justice. The report stated:

Twenty six Irish men were not afforded the opportunity of an appeal to the King, had no military commanders pleading for pardons on their behalf, and received no retrospective leniency for their actions, no matter how deserving they may or may not have been. A military system of law that provides one form of justice to the lower ranked troops on the front line, and another to the officers and upper echelons, cannot be deemed to be just and must be seen for what it evidently was: biased.[15]

It is clear that the court martial system was simply mirroring a class divide that existed in Britain at the time, and this division was at play on the fields of France and Flanders. It is a point that Cathryn Corns and John Hughes-Wilson acknowledge, with some reservations.

The courts martial merely reflected the paternalistic standards and mores of their age, and the hierarchy of society of the day. Crucially, no one at the time felt there was a vendetta against working class soldiers. Such ideas are a later invention of modern social commentators looking back in indignation at some of the stranger ideas of the early social and racial theorists.[16]

———

One officer who was executed during the Great War was Sub-Lieutenant Edwin Dyett. He had enlisted in the Royal Navy and had not expected to be subjected to trench warfare. However, in November 1916 he was in action on the Western Front with the Royal Naval Division. During the fighting, as he and his comrades came under attack, he became separated from his comrades. He came across another officer, who insisted that he return to the front line. An argument broke out, Dyett refused the officer's instruction, and he was reported for refusing an order. When he was later discovered he was charged with desertion and found guilty by a court martial. He was shot in January 1917.

Dyett's case became a cause célèbre. It was raised in Parliament and attracted much press attention. Leading Seaman MacMillan, who worked as a clerk at brigade headquarters and who processed Dyett's trial papers, would write about the case in his diary. He wondered whether Dyett had been executed as a token officer.

Was he, I wondered to be the first martyr to the clamour from the ranks for an example to be made of an officer for desertion or cowardice? 'How is it' the men were asking and rightly so, 'that only rankers are being shot for cowardice? How many officers have been guilty of this offence and why have they not been able to answer for it with their lives, as we have to do?' The Higher Command must have heard this grouse grow louder and could not fail to admit the justness of it. If however they were forced to act, why did they select a mere boy for their first victim?[17]

While there was no concerted campaign to single out working-class soldiers, the issue of class was often raised by officers. In October 1915 Major-General Oliver Nugent, commanding officer of the 36th (Ulster) Division, wrote to his wife about his unhappiness with the quality of his latest officers.

I don't think they are fit for service and I should be very sorry to have to trust them. It is all due to putting a weak man in command of the Brigade to start with and giving commissions to men of the wrong class.[18]

However, it was not just the issue of social class that concerned Irish investigators when they began to examine the detail of the executions in 2003. A study of the number of deaths involving Irish-born soldiers led officials of the Department of Foreign Affairs to believe that there was a disparity in the treatment of soldiers from Irish regiments. Research suggested that Irish soldiers were three to four times more likely to be sentenced to death than any other men in the British Army, with the exception of non-European recruits. Figures showed that in most British formations one in every 3,000 soldiers was sentenced to death, yet for every 600 Irishmen who enlisted one would be sentenced to death following a court martial.

Comparisons with recruiting rates were also considered. In New Zealand, where the number of recruits was comparable to Ireland, only twenty-three soldiers were given the death sentence, whereas the figure for Irishmen was ten times that figure. About one in every fifty recruits to the British Army was Irish—yet one in every thirteen men condemned to death was Irish.

This issue of perceived bias was raised by the Irish government in formal exchanges with the British government. The Minister for Foreign Affairs, Dermot Ahern, outlined his thinking during an interview for BBC Northern Ireland's 'Spotlight' programme in 2005:

If you were in the lower ranks of the army at the time, the punishment that was meted out for quite insignificant misdemeanours was excessive and was used as an example to others, and we also noticed that if you happened to be Irish there seemed to be a much higher proportion of punishment meted out to Irishmen rather than other nationalities.

Asked whether he thought this was institutionalised he replied:

Well, we think it went right through the system from what we see.[19]

The Irish investigation relied on research carried out by Dr Gerard Oram, a lecturer in modern European history and research fellow at the Centre for First World War Studies at the University of Birmingham. Oram chronicled the details of more than three thousand soldiers who were sentenced to death during the Great War. He found the disproportionately high number of Irish death sentences puzzling and as part of his research analysed army divisions where Irish units served alongside English, Scottish and Welsh units.

In the Guards Division the highest number of death sentences passed on one battalion was the six passed on the 1st Battalion of the Irish Guards. Similarly in the 8 Division the seventeen death sentences passed on 1 [1st Battalion] Royal Irish Rifles is the highest in the division. The situation was not much better for Irish units in the other three divisions: Irish battalions received either the second or third-highest number of death sentences. In short Irish units in these divisions consistently came off worse than others. The overall average for English, Scottish and Welsh units in these division is four death sentences per battalion. However, the overall average for the Irish units in these divisions is seven per battalion.[20]

Oram says the most likely explanation for these figures is that Irish soldiers were regarded by the military hierarchy as troublesome and needed firm handling. Though he says there is no evidence of a deliberate anti-Irish policy in the court martial system, he believes there is much anecdotal evidence that senior political and military figures viewed the Irish as unreliable and difficult to manage. The Irish government report in 2004 supported this view:

There is nothing to indicate a deliberate policy against the Irish ranks in the transcripts of the trials themselves. However, the pervading British attitude towards the Irish at the time is well documented as one of mistrust and suspicion.[21]

Timothy Bowman, who has investigated the issue of discipline in Irish units, also accepts that the image Irishmen had before and during the Great War may have contributed to the frequent use of courts martial.

The stereotypical image of the Irishman in early twentieth century Britain may have meant that officers were prepared to have men serving in Irish regiments tried by courts martial for crimes such as drunkenness, much more readily than their counterparts in English, Scottish or Welsh regiments. This stereotypical view of Irish soldiers may account for the relatively high number of courts martial in Irish units, even from 1916 to 1918, when they contained large numbers of non-Irish personnel.[22]

Bowman's analysis is worth examining. Though 1916 had the highest number of Irish executions, with ten men facing firing squads, the deaths continued into the final two years of the war, even though the make-up of the Irish regiments meant they were not exclusively Irish. In fact two members of Irish regiments who would be shot were not Irish: Private Albert Rickman of the Royal Dublin Fusiliers, shot in 1916, was English, and Private Henry Hendricks of the Leinster Regiment, shot in the final months of the war, claimed to be an American.

By the late summer of 1916, following the slaughter of the Somme and the political unrest in Ireland, the composition of many Irish regiments had begun to change. The 36th (Ulster) Division and the 16th (Irish) Division were short of reinforcements as a result of casualties and a reduction in the number of volunteers from home. Recruitment in Ireland was in crisis, and in some parts of the country the number of men coming forward had halved or the supply had even stopped completely. Conscripts from England were drafted into Irish units, and it was suggested that the 16th and 36th Divisions might have to merge. The Irish infantry units needed nearly 18,000 men to bring them up to fighting strength.

By 1917 the prospect of conscription loomed large over Ireland, and as the manpower crisis took hold the military authorities wanted to get every able-bodied man into uniform. For three experienced Irishmen, who had once deserted the trenches, that meant an unexpected return to the front line.

Chapter 12 ∼

ONE LAST CHANCE

I see no reason why the maximum penalty should not be enforced. In fact I am of the opinion that an example would be beneficial.
—LIEUTENANT-COLONEL BAGGALLAY, 1ST BATTALION, IRISH GUARDS

In the late summer of 1917 Private George Hanna's war was not going well. It had been some time since he had last heard or seen the enemy's guns, let alone fired a shot in anger. As his countrymen fought in France and Flanders, the young Belfast man was living a solitary life tucked away in the safety of Kent. Detained at His Majesty's pleasure, Private 12609 was spending his days and nights inside a cell at Maidstone Prison.

Since he volunteered in Armagh in 1914 the Ulsterman was no stranger to being in custody, as he had developed an uncanny habit of absconding at crucial moments during the war. The 26-year-old member of the Royal Irish Fusiliers had become a serial absentee and was serving a seven-year prison sentence for desertion—the second time he had been found guilty of abandoning his colleagues. However, in the middle of the summer the young Irishman was offered a reprieve, a last chance to prove himself as a soldier and change his ways. On 7 August a letter arrived at the prison from the War Office suspending his sentence and informing him that he would be returning to his regiment forthwith. Hanna was released as part of a plan to secure reinforcements for battle. By the autumn of 1917 men would be badly needed, particularly during the Battle of Ypres.

Within days of the letter arriving in Kent, George Hanna was making the journey back to duty to the depot of the Royal Irish Fusiliers at Clonmany, Co. Donegal, in preparation for service in

France. He would eventually join the men of the 1st Battalion, the same unit he had abandoned twice before.

By now Hanna's reunions with his old comrades were becoming regular affairs. Two years earlier, in August 1915, he had taken part in the landing at Gallipoli, but his experience in the Dardanelles, like that of so many of his countrymen, was not a happy one. He had originally set sail from Devenport Docks on the *Canada* to take part in the assault that the Allies hoped would push the Turkish forces out of the war.

During the journey the men, many of whom were about to experience their first taste of battle, were in good spirits. There was a great sense of camaraderie and the regimental bands kept spirits up with renditions of 'God Save Ireland' and 'Brian Boru'. As they reached their destination the mood changed. When the thousands of Irishmen finally went ashore at Suvla Bay they were at the centre of a bloodbath. Under constant shell fire, they were outgunned and outmanoeuvred. The Allied attack had been poorly planned and badly organised and within weeks it would be apparent that the bold battle plan conceived by Lord Kitchener and Winston Churchill would not work.

George Hanna was clearly affected by the carnage he witnessed on the beaches and on the hillsides during those frenetic opening days of battle. After two days of fighting he had simply had enough, and he fled the ranks. Under the heat of the Mediterranean sun he absconded as his battalion fought with the Turkish defenders in an area known as Hill 70. In the confined space surrounding Suvla Bay, and with little opportunity to travel any distance, his disappearance was predictably short-lived. He was quickly arrested and brought before a military court. He was found guilty of desertion and, as military law dictated, sentenced to death.

Hanna's life lay in the hands of another Irishman: Lieutenant-General Brian Mahon from Galway, commanding officer of the 10th (Irish) Division. Perhaps influenced by the losses he had witnessed, Mahon may well have been keen to keep another fighting man alive, and he spared his countryman's life. The death sentence was commuted to ten years' imprisonment and then suspended.

It appears that Hanna quickly understood that he had been given another chance and knew that his behaviour had to change. In the weeks that followed he learnt what he needed to do to escape a firing squad in the future. With the death sentence still hanging over him, he was allowed to resume his soldiering and set about trying to impress his superiors with his work.

In late September he was transferred to Salonika, and he continued to fight there with his battalion as part of the 10th Division. Now the fusilier caught the eye of his officers for all the right reasons. His hard work and good conduct were rewarded when he was given remission by Brigadier-General Morris in September 1916, and complimentary remarks were written on Hanna's file. But if the brigadier believed the Belfast man had turned a corner, he would be disappointed in a matter of weeks.

Two months later, as members of the 10th Division suffered frostbite and exposure during preparations to fight the Bulgarians at Kosturino, George Hanna once again left the ranks. As with his unsuccessful escape on the Gallipoli peninsula, he was arrested quickly and charged with attempting to desert His Majesty's service. After five witnesses gave evidence to the court martial, the fusilier was found guilty and, as before, sentenced to be shot by firing squad. But luck was again shining on the defendant, and his life was spared for a second time, on this occasion by Lieutenant-General Wilson, who commanded the forces in Salonika. Hanna was given seven years' imprisonment—the sentence he was serving when he was released from Maidstone Prison in 1917—and ordered to rejoin his regiment on the Western Front.

It was in France in late autumn that Hanna's good fortune would finally end.

By late August, Fusilier Hanna was in camp with the 1st Battalion of the Royal Irish Fusiliers in Le Havre. On the morning of 29 August, just after daybreak, he made a desperate bid for freedom. He broke out of the base, evaded guards and remained at large for seven hours, eventually being caught by the military police at Rouelles in mid-afternoon. Returned to the camp, he was brought before a court martial on 1 September. He was docked one day's pay and given field punishment no. 1.

This very public and humiliating punishment did little to discourage the Ulsterman from deserting in the future: in fact his seven-hour unofficial leave of absence simply appears to have spurred him on to try again. Four weeks later, as the battalion was preparing to go into the trenches, Hanna disappeared for a second time, as Company Quartermaster-Sergeant McLaughlin would recall.

On 28th September 1917, a draft of 7 men were posted to my company, the accused was one of the draft. I warned them to parade at 6.30 p.m., to proceed to the trenches, the accused was present when I warned the men of the draft. I fell the draft in at 6.30 p.m. and the accused was absent.[1]

As his comrades were on their way to the front line, George Hanna was going in the opposite direction, towards the city of Amiens in the Somme region. He spent the next few days walking and sleeping rough, eventually arriving in Amiens on 1 October. At the tramway terminus at Saint-Acheul he was hungry and weary, and he approached a fellow-soldier, Quartermaster-Sergeant Crossley.

The accused came to me and asked me for some food. I asked him why he wanted food at that hour of night. I then took him to the cookhouse and ordered the cook to give him some food. He complained he was hungry. I asked him if he was on a pass and had missed a train. He said 'No.' I said 'What are you?' He answered, 'I am an absentee.'[2]

Hanna was then put in the guardroom and handed over to the military police. He was returned to his unit and charged with desertion, and on 19 October he faced his final military trial.

I had absolutely no intention of deserting. If I had not been detained I should have returned to camp. I have been three years in service, two of my brothers have been killed in France and one at sea. I was refused leave to go and see my people. My last leave was in December 1914.

He then told the hearing why he left the camp:

I absented myself because I was upset at not being able to get leave and had heard from my sister to say that she had been expecting me home and when I did not come, it upset her and she was not well.

He would later add:

My home is in Belfast. I wanted leave to go to Belfast.[3]

Hanna was found guilty and sentenced to death. This time there would be no leniency or last-minute reprieve: those who sat in judgement on him clearly believed he had been given one chance too many. It was the fourth time he had gone absent, and it would be his last.

Julian Putkowski, who investigated Hanna's trial and execution, is convinced that the Ulsterman's fate was decided before the court martial was convened.

Field General Courts martial were highly likely to sanction the execution of recidivists who had already been found guilty of a capital offence. So even before proceedings opened all concerned must have known that Hanna's chances of escaping the death sentence were pretty nearly nil.[5]

In the early hours of 6 November 1917, Private George Hanna was shot by a firing squad at Barrosa Hall at Metz-en-Couture.

His death was examined by the Irish government in 2004. The officials concluded:

Private Hanna's absences seem to stem from family problems, in that he had apparently lost three brothers to the war and was understandably worried about his family in Belfast. At the time of his execution he had not been home in almost three years and this undoubtedly influenced his decision to get back to Belfast to see his family.[6]

The Irish government's study of George Hanna's case was sympathetic. However, it takes little consideration of the difficulties faced by Hanna's commanding officers as they tried to manage him. His final disappearance was his fourth unofficial absence, if the seven-hour break for freedom is included. The Ulsterman had twice before been sentenced to death for desertion, and twice that sentence had been commuted. By 1917 his actions had well and truly tested the patience of his officers, who did not know how to keep him in the trenches.

His story of losing his two brothers may be true. One brother, David Hanna, a member of the Royal Inniskilling Fusiliers, is recorded as having died in August 1916. However, Hanna's family circumstances extracted little sympathy at the court martial. His unofficial walk to Amiens was one trip too many, and senior officers in his division clearly believed that the time for leniency was over.

——

The policy of suspending sentences had begun two years earlier as the military authorities strove to use every available man in the war effort. Men were desperately needed as new assaults were planned on the Western Front, including the third and final Battle of Ypres, which began in July. Rather than see fighting men locked up, commanders were happy to gamble that those who had once deserted the battlefield might now be prepared to change their ways.

One of those deserters released from prison and then sent to fight at Ypres in October 1917 was 21-year-old John Seymour, a private in the Royal Inniskilling Fusiliers. Like his fellow-Irishman George Hanna, he had a record of disappearing from the trenches at important moments.

Seymour joined the 1st Battalion of the Royal Inniskilling Fusiliers in April 1915, but within a month of signing up he had fallen foul of his superiors. On 5 May he left his post without permission. He was found guilty by a court martial and given two years' hard labour, but the sentence was later commuted and then finally suspended. Seven months later Seymour deserted the ranks. Again he was found guilty, but this time the sentence was severe: he was sentenced to death by firing squad, as military law dictated. However, the officer commanding the 4th Army showed the Irishman considerable leniency, first commuting the sentence to ten years' imprisonment and later reducing it to two years' hard labour.

By March 1916 it seemed that John Seymour's role in the war had come to an abrupt end when he was sent to prison. His reputation was now in tatters, as Regimental Sergeant-Major McGuire would later recall.

I knew Private Seymour when he originally joined the battalion. At Cuinchy he left the trenches without orders, and it was there he first came to my notice. Again early in 1916 he left the trenches opposite Thiepval during an enemy bombardment. The general opinion in the battalion at the time which I myself shared was that the offences had been deliberately committed.[7]

Seymour's time in jail lasted nearly twenty months, up to the autumn of 1917, when, like George Hanna, he was offered one last chance. On 13 October his sentence for desertion was suspended, and three days later he was back in the line with his comrades of the 2nd Battalion of the Royal Inniskillings.

This was to be Seymour's final opportunity. In late November members of his battalion readied themselves to take part in an assault on German lines. At daybreak on 27 November, Seymour's platoon was called to duty at Hurst Farm as it prepared to go into the front line. When the roll-call was taken Seymour was nowhere to be found.

The young fusilier would later claim that his disappearance could be explained:

On the night of 26 November I was sent for some rations. I met some men who gave me some rum. I do not remember anything more until I found myself the next morning in a hut alone about 3 kilometres west of Poperinghe. I tried to find the regiment but I failed to do so. I can not account for my movements on the days I was absent.[8]

Seymour's absence would last more than a few days. His unofficial leave would stretch to a month before he would eventually be discovered by a member of the military police late one evening in the town of Poperinghe, near Ypres. The arresting military policeman would later recall:

I was on duty on the Rue du Ypres, Poperinghe, and I visited the YMCA hut there. I saw the accused in the YMCA hut. I questioned him. He replied, 'I come from hospital this morning and I am joining my battalion in the morning.' I arrested him.[9]

The Irishman was charged with desertion and kept under guard. When his court martial began in the new year he was given an opportunity to explain why he was missing for so long from his colleagues.

I did not report during this month to anybody. I can not give any reason why I did not. I went to the Canal but could not find my battalion. I am 21 years old. I have never reported sick because my nerves have been upset, or for any reason.[10]

Later he told the hearing:

My nerves get the better of me sometimes.[11]

Seymour's explanation did little to convince the four-man court martial, which found him guilty of desertion and recommended that he be shot by firing squad. Senior officers charged with examining the court's findings agreed. On 13 January the brigadier-general wrote:

There have been too many cases already of desertion in this battalion. An example is needed as there are many men in this battalion who never wished to be soldiers but were combed out . . . and who do not understand the seriousness of the offence of desertion.[12]

The lieutenant-colonel who commanded Seymour's regiment concurred. He said that the character of the accused from a fighting point of view was bad. He was worried that any leniency in this case would adversely affect discipline, particularly as a large number of new recruits had just joined the regiment.

The final decision rested as ever with Haig. He endorsed the death sentence on Monday 21 January and simply wrote on Seymour's court martial file the word *Confirmed* and then signed his name. Three days later, at dawn on 24 January 1918, John Seymour was brought before a firing squad and shot.

Seymour's case was studied by Irish government officials in 2004. They concluded that he had been shot to warn other members of the regiment who might have been tempted to quit the ranks.

The fighting character of Private Seymour, in the opinion of his regimental Sergeant Major provided a negatively influencing factor in the deliberations of those in the confirmation process. There is clear reference here to Private Seymour being executed as an example to others, and as a consequence of previous desertions not being dealt with so severely.[13]

James Seymour was the only British soldier to be placed before a firing squad during January that year. The rest of the year would not be so quiet, and up to the Armistice in November an average of five executions would take place every month on the Western Front. Most of those shot in 1918 had a similar background to Seymour and Hanna, men who had previously absconded and had served prison sentences for desertion. Such men as William Scholes of the South Wales Borderers and John Swain of the Royal Berkshire Regiment were shot as they served under suspended sentences. Scholes and Swain were executed in August 1918, the year's bloodiest month for executions. The same month a soldier from Co. Wexford faced a firing squad.

———

Benjamin O'Connell's disciplinary record was like that of his fellow-Irishmen John Seymour and George Hanna. A member of the Irish Guards, he had deserted on a number of occasions before and would be released from prison as the war moved slowly towards the Armistice.

An examination of his disciplinary record suggests that the 21-year-old was more interested in womanising and socialising than in soldiering. From Tinarath, near Foulkesmill, Co. Wexford, he was the son of James and Mary O'Connell, and it seems likely that he had little formal education. Even in his twenties he could not read or write, though he could recognise and write his own name.

The new recruit first began to disappear from duty after he left Ireland and was based at Caterham army camp in Surrey. In December 1915, four days after Christmas, he ended up losing three weeks' pay and being put in a cell for fourteen days after he left the camp and went missing for a number of hours.

Four months later he vanished again and, as before, was locked up as a punishment, this time for eighty-four days. No sooner was he released from custody, however, than he skipped the confines of the camp again, this time in plain clothes. The civilian attire did little to aid his escape, however, as he was arrested quickly and returned to the camp.

The young volunteer must now have been very familiar with what was about to happen. He was once again brought before a court martial, found guilty, and locked up for three weeks, with the loss of ten days' pay.

Sympathetic observers might suggest that O'Connell's earlier absences were nothing more harmless than a young soldier going out to a nearby town to enjoy a few drinks and the company of the opposite sex. That may have been true in the early stages of his career, but in October 1916 his absences became more serious.

On the first occasion he broke out of the camp at Caterham and went missing for nearly two days before he gave himself up to the police in Old Malden. He then made the familiar journey back to the camp under guard and once again found himself locked up. Four days later he committed the same offence, escaping from his cell, evading the guards, and remaining absent for a total of seventeen days. This lengthy disappearance meant that O'Connell was detained for twenty-eight days and lost eighteen days' pay.

By December 1916 O'Connell's training days were over and he and his regimental colleagues were on French soil, preparing to go into action. As his comrades celebrated Christmas as best they could, O'Connell clearly wanted a change of scene. On Christmas Day, as the regiment marked the festive season in the coastal city of Le Havre, O'Connell used the occasion to slip away from camp. Ten days later he appeared before a court martial, and after two of his colleagues appeared as witnesses to his disappearance he was found guilty of desertion and sentenced to two years' hard labour. The sentence was quickly suspended by Haig, and the young guardsman narrowly avoided prison.

O'Connell's return to duty was characteristically short-lived and with the new year a month old he went missing again. On 31 January he abandoned his comrades when they were in action and later compounded the offence by trying to escape when he was arrested. He was later charged and again brought before a court martial. Predictably, this hearing did not go as well as his last, and he was found guilty. He avoided the death penalty, though the alternative was not an easy option, as he was sentenced to ten years in prison. Five months later his case was reviewed and his sentence was commuted to two years' hard labour.

As hostilities on the Western Front dragged on, O'Connell must have thought he would have to spend the rest of the war behind bars. However, in 1918, just like George Hanna and John Seymour before him, O'Connell was given one last chance. He was freed and returned to duty. He joined the 1st Battalion of the Irish Guards, which by the middle of the summer was preparing for an assault on the western edge of Château Wood, near Hendecourt.

For the soldiers it was not just constant training: there were other distractions. The battalion war diary records that the Duke of Connaught paid a morale-boosting visit to the men and the men also had time to challenge their colleagues in the Munster Fusiliers to a series of athletic events. The diary records that the Irish Guards triumphed at every event except the 100-yards sprint!

On 5 July the Irish Guards were on the move and, to the beat of the drums, O'Connell and his comrades marched to Bavincourt station. The next day the weather was hot and there was little shelling as they waited in trenches near Ransart, known as the intermediate line.

On 7 July they were briefed about what was about to happen and were expected to go into the front line for four days. That night, when the roll was called by Lance-Corporal Casey after 6 p.m., O'Connell was absent.

His break from the ranks would last until 10 July. On that day at Warlincourt, some 8 kilometres from Ransart, O'Connell was spotted by a British soldier, Private Jefferson, who was on sentry duty. When Jefferson challenged the Wexford man he was wearing Royal Engineers insignia and he claimed he was a private called Fitzgerald. However, the story did not ring true and Private Jefferson was suspicious, and when O'Connell could not produce an identity disc he organised his arrest.

At his trial O'Connell was charged with desertion and pleaded not guilty. Unusually, he had the services of a prisoner's friend during the trial and in his defence he attempted to explain what had led to his disappearance.

> I can't read or write except my name. I did not realise it was a serious offence to leave the company nor that I would be punished. I left to find a woman in one of the villages. I intended to return to the battalion. I was wearing a Royal Engineers badge to avoid being taken for an Irish Guardsman. This was my first tour in the line. I did not know the company was going into the front line.[14]

O'Connell was found guilty by the court martial of deserting His Majesty's service, and the punishment was to be death by firing squad.

When his senior officers were asked to give an opinion on the court's finding there were no words of comfort for O'Connell. Lieutenant-

Colonel Baggallay, who commanded his battalion, wrote: 'I see no reason why the maximum penalty should not be enforced. In fact I am of the opinion that an example would be beneficial.'[15] The brigadier-general commanding the 1st Guards Brigade wrote:

> I consider that the sentence of death should be carried out, considering the man's character and the number of cases of desertion and absence in this battalion and brigade during the past 12 months. The discipline of this battalion is very good.[16]

This comment appears to be self-contradictory: on the one hand the brigadier-general is suggesting that O'Connell's death needs to take place to stop men deserting, and he then states that the discipline in the battalion is good. This statement appears to have confused others also. On O'Connell's court martial file, which remained secret until 1994, a question mark has been written against the brigadier-general's comments, and his words have been underlined.

Is it possible that these marks were made when O'Connell's punishment was being decided in 1918? Is this the work of Haig or another senior officer as he reviewed O'Connell's fate? We do not know who marked the text, or when it was done, but clearly someone reviewing O'Connell's file had spotted this discrepancy and had marked the file accordingly.

What is missing from O'Connell's court martial file is also revealing. Often senior officers in their statements would note how many desertions had taken place in order to illustrate problems of discipline, yet in O'Connell's case no details are given concerning the number of soldiers who had deserted from the battalion.

The confusion of the brigadier-general's statement was highlighted by the Irish government in 2004 when civil servants in Dublin reviewed Benjamin O'Connell's trial papers. In their examination of his file they concluded that the brigadier-general's statement requires a full and complete examination.

> It is clear that an example to other men played a contributory factor in the deliberations of the confirming officers, but if discipline was good then why was an example necessary?[17]

Benjamin O'Connell spent his last night under armed guard on Wednesday 7 August, a month from when he quit the trenches. The next morning at 4 a.m., before first light, he was taken from his cell and tied to a post at Bailleulmont. He was shot at 4:24 a.m., and his death was recorded by the medical officer as instantaneous.

At the very moment that Benjamin O'Connell was being shot, other British soldiers were taking aim, but this time their targets were German. That morning the Battle of Amiens had begun. Regarded as one of the greatest British victories in the Great War, the surprise assault began at 4:20 a.m., just as O'Connell's firing squad was in action on another part of the Western Front.

With the German defences weakened, the Amiens fighting resulted in the Allies being able to advance up to eight miles, the biggest gain seen on the Western Front in a single day. It would be a turning-point in the war and would be viewed later by the Germans as one of the blackest days in their military history.

On 8 August, six hours after the Amiens attack began, Douglas Haig wrote to his wife:

Who would have believed this possible even two months ago? How much easier it is to attack, than to stand and await an enemy's attack! As you well know, I feel I am only the instrument of that Divine Power who watches over each one of us, so all the Honour must be His.[18]

By the late summer of 1918, Haig was understandably optimistic. The successful Battle of Amiens would be followed by an offensive at Albert on the much fought-over Somme battlefield. With each passing week it seemed more and more likely that there would be an Allied victory. Yet there would be no relaxation of military discipline on the Western Front. In the Great War's final months, soldiers would continue to be executed, among them men from Ireland.

Chapter 13 ~

THE FINAL EXECUTIONS

If you desert and let your friends down, and left them to do your fighting for you, you deserved what you got.
—CAPTAIN LESLIE WALKINTON, MACHINE GUN CORPS

O n a cold, wet September evening near the old monastery at Labeuvrière, a young Irish soldier and a Catholic chaplain sat together inside a cramped cell. As the night wore on, the two men talked at length within earshot of the guards, standing behind the ironwork door with their bayonets fixed.

Aware of what the next day would bring, both men knew this was their last opportunity to speak. For the condemned soldier it was a final chance to talk about his life and his family. He made his confession and was given absolution and seemed calm and resigned to his fate. It was an attitude that impressed his guest, who found the scene reminiscent of the days of the Catholic martyrs, prisoners who were put to death for their faith.

As the conversation came to a natural end, the chaplain got up to leave. The young man said his goodbyes and then earnestly told his visitor that he was ready for what lay ahead. 'Father, I am glad I am a Catholic, and I am not afraid to die.'[1]

Within hours of these defiant words the soldier's life would end at the hands of his comrades. Only a handful of people would witness the execution: a doctor, the provost-marshal, a chaplain and members of the firing squad. His killers, six men handpicked from his regiment who had all seen much service on the Western Front, would never know whether they had fired one of the fatal bullets, as one of their number had been issued with a blank round.

The prisoner, described by the officer in charge as 'a nice, quiet, friendly sort of chap,' was polite to the end. He smiled as he told his comrades that he bore them no ill will. He had asked not to be blind-folded, but his request was ignored and his face was covered after he had been tied down. A piece of paper was then pinned onto his clothes near his heart for the firing squad to aim at; then the prisoner, seeking some last-minute comfort, called out:

'Where is the priest?'
'Here I am, dear boy, just beside you.'[2]

The two men shared final prayers, and then the young recruit said, 'Goodbye, Father.' The time for talking was over. The priest stepped aside, and the order to fire rang out.

The firing squad were understandably uneasy and nervous. Within seconds their bullets had shattered the stillness of an autumn morning. The prisoner's head was now slumped on his chest and the priest stepped forward and anointed the warm body. A stretcher was pro-duced and the body, wrapped in blankets, was placed in an ambulance. Then the firing party marched off, back to other duties. Their job was done. Private Patrick Murphy would never abscond again.

The priest who watched Murphy die and who had tried to comfort him in his final hours was Father Benedict Williamson. An eternal optimist, he was known throughout the ranks by the nickname 'Happy Days', as he seemed always to see the positive side of every experience. One colleague said he lived in 'a world of sunshine destitute of shadows.' Even amid the horror and sadness of that morning in September 1918 he found comfort.

The boy's death and his fine courage made a great impression on all who assisted at that sorrowful scene, and bore striking testimony to the power of the Catholic religion in the most terrible circum-stances. I have never in the course of my experience assisted at a death more consoling or one [at] which I felt more absolute assur-ance of the state of the soul going forth to God.[3]

Patrick Murphy's crime had been to abandon his colleagues as they came under attack from German artillery. The Irishman and his com-rades were all members of the 47th Battalion of the Machine Gun Corps, part of the London Division, which was in the trenches on 31

July when they were fired on. After shells landed close to their position, Murphy and his comrades dived for cover. When the firing ended, calm was restored and the soldiers regrouped. An officer then conducted a roll-call to assess the number of casualties. When the names were read out, Private Murphy did not respond.

His disappearance that July evening amid the noise, panic and confusion of the shelling was characteristic. The 22-year-old private had chalked up quite a disciplinary record, having deserted from duty on three previous occasions. Despite his tender years he was an experienced soldier, well aware of what army regulations dictated.

Life in uniform for the volunteer had begun shortly after the outbreak of war in September 1914, when he joined his home regiment, the Royal Dublin Fusiliers. He saw action with the regiment for more than three years, and his service record during that time was unblemished. The only report about his service with the regiment notes that he was wounded in December 1916. A year later he was in a different regiment, and it seems he became a different soldier.

In October 1917 Murphy deserted for the first time, and in the process of escaping he lost his equipment and regimental accessories. He was found guilty of these offences and given six months' detention and ordered to pay for the lost equipment.

The young Dubliner did not stay out of trouble for long. Four months later he went missing again, but this time when he was caught and later faced a court martial his sentence would be more severe. He was found guilty and, under military law, was sentenced to death. The execution, like the great majority of capital cases, did not take place. First his sentence was commuted to five years' in prison, and then it was suspended completely.

Yet Murphy would not enjoy this last-minute reprieve, because by the time it was officially granted he had made his own attempt to be free. Before the word arrived at Longueval, where he was being held, Private 15161 had escaped from his prison cell. For nearly two months he was on the run in northern France. When he was finally recaptured, in May 1918, the absentee was discovered at Étaples, on the coast close to Boulogne.

Étaples was home to thousands of British soldiers as they rested and trained. It was the army's biggest base in France and at one point during the war played host to fifty thousand men. Perhaps Murphy believed that at Étaples he could pretend he was wounded, in the hope that he would be shipped home, or he may have thought he could sneak onto a troopship and sail back to the safety of England. Either way his plan failed, and after a week's custody he was escorted from the camp and back to his old unit.

As he was being moved the impatient young Dubliner managed to give his guards the slip and broke free. For a month he would remain undetected. He did not travel far and it seems he spent his time hidden in the camp where he had previously been held. In late June he was discovered, still at Étaples, close to where he had earlier been arrested.

In July his two escapes were disciplined with ninety days' field punishment, when he was tied up and displayed in front of his colleagues, and he was also docked pay for the time he was on the run.

The punishment did little to deter him. At the end of the month Murphy would abscond again; but this time it would be his last escape. When he left the trenches on 31 July he was not seen for five days. On 5 August, without a rifle or any other equipment, Murphy approached a military policeman on duty at Pont-Rémy. He said he could not find his comrades and claimed he had been missing for two or three days. He was arrested, charged with desertion, and held in custody until his court martial.

During the hearing, before a major and three captains, Murphy offered no explanation for his behaviour. He had the services of an officer as a prisoner's friend, and he pleaded not guilty to the single charge of desertion. Though he did not speak at his court martial, in a conversation with Father Williamson he challenged the official version of events surrounding his desertion and claimed that when he left the ranks there was no shelling. 'It wasn't that I was afraid, Father . . . There was nothing to be afraid of; there were no shells coming over.'4

The court martial found him guilty and sentenced him to death. The sentence was then considered by senior commanders, and there was a unanimous verdict. A major-general in the division wrote:

I recommend that the extreme penalty be inflicted in this case—in view of this man's bad record, which shows that in his case leniency is of no avail. The state of discipline of this unit as a whole is good: but there are individuals (such as the accused) in the unit who take advantage of leniency and for whom an example is necessary.

The brigadier-general commanding the 141st Brigade would add: 'This man's value as a fighting soldier is NIL.' He later added: 'I regret that I am unable to recommend mitigation of sentence in view of the original intention not to carry out these duties.'5

The general commanding the Fourth Army, Henry Rawlinson, simply wrote that the sentence should be carried out, and after Haig confirmed that the shooting should go ahead, the final preparations were made.

One of those asked to assist in Murphy's killing was Captain Leslie Walkinton.

> It came as a great shock, however when the Colonel sent for me and told me that I was to provide a firing party from my company to shoot a man who had been convicted of desertion on three separate occasions. No one in the company could remember him. It seemed that on the final occasion he had joined it one day and deserted it the next, when on the way up the line.

Walkinton clearly had little sympathy with those who went missing.

> This was all part of the Army way of things and it was accepted by everybody I knew as being just and fair. If you deserted and let your friends down, and left them to do your fighting for you, you deserved what you got.6

While everyone knew what the consequences of desertion were, the reality of seeing a comrade being executed still aroused strong emotions, as Father Benedict Williamson recalled in his diary.

> I saw the Assistant Provost Marshal, a kindly hearted man who was really much distressed over the affair, as indeed I think everyone was; for there is an immense difference between seeing a number of men slain in battle and seeing one shot with all the cold deliberation that follows in such a case as this.7

At ten minutes past six on 12 September 1918, Patrick Murphy was tied to a stake, blindfolded and then shot by a firing squad. The men who killed him then returned to duty, as Walkinton recalled.

It was a very quiet and thoughtful party that returned to the Company. At their own desire they immediately joined in with the normal parades and tried to forget their unpleasant experience. The rest of us tried to treat them as if nothing abnormal had happened.[8]

Nine decades later, what are we to make of Patrick Murphy's court martial and execution? His court martial file, which was secret until 1994, was examined by Irish government officials in 2004. They concluded that the court martial panel failed to take a full account of Murphy's fighting character before he joined the Machine Gun Corps, which may have been good (though no records indicate this) and also argued that members of Murphy's court martial failed to investigate whether his injury sustained in 1916 contributed to his absences.

It is possible that Murphy's last disappearance was brought on by the shell attack and that he was genuinely affected by it. However, the issue of health was never raised during proceedings; interestingly, Murphy made no comment during the trial and this defence was not used or explored by his prisoner's friend.

Murphy's conversation with Father Williamson states that when he disappeared there was no shelling—so we can perhaps discount this.

Like so many of the executed men, what damned Murphy in the eyes of his superiors was his past behaviour and his long record of other escapes; and those absences clearly sealed his fate. Murphy's commanding officers clearly believed they had shown the Dubliner enough leniency.

———

Patrick Murphy, who would become the last Irishman to face a firing squad in the Great War, was one of three Irish-born soldiers to be executed in 1918. Earlier in the year John Seymour of the Royal Inniskilling Fusiliers had been shot, and in August the Co. Wexford soldier Benjamin O'Connell had faced a firing squad.

However, the Great War's dying months would also witness one of the most unusual desertion cases involving a soldier from an Irish regiment when Henry Hendricks was shot in August. Some weeks earlier Brigadier Bernard Freyberg of the 88th Infantry Brigade had written:

This man is one of the worst characters in the army, he openly defies all authority and deliberately commits crime. He is the worst influence in his regiment and is valueless as a soldier.[9]

When these words were neatly handwritten in pencil, folded into an envelope and then sent to the officer commanding the battalion, Henry Hendricks's life was over. This damning indictment and most cutting of character references was sent in late July 1918. Like a successful sniper's bullet, it reached its target with devastating effect. Four weeks after the brigadier-general wrote this critical assessment the subject of his ire, a veteran of the Boer War, was taken from his cell, brought before a firing squad and shot.

Henry Hendricks of the 2nd Battalion, Leinster Regiment, stands out from the rest of the Irish cases because of his age and background. Hendricks claimed to be an American citizen and at forty-six was the oldest soldier to be executed during the First World War.

By the middle of 1918, hearing American voices in some parts of the Western Front was an everyday occurrence, as the United States had officially entered the war a year earlier. Hearing American accents among British uniforms, however, was not so common; and seeing an American in the uniform of an Irish regiment was particularly rare.

However, despite his unusual route to the ranks of the Leinster Regiment, Hendricks had experience that corresponded with his age, having seen action previously during the war and also in the Boer War for nearly three years.

A small man, Hendricks was five foot five, with blue eyes and fair hair and a round, bony face. His association with the Leinster Regiment began in the summer of 1917, when he sailed to France. In August, he had his first brush with the authorities on what was a trivial matter. The veteran private had been warned not to gamble in his billet and had been instructed that such behaviour was against regulations; but as he and his comrades relaxed after duty Hendricks rather unwisely ignored the instruction. He was discovered breaking the rule and was subsequently docked fourteen days' pay.

It is not known whether this affair triggered Hendricks's next move, but within weeks he was in trouble again. This time it was a more serious misdemeanour. On 16 September, when Hendricks's platoon was close to Bailleul, a roll-call was taken at 9 p.m., and the American veteran was reported absent. As his comrades were readying themselves for duty, the missing private was on the march to the coastal city of Boulogne. For the next two weeks he was on the road, walking and sleeping rough as he made his way northwards to the sea, still in uniform and with his rifle and kit.

He arrived at the coast on 3 November and on that day at Marlborough Camp in Boulogne he was stopped by a Sergeant Elliot of the Royal Irish Rifles. Elliot handed him over to the assistant provost-marshal, the unit's head of military police.

The American was detained and placed in the detention barracks, where he stayed until 9 November, when he was sent to hospital complaining of being ill. For the next four months he would remain a patient at No. 7 Stationary Hospital, where he would be subjected to regular tests.

> I had a medical board. I was passed unfit for foreign service, a month after I was passed fit again by another medical board. Then I was discharged and sent to the Assistant Provost Marshal. I waited for an escort for 26 days. On the 27th day I took sick. I was sent back to hospital.[10]

After weeks in hospital Hendricks was eventually sent back to his regiment in the summer of 1918. In May medical opinion on his condition was sought. A lieutenant from the Royal Army Medical Corps based at the hospital that had originally treated Hendricks wrote this report:

> He has no physical signs in his chest but declares he expectorates to the extent of a spittoon full every night. The contents are very watery and always produced at night. I believe he adds the contents of spittoons belonging to other patients with perhaps rinsings from his own mouth to create the bulk.[11]

Then the doctor delivered a concluding line to his diagnosis, which would be devastating.

> I suggest he is a malingerer and should be treated as such.[12]

No sooner had Hendricks's superior officers digested the contents of this report than the story took another turn. In June, only weeks after he had been returned to his regiment, Hendricks disappeared again.

He again made a break for the coast, this time with an accomplice, who is referred to in official documents as Private Murphy. The two men would sleep rough in fields and also take shelter in barns and farmers' sheds. They were quickly spotted by French villagers who saw the soldiers walking from a wood and then taking shelter behind a hedge. The gendarmerie were called and two policemen on horseback searched the fields for ninety minutes before they discovered the two absentees hiding on farmland. They arrested them for desertion and then called on the services of a British lance-corporal, who acted as an interpreter.

It quickly became clear how Hendricks and Murphy had survived while on the run. They had bought bread from a local farm and when they were arrested they had boxes of preserved meat and supplies of sugar, rice and tea. The fugitives had no identity discs or papers, and when he was questioned Hendricks claimed he was an Australian soldier. He told the gendarmes he was a member of the Australian Pioneer Battalion and said his name was Harry White, son of Jack and Annie White of Newcastle, New South Wales. The French police passed the two escapers on to the British authorities and within hours Hendricks's identity was uncovered.

His co-accused, Murphy, has never been fully identified. It is possible he is the same Private Murphy from the 2nd Battalion of the Leinster Regiment who was later charged with two counts of desertion and given ten years' imprisonment in November 1918.

Hendricks would not be so fortunate. When he was returned to his unit his officers believed he would escape at any opportunity, so the prisoner was placed in handcuffs. He was then charged with desertion, escaping when in confinement, and going absent without leave. Before the court martial took place a series of reports was commissioned, including one from Brigadier Bernard Freyberg, officer commanding Hendricks's brigade. It could not have been more damning. 'He has to be hand cuffed while under arrest to prevent him from escaping. I consider the sentence should be carried out.'[13]

Freyberg's belief that the punishment should be carried out is particularly interesting, as his report was written before the court martial had met. This raises suggestions that the court martial's verdict was a *fait accompli*. Other senior officers would later support the brigadier's call.

On 30 July Henry Hendricks was brought before a court martial made up of a major, two captains and a lieutenant. He faced three charges deserting His Majesty's service, escaping from confinement, and being absent without leave.

Hendricks pleaded not guilty to deserting but said he was guilty of the other two offences, of escaping and being absent. He was found guilty of all three charges. The next day the major-general commanding the 29th Division wrote to endorse the conviction and sentence. 'Though the state of discipline in the battalion is very good, I consider that the accused's crime appears to have been deliberate and the sentence should be carried out.'[14]

After senior officers had given their opinion, the case was naturally referred to Haig, but it would be nearly three weeks before he would get a chance to consider Henry Hendricks's offences. August was a busy month for the army's most senior officer. It was the fourth anniversary of Britain's entry into the war and the early part of the month would be taken up with final plans for the successful Battle of Amiens.

On Monday 19 August, the day Haig met senior commanders to discuss tactics for the forthcoming Battle of Albert, he considered the American's fate. He confirmed that he believed the soldier was guilty of desertion and escaping but not guilty of going absent without leave. He endorsed the death sentence and then signed Hendricks's court martial papers accordingly.

Four days later the Commander-in-Chief's wishes were followed. Henry Hendricks was woken early on 23 August at La Kreule, and at 5 a.m., in the stillness of a summer's morning, he was shot.

At the distance of ninety years, and with the luxury of hindsight, what are we to make now of the trial and execution of Henry Hendricks? His death warrant was in effect written by Brigadier Freyberg when he described him as one of the worst characters in the army, who was valueless as a soldier.

As we know, Hendricks was the oldest and also one of the most experienced soldiers to face a firing squad during the Great War, yet we know little of his past soldiering. Did the 46-year-old veteran behave well during the Boer War? Was he a model soldier in other regiments? Had he a long history of desertion, or had he behaved with valour elsewhere?

All this information might help us to decide whether he was unjustly treated. His court martial file, which was kept secret until 1994, reveals little of his past army experience. It does seem that the American had health problems. Though the army suggested he was a malingerer, he did receive prolonged medical treatment and it is unlikely that he would have been hospitalised for so long if he was simply pretending. The issue of health was quickly dismissed by his superior officers, despite the fact that by 1918 the army hierarchy were becoming more attuned to the health problems faced by soldiers in the front line.

The statement made by Brigadier Freyberg before the sentence was handed down also raises a suggestion that the court martial was being guided to come to a certain conclusion.

So why was Hendricks shot? In simple terms, because he repeatedly broke the rules of soldiering and abandoned his comrades. However, it cannot be argued that he was executed as an example to others, as one officer reported that discipline in the battalion was very good. It seems that Hendricks simply tried the patience of his superiors, continually broke military law and had become a nuisance to his commanding officers, who were unable to manage him. His death in the war's final months now seems needless and pointless.

Ironically, as the war was coming to an end many officers about to lead their men into battle were desperate to get their hands on experienced soldiers such as Hendricks. In other circumstances the Boer War veteran would have been welcomed into service by some senior officers, who would have seen his experience as an asset to their battalion.

With hindsight it would seem that having his sentence commuted to imprisonment might have been a better alternative. But the court martial system was clearly a lottery, and its vagaries can perhaps be poignantly illustrated by events involving Hendricks's own regiment that occurred only days before the Armistice in November 1918. Two of his battalion colleagues who had six cases of desertion between them were later found guilty of leaving the ranks and were sentenced to death, but the men's sentences were commuted to imprisonment. The difference between dying and surviving on the Western Front rested with timing and circumstance—and often with luck.

Chapter 14

THE FIGHT FOR CHANGE

For years after the Armistice successive governments of all colours have smothered the details of a national scandal.
—WILLIAM MOORE, *THE THIN YELLOW LINE*

After four years of fighting, the First World War finally came to an end on a chilly, dull Monday morning in November 1918. For three hours that day, before dawn broke, Allied and German commanders held negotiations inside a railway carriage in the Forest of Compiègne used by the supreme Allied commander, Marshal Foch. The discussions were formal, the mood was businesslike, and the atmosphere was understandably frosty. The terms were first presented in English by the Allied delegation and then translated into German for the visiting officers. Foch's guests had little choice but to accept the detailed conditions for surrender, which had been fine-tuned in the days before by the British and French political hierarchy.

By the late autumn of 1918 the war had not been going in Germany's favour on several fronts. Its disorganised and disheartened battalions were conceding ground on the all-important Western Front, and both the Turkish and the Austrian armies had capitulated. At home, Germany was experiencing a domestic uprising, and sailors of its fleet had refused to go into battle and had subsequently mutinied.

The war was lost, and at 5 a.m. on 11 November the Armistice was signed, to come into force some six hours later. The news was greeted with joy by British and Commonwealth forces at the front line. Sergeant Robert McKay of the 109th Field Ambulance, who had seen action on the Somme with the 36th (Ulster) Division, would record in his diary:

Hostilities ceased at 11 o'clock a.m. today. Guns in the distance kept firing away up to the last minute. Great rejoicing.[1]

There were scenes of jubilation in London, Paris and New York as crowds took to the streets. In London the Prime Minister, David Lloyd George, boldly declared to the House of Commons: 'I hope we may say that thus, this fateful morning, came to an end all wars.' For the British soldiers from all parts of the Empire there was now only one thing on their mind: going home. When they were eventually reunited with their families much had changed personally and in some cases politically.

This was particularly true of Ireland, and when the men of the 10th and 16th (Irish) Divisions finally returned they set foot in a very different country. In the south of Ireland the mood had changed dramatically after the Prime Minister had called a general election. The result in Ireland had caused a political sensation.

Sinn Féin won a resounding victory and took 73 of the 105 Irish seats. The party refused to send its MPs to London; instead, buoyed up by their success in January 1919, republicans established a new parliament, Dáil Éireann, and planned to legislate for the entire island. This direct political challenge to years of British rule in Ireland came with military muscle, and in the same month two RIC members were shot dead in Co. Tipperary. Ireland was changing day by day, the trappings of empire were being rejected, the mood was restless and rebellious and more bloodshed seemed certain.

As nationalists promoted the idea of a free and independent Ireland, devoid of outside interference, it was an anxious and difficult time to be a former servant of the Crown. Ultimately it was not the returning soldiers who would influence Ireland's destiny but the men who had stayed behind, the men of Easter 1916, who had fought the Crown. History would be written about those who took to the streets of Dublin, not about the Irishmen who died in the mud of Flanders and France. For the veterans of the conflict, postwar Ireland was a confusing place to be. Many ex-soldiers felt disillusioned about their war service, unsure why they had volunteered. Some felt they had fought the wrong war, against the wrong enemy, and began to doubt the intentions of a British government that they had entrusted to grant Home Rule after hostilities with the Germans had ended. Stephen Gwynn, a writer and Irish Party MP who had served with the Connaught Rangers, summed up the mood in postwar Ireland.

And when the time came to rejoice over the war's ending was there anything more tragic than the position of men who had gone out in their thousands for the sake of Ireland to confront the greatest military power ever known in history, who had fought the war and won the war, and who now looked at each other with doubtful eyes.[2]

Unlike the doubts expressed by some nationalists, unionists viewed their war service with a degree of certainty. Unionism's political leadership argued that it was pay-back time from the British government. In simple terms, they argued that since they had fought the war for England it was now time for England to fight for Ulster. Increasingly the postwar commemorations of the 36th (Ulster) Division would be interpreted as events that reinforced Ulster's 'Britishness'. Similarly, the Orange Order would lay claim to a role in the fighting of July 1916. Some members of the Ulster Division at the Somme went into battle wearing Orange sashes, as the Battle of the Boyne had taken place on 1 July in the old calendar.

As Cyril Falls wrote in his history of the 36th Division, some men saw parallels between fighting by the Somme and the Battle of the Boyne:

For it was upon July the 1st, the anniversary of the Boyne, that the sons of the victors in that battle, after eight generations, fought this greater fight. To them it had a very special significance. A stirring in their blood bore witness to the silent call of their ancestors. There seemed to them a predestination in the affair.[3]

The events of July 1916 were woven into the fabric of Ulster unionism and when partition finally arrived many Unionists claimed that it was the slaughter on the Somme that secured the link with Britain and helped found the new state of Northern Ireland. Throughout the country, north and south, the old arguments over participation in the war had now been replaced by the politics of remembrance.

In 1919, just as they had done at the outbreak of hostilities in 1914, both republicans and unionists used the Great War experience to suit their different agendas. Unionists wanted the British people to remember; republicans thought the Irish people should forget.

In postwar Britain there was a much different atmosphere and the questions about the war remained simple and straightforward. The trauma and suffering of the conflict, evidenced in the thousands of war widows and the hospitals full of injured, became the subject of much debate. Why had Britain gone to war? What was achieved? Parliament then began to turn its attention to matters that had largely remained secret during the four-year conflict. The issue of military executions raised its head again, and this time, despite the previous parliamentary attempts, the demand for answers was so great that a committee was set up under the chairmanship of a senior judge, Sir Charles Darling, to investigate the law and rules surrounding courts martial and to bring forward recommendations.

The committee included Horatio Bottomley, an MP with an interest in military executions and an understanding of how the court martial system worked. In 1918 Bottomley had come to national attention as the editor of the weekly magazine *John Bull* when he published the story of Edwin Dyett, a sub-lieutenant in the Royal Naval Volunteer Reserve who was executed for desertion.

Bottomley and four other MPs sat on the committee, which met for twenty-two days and heard evidence from a series of witnesses. The evidence was never published, though the report was. It concluded: 'We are satisfied not only that members of courts martial intend to be absolutely fair to those who come before them, but also that the rank and file have confidence in that fairness.'4

Bottomley and two of the other MPs would not sign the committee's findings and issued their own minority report, which was critical of the judicial processes and recommended that a Court of Appeal be established.

The Darling Committee was not the only group charged with learning some lessons from the experience of the Great War. A fifteen-member committee under the chairmanship of Lord Southborough, including eleven doctors, was established to investigate shell-shock. The committee concluded that shell-shock had been a 'costly misnomer', that it was not a new form of mental illness, and that warfare had led to complaints being exaggerated. The report stated that 'nerve disorders' could be placed in three categories: emotional shock, concussion and mental exhaustion. Witnesses told the committee that it was right to view cowardice as a military crime and that it should be punished on occasion. However, the committee concluded:

That experienced and specialised medical opinion is required to decide in possible cases of war neurosis of doubtful character;

That a man who has already proved his courage should receive special consideration in case of subsequent lapse.[5]

There was criticism of the way the services had recruited men, and the Southborough Committee recommended that screening procedures be established to prevent would-be recruits who were mentally unsuited to fighting from joining up.

If the military hierarchy had hoped that the Southborough and Darling investigations would end the debate over the death penalty they would be disappointed. The two investigations simply whetted the appetite of campaigners who wanted the death sentence abolished for military offences. In the 1920s the abolitionists continued to press for change and the leading campaigner was a former soldier who had become a member of the House of Commons.

Ernest Thurtle, a Labour MP from east London, had enlisted when war broke out in 1914 and was later commissioned as an officer. He served in the trenches in France, and in 1917 at Cambrai he was seriously wounded in the throat. In May 1919 he was discharged and on his return to civilian life he developed an interest in the welfare of former soldiers. A son-in-law of the pacifist MP George Lansbury, Thurtle was keen to pursue a political career, and after a number of attempts he succeeded in being elected to the House of Commons in 1923. He would become a thorn in the side of the military establishment and became a staunch opponent of the use of the death penalty for military offences.

Two years after he won his parliamentary seat Thurtle brought forward a proposal to abolish 'shootings at dawn.' The proposal had the support of the Labour Party and nearly made it onto the statute book. It was narrowly defeated; but he had struck a blow for the abolition campaign, and his move was garnering support and momentum. His pamphlet *Shootings at Dawn* made a powerful case for reform, and the inclusion of letters from soldiers describing executions in detail convinced many that the law needed to be overhauled.

In response, significant changes were made to the way military law would be implemented in the future. In 1928 the government proposed that the death penalty be abolished for a number of offences, including sleeping on duty, disobedience and assaulting superior officers. Few soldiers were in fact shot for these offences during the Great War and the government planned to keep the death penalty for desertion and cowardice, two offences that had led to hundreds of deaths between 1914 and 1918. For the abolitionists it was a start, and a year later Ernest Thurtle's campaign would be complete.

However, before the debate was finished it would witness a bizarre contribution from Brigadier-General Frank Percy Crozier, the man who had witnessed the execution of his namesake James Crozier in 1916. Crozier, now retired from the army, was becoming known for his controversial opinions, and in an article in the *Daily Express* he did not disappoint his regular readers.

> I suggest that a paragraph be inserted in the Army Act to the effect that, whenever possible, executions be carried out by machine-gun fire. It is not fair to men to have to be put to such a terrible strain as is entailed by the execution of a comrade in any case, but, in these days, to neglect to rely on the scientific accuracy is short-sighted and inhuman.[6]

Crozier then suggested that if ordinary soldiers were to be shot for showing cowardice on the battlefield, generals who exhibited similar behaviour should also be executed:

> If cowardice is a triumph of matter over mind, then I know of one general, who should undoubtedly have been tried for cowardice, instead of which he was promoted.[7]

Crozier's contribution may have made headlines and raised some eyebrows, but it did little to affect the public debate.

Within months the political landscape would change and with it would come a victory for the campaigning former soldier from east London. The 1929 general election ushered in a Labour government and the parliamentary mathematics would be in Thurtle's favour. His motion to abolish the death penalty for all military offences, excluding mutiny and treason, won on a free vote of 219 to 135.

Thurtle's lobbying had paid off; but the battle was not over. His victory in the House of Commons was challenged by the House of Lords, and when some peers argued that the death penalty should be retained for those soldiers who deserted, showed cowardice or quit their posts, Thurtle now had another fight on his hands. Some members of the House of Lords, especially retired military personnel, did not take kindly to the proposal and suggested that such a move would hamper the army's effectiveness and lead to widespread disciplinary problems. Despite these arguments and the opposition, Thurtle's bill was passed and became law in April 1930. His ten years of campaigning, leafleting and lobbying had paid off.

The death penalty would still be used for those servicemen and women who were found guilty of treachery or mutiny, but never again would a British Army firing squad shoot one of their own men for deserting, showing disobedience or exhibiting cowardice.

When the Second World War broke out in 1939, Britain's soldiers would go to war under a different regime. Unlike their forefathers, the men who once again travelled to France to engage with the German army did so without the threat of execution—though four soldiers were shot for military offences.

The Second World War, like the First World War some three decades earlier, would again see the Allies triumph. Those who had opposed the removal of the death penalty had warned that its abolition would encourage desertion and could lead to serious disciplinary problems. The six-year conflict between 1939 and 1945 became the place to test that argument, and as Anthony Babington, a member of the Royal Ulster Rifles and Second World War veteran, discovered, the warnings of the death-penalty lobby were unfounded.

Throughout the Second World War the spirit and pride of the British Army remained inviolate. One reason for this might have been that most of the higher commanders had learned the lessons of leadership whilst serving as junior officers on the brutal and blood-sodden wastes of the Western Front. Perhaps they realised that there are better ways of controlling men in action than by resorting to a discipline of fear.[8]

Babington's opinion is worth considering when one studies his own experience and record. During the war he was wounded twice and awarded the Croix de Guerre with Gold Star for bravery. After his military career ended he entered the legal profession, and in 1972 he became a circuit judge. His interest in the law and his military background combined in the 1980s when he was the first author to be granted access to the court martial records. He was allowed to write about the cases of those shot for desertion and other military offences only if he did not identify the soldiers' names. His resulting book, *For the Sake of Example* (1983), following William Moore's less detailed account some years earlier, was a breakthrough and for the first time gave eye-witness accounts and personal testimony of how some three hundred British soldiers met their deaths.

For most of the twentieth century the only place where the court martial details were recorded was in the files stored away in government archives in London. Such official secrecy meant that the descendants of the executed men received only piecemeal information about their relatives' death. Subsequent generations had existed on stories handed down by their forefathers, and inevitably the tales of how their great-uncle or grandfather died sometimes became embroidered or confused and in some instances were wrong.

The rationale for such secrecy is worthy of analysis. Why was it needed and in particular why was such a lengthy embargo placed on the release of information to the public? Like the debate over the pardons issue, there are two opposing views relating to the decision to keep the details confidential for decades. The writers Cathryn Corns and John Hughes-Wilson, staunch opponents of the pardons campaign, argue that such secrecy was maintained to protect the feelings of relatives. They maintain that the files stayed shut to avoid families suffering any stigma about their loved one's death.

If a Labour MP had been successful thirty-five years ago we would never have known the full story of those who were shot at dawn, as their records would have been shredded. Don Concannon, a former soldier, rose in the House of Commons in May 1972 to highlight the subject of the surviving trial records. He suggested that the details be destroyed to prevent the names ever being released. In response Geoffrey Johnson-Smith, a Minister of State for Defence, said he was not prepared to see the records being destroyed and explained that the reasons were essentially twofold: 'to strike a balance between the protection of the innocent from unnecessary pain and the preservation of material that is part of our history.'[9]

The Shot at Dawn campaigners say the establishment simply wanted to keep the awfulness and the inequality of the executions under wraps and to protect the officers who sanctioned the killings. The government's decision to keep the details of the killings private for such a length of time inspired some historians and academics to try to uncover what lay inside their locked cabinets. It prompted writers to criticise the embargo, and for many the campaign to have the files released became a simple quest for truth. As William Moore wrote, 'for years after the Armistice successive governments of all colours smothered the details of a national scandal.'[10]

Like Moore, Anthony Babington did not name in his book the men who were executed, but in 1989 two researchers did. Julian Putkowski and Julian Sykes used Babington's book, war diaries, newspaper reports and personal accounts and with resourceful detective work managed to put names to those who were executed during the Great War. Their ground-breaking work did more than cast light on one of Britain's darkest military secrets: it spawned a campaign to have the executed soldiers pardoned.

Soon the Royal British Legion backed the idea of pardons for the executed men, and a lobby group founded by John Hipkin and simply named Shot at Dawn came into being. Hipkin, who went to sea as a fourteen-year-old merchant seaman and was taken prisoner during the Second World War, first became interested in the cases after reading an article in a local newspaper.

After the courts martial files were made public my local newspaper published details of the soldiers from Northumbria who had been executed. I noted that one of the executed soldiers was seventeen. I thought it was a misprint, because I thought you don't shoot boy soldiers, so it must be a mistake. I then looked into all this and discovered there were three other boys who were shot. It made me so angry that young boys were shot. To me it went against everything that I thought the British people believed in: that sense of fair play and common sense; and I just realised that those boys deserved justice.[11]

As Hipkin stepped up his campaign and the issue generated public attention, Britain went to the polls to decide if John Major should continue as Prime Minister. The Conservative Party won the 1992 general election, but they didn't get everything their own way and were returned to power with a reduced majority. In the constituency of Thurrock in Essex, a Conservative seat, the Labour Party candidate surprised the odds and defeated the sitting MP. Victory for Andrew Mackinlay was particularly sweet and as a serial parliamentary candidate it was a welcome reward for years as a political also-ran. A local government trade union official, he had tried on four previous occasions to become an MP and now on his fifth attempt was at last making the journey to the Palace of Westminster.

Exhausted by the hustings, the successful candidate, his wife and daughter were in need of a holiday and after the election they travelled to Belgium for a few days' rest. It was a chance for the family to unwind and take stock of their new circumstances. It also gave the new MP, a First World War enthusiast, an opportunity to visit the landmarks and cemeteries along the Ypres salient.

It was in the Flanders countryside, surrounded by the memories of war, that Mackinlay's first act as an MP took shape. As he walked through one of the many Commonwealth war graves that mark this part of Belgium he came across the final resting place of one of the executed men. Moved at what he had discovered, he pledged to investigate the case on his return to London.

After some research he became convinced that the executions deserved further investigation and he tabled a motion condemning the men's deaths and calling for them to be pardoned. His move garnered support and led to a correspondence with the Prime Minister, John Major, who instructed officials to examine a number of files. Though Major conceded that some of the soldiers might have been suffering from shell-shock, he suggested that the files contained little information about their medical state. He also cautioned that it would be wrong to try to rewrite the past with modern philosophies and outlooks. Ultimately the discussions with Major did not change policy; neither did the private member's bill that Mackinlay championed. It failed to get parliamentary approval on a number of occasions.

By the early 1990s the climate of secrecy that had surrounded the pardons debate for decades began to change as some of the files were being made public. The release of the court martial documents was a historic moment, a watershed when a bloody chapter of Britain's military past was at last laid bare. The move also gave hundreds of families their first chance to discover their own personal history.

An east London teacher, Eileen Hinken, became aware that her great-uncle James Templeton had been shot for desertion only when she started to research her background. A member of the 15th Battalion of the Royal Irish Rifles, the twenty-year-old from Belfast was executed along with his battalion comrade James McCracken in March 1916:

> I only started to find out about this because I was looking at family history, so it was all a bit of a surprise to find out that I had a rela-tion who was executed. And at the time you think, it must have been for a good reason; but when I started to look into it I realised that it wasn't. I managed to get some of his papers, and gradually the story unfolded over a few years.[12]

As the public began to read stories and hear news reports about the executed men, Andrew Mackinlay secured backing from an important quarter. Tony Blair, then leader of the opposition, pledged that a Labour government would look at the issue sympathetically and would initiate a review of the cases. When the Labour Party took power in 1997 the Minister of State for Armed Forces, John Reid, was charged with carrying out the review; but when he examined the files he concluded that the government could not grant pardons.

Before Reid made his announcement in the House of Commons he asked Mackinlay to come and see him in his office and hear the news privately. The meeting left the backbench MP puzzled.

> I was stunned when he told me that there would be no pardons. I couldn't believe it. After all, I couldn't think of a Labour MP who was against the idea of pardons; yet here we had a Labour Minister telling me it wasn't possible. I was dismayed. He told me he had tried very hard but it just wasn't possible and then explained the reasons; and then he said that I shouldn't keep on at this issue—that it was over—and I should move on. In cricketing terms, he made it clear I should draw stumps.[13]

John Reid then went public with his thoughts, and in the House of Commons he told MPs that the grounds for a blanket pardon on the grounds of unsafe conviction just did not exist. He said he had person-ally reviewed approximately one hundred of the cases and while it was

a moving experience, regrettably many of the files had limited information. He said there was insufficient evidence to overturn original
judgements, and it was impossible to distinguish between those who
deliberately deserted and those who were innocent.

He then argued that if the government was to consider individual
pardons the vast majority of cases would remain condemned or in some
cases re-condemned eighty years after the event. He argued that by
addressing one perceived injustice he could end up creating another.

Deflated and disappointed, Mackinlay had few options when he rose
in the House of Commons to respond to Reid's analysis. He began by
remembering a parliamentary predecessor, Ernest Thurtle, who had
fought to remove the death penalty for desertion and other offences
some seven decades earlier. While he accepted some of what John Reid
had to say, Mackinlay said he wanted to reserve his position on the issue
of a formal legal pardon and hoped he or others could bring in draft
legislation that would make that possible.

The parliamentary debate attracted the interest of a number of
Ulster Unionist politicians. The Rev. Martin Smyth MP said he hoped
those who were executed would have their names restored to war
memorials. The leader of the DUP, Ian Paisley, clearly felt that John
Reid's announcement had fallen short and he asked for pardons to be
introduced to finally lift the stigma felt by the relatives.

Others were more supportive of the Minister's statement. While the
Conservative MP Keith Simpson, a historian with an interest in the
Great War, endorsed Reid's conclusions, he was worried that the
Minister's expression of regret could set a precedent.

> Last year, the Prime Minister expressed regret over the Irish potato
> famine, an action many people agreed with. However we have to
> consider: where does this begin and end? I say in all seriousness: are
> we to consider giving expressions of regret for those people who
> were executed after the battle of Culloden by the forces of the
> Crown? Are we to express regret for those people who were executed
> by forces of the Crown after the Indian mutiny? Those are questions
> that involve us looking back into history and making value judge-
> ments. My fear is that the Minister's statement has not drawn a line
> under this issue.[14]

Simpson's prediction would prove to be correct, and eight years later MPS would return to the issue; but in July 1998 the parliamentary argument for the introduction of posthumous pardons had been lost.

The government's announcement shattered the families of the executed men and the Shot at Dawn campaign, including its chief organiser, John Hipkin:

We were at a loss. John Reid had been supportive whilst in opposition, but in government, as politicians do, he had changed his mind, and we just felt dreadful.[15]

The refusal to grant pardons privately angered Andrew Mackinlay, who felt let down both by his party and by the government. The Reid statement halted the pardons lobby in its tracks, and for the next few years there seemed little prospect of a change of heart at Whitehall or Westminster.

In the months that followed, Andrew Mackinlay moved his private member's bill again, but without success. Though there were those in the House of Commons who supported his efforts, some of his parliamentary colleagues were irritated by his stance on the pardons issue. He had clearly rubbed some of his colleagues up the wrong way, and in the competitive world of the Parliamentary Labour Party some wanted revenge. When a vacancy arose on the Commonwealth War Graves Commission, Mackinlay, keen to put his interest in First World War matters to good use, informed a Cabinet Minister that he would be interested in the position. The Minister suggested that Downing Street was unlikely to approve his nomination because of his stance on the executions, and even if he was successful he would 'have to promise not to do any of that pardons nonsense.' When Mackinlay's name was later mentioned at a meeting in the House of Commons one Labour MP quipped that he could have a place on the commission 'provided he took a permanent plot in the war graves as well.' Ultimately the vacancy on the commission, an unpaid voluntary position, went to someone else.

By the late 1990s the pardons issue had largely dropped from the political landscape, and it was events outside Britain that would ultimately keep the issue alive.

In 2000 the New Zealand Parliament passed legislation that granted a pardon to five soldiers who had been executed during the Great War.

The act, which had begun as a private member's bill, was later adopted by the government. In Canada politicians offered a formal apology in December 2001 to twenty-three Canadian soldiers who were shot after they had appeared before courts martial. However, the Canadian government stopped short of granting a pardon to the men concerned.

Members of the Shot at Dawn campaign in Britain watched the unfolding events in Canada and New Zealand with fascination, ever hopeful that the British government would be prepared to reconsider the pardons issue. Then a development closer to home gave the flagging campaign a boost.

Chapter 15 ∾

IRELAND'S CALL

You are a fucking coward and you will go to the trenches.
—COMMAND GIVEN TO PRIVATE HARRY FARR, LATER
EXECUTED FOR COWARDICE

Iveagh House sits grandly overlooking St Stephen's Green in the commercial heart of central Dublin. With its sweeping staircase, ornate ballroom, gilded mirrors and Italian statues, it contains some of the finest rooms to be found in the Irish capital. Once a bishop's residence, it is a rabbit warren of corridors and secret passages and makes an impressive home for the staff of the Department of Foreign Affairs.

In 2002 a smartly dressed man in his fifties arrived at the steps of the building carrying a briefcase and then walked into the reception area. In the long-running battle to win pardons for the executed British soldiers, a Dublin bus-driver was about to try a new tactic.

Peter Mulvany, a former merchant seaman who now earned his living ferrying passengers around Dublin's congested streets, had recently established the Irish branch of the Shot at Dawn group. His efforts had already proved successful and he had begun to attract the support of politicians from all parts of the country. He quickly secured unionist and nationalist backing in Northern Ireland and all-party support in the Republic. When he wrote to the Department of Foreign Affairs explaining that twenty-six Irish-born soldiers had been executed in the Great War, officials took note, as one would later recall:

We get lots of people writing to us asking for meetings, but when Peter's letter arrived it really made an impact. Right away we knew there was something here worth looking at. So we met him, and the first thing we noticed was Peter's energy. He came across as someone so passionate in what he believed in. He told us about the Irish cases and explained how they had been victims of a miscarriage of justice. We listened and then we went away to consider what he had told us.[1]

The Irish officials did more than simply listen to Peter Mulvany. Convinced that the British government had a case to answer, officials in Iveagh House did some initial research and then briefed the Minister for Foreign Affairs, Brian Cowen. He examined the arguments and in November 2003 announced that the government was supporting the Shot at Dawn campaign and wanted the British government to pardon the twenty-six Irish-born soldiers.

In February 2004 officials met their counterparts in the Ministry of Defence in London and asked to see the files pertaining to the Irish soldiers. The British officials seemed surprised at first by the Irish approach but did not refuse the request, and within a month copies of the files—excluding that of Private Wilson from Canada—were on their way to Dublin.

Over the next six months staff at Iveagh House pored over the court martial files of the Irish-born soldiers and began to compile a report. By the time it was complete there had been a reshuffle in the Irish government, and the report's authors had a new superior to report to. Brian Cowen had been replaced by Dermot Ahern, and the incoming Minister for Foreign Affairs needed time to get to grips with his new portfolio.

Ahern, a Fianna Fáil TD from the border town of Dundalk, was sceptical at first about the idea of backing the campaign. However, after he read his officials' work he changed his mind and was four-square behind the move. He realised how significant the issue was to the families, to the campaigners and to Anglo-Irish relations. However, he was also conscious that the issue needed to be handled carefully and that it should not be about 'raking over old sores' or 'getting at the Brits.' He simply wanted a resolution that recognised how twenty-six Irish soldiers had been unjustly and unfairly treated.

The Irish report, which analysed each case, allegations of class bias and the perceived disparity in the treatment of Irish soldiers, was completed by the autumn of 2004. The finished document was sent to the Irish embassy in London and then passed on to the British government.

If the Irish government had expected a speedy response to their overture they would be disappointed, as officials in Dublin would have to wait months for a reply from London. Though the issue was raised in Anglo-Irish meetings in 2005, a year later the British government had still not formally responded.

In the House of Commons in November 2005 the Minister for Veterans' Affairs, Don Touhig, was pressed for some answers. He said nothing of note except to acknowledge that discussions were continuing between the two governments, and he confirmed that the British government had still not completed its response to the Irish report. For the officials in Dublin the delay was frustrating; but by this time the Irish cases were not the only ones preoccupying officials of the Ministry of Defence. Six months earlier, in May, a landmark legal case had begun involving the family of Private Harry Farr, who was shot for cowardice in 1916.

For fourteen years Farr's family, including his 93-year-old daughter Gertie and granddaughter Janet Booth, had campaigned for a pardon, and after the government rejected their appeal, relatives brought an action in the High Court. The family insisted that Harry Farr, who had been serving with the West Yorkshire Regiment, had shell-shock and had not been given a fair and just trial. At his court martial Farr said he was sick and had been shell-shocked. He said he was ordered to go to the front line by his sergeant-major.

You are a fucking coward and you will go to the trenches. I give fuck-all for my life and I give fuck-all for yours, and I will get you fucking well shot.

Instructing Farr to go to the front line, the sergeant-major then told him:

I will blow your fucking brains out if you don't go.[2]

Harry Farr's relatives had first been told there were no legal grounds on which to challenge the government's refusal to grant a full pardon. However, during the legal proceedings Mr Justice Stanley Burnton said there was 'room for argument' that the family had been wrongly refused a conditional pardon.

The case began to take on some significance, and it became clear that if the family were successful the Ministry of Defence would have to reopen the remaining 305 cases. The case was adjourned after the

Ministry of Defence announced that the Secretary of State for Defence, John Reid, would reconsider the case if he received new evidence.

As the Farr case placed the issue of pardons in the public eye, discussions were taking place away from the gaze of the cameras. Don Touhig, the Minister for Veterans' Affairs, had come to the private conclusion that the Ministry of Defence should prepare the ground for a U-turn on pardons. He was convinced that the matter could be satisfactorily dealt with only through a parliamentary bill and he asked his staff to begin drafting legislation.

The work was slow, and Touhig was becoming frustrated at the lack of progress in his own department. He was concerned that even when legislation was drafted it would not find favour with his superior, John Reid. He went looking for allies who would support the pardons legislation and who carried political influence. He met Dáithí Ó Ceallaigh, the Irish ambassador to Britain, and in the breakfast room at the Irish embassy in London the two men discussed the Irish government's desire to see pardons introduced for all the executed British soldiers, including the twenty-six Irish-born soldiers.

Breakfast meetings were the ambassador's speciality; his previous guests had included the Taoiseach, Bertie Ahern, and the leader of the DUP, Ian Paisley, who famously broke bread at Ó Ceallaigh's table in 2004.

In 2006 Touhig and Ó Ceallaigh spoke for ninety minutes and the two men shared much common ground. Touhig suggested to his host that it would be helpful if Bertie Ahern raised the issue of pardons at his next meeting with Tony Blair. The ambassador agreed to brief the Taoiseach before his next meeting and on Touhig's suggestion agreed that the Irish government should send a letter to John Reid to increase the political pressure.

On Wednesday 3 May Dáithí Ó Ceallaigh stepped into his official car and was taken the short journey to the Ministry of Defence in Whitehall. He took with him a letter from Dermot Ahern, who was asking for a response to the Irish government's report and was also seeking pardons for the twenty-six Irishmen. Once inside the Ministry building Ó Ceallaigh was taken to the office of Bill Jeffrey, the department's permanent under-secretary.

Jeffrey was an experienced civil servant and no stranger to receiving Irish visitors. He was well known on the Anglo-Irish circuit, having been political director at the Northern Ireland Office for four years. He had advised the Prime Minister and successive Secretaries of State on the Northern Ireland political process and had been involved in the Belfast Agreement. He knew how the pardons campaign in Ireland had attracted cross-party support and was struck by Ó Ceallaigh's personal involvement. He told the ambassador that the British government was taking the Irish government's arguments very seriously. He passed on the letter to his Minister; but John Reid had little time to draw up a response.

Two days later, on 5 May, Tony Blair was suffering from a political hangover and embarked on the biggest reshuffle of his premiership. In an attempt to regain political momentum following a disastrous local election campaign he initiated a game of musical chairs around the Cabinet table. But it was the sacking of the Home Secretary, Charles Clarke, that would have the greatest impact on the pardons issue. John Reid, highly regarded by Downing Street, became his replacement. In Reid's place at the Ministry of Defence came a fellow-Scotsman and Blair loyalist, Des Browne, who had experience in the Home Office, the Northern Ireland Office and the Treasury.

The Browne appointment would transform the atmosphere in which the pardons campaign was now being fought. As Browne arrived, Don Touhig became another casualty of the Downing Street cull and was sacked as Minister for Veterans' Affairs. Instead of being central to the pardons debate, Touhig was reduced to observing proceedings from the backbenches.

Browne, who had been a barrister in Scotland before he entered politics, quickly got to grips with the legal intricacies of the Farr case. His legal background was obviously useful, but so too was his previous ministerial experience and in particular his time at the Northern Ireland Office. Browne, whose mother comes from Warrenpoint and who has an extended family in Northern Ireland, enjoyed his time in Belfast. One of his final duties in Northern Ireland as Minister for Victims brought him into contact with hundreds of relatives whose loved ones had been killed in the Troubles. This experience of dealing with grieving families and his exposure to a society trying to come to terms with the injustices of the past would be relevant when he came to consider the war pardons debate.

Nobody can come out of Northern Ireland without having a clear sense of how victimhood in Northern Ireland can pass over generations. People who are long disconnected in time and personal experience from things that have happened in Northern Ireland have a very strong sense of victimhood because of what their family suffered and the absence of any redress for that or justice. My own professional background in dealing with victims also gave me a start.[3]

However, when he arrived at his new desk in Whitehall he brought more than this experience. The MP for Kilmarnock and Loudoun had some interesting political baggage. When he was first elected and before he had started to climb the ministerial ladder, he had signed one of Andrew Mackinlay's early-day motions expressing support for the families of the executed men. Browne rarely endorsed such motions, because he believed they served little purpose, but on this occasion he felt strongly about the pardons campaign. When he started work at the Ministry of Defence his views on the Great War executions were already mapped out:

I came to the job with a sympathy for the families and a sense of injustice. There was a focus on it because there was the outstanding Farr case and I had decisions to make in relation to it, so that caused me to look at it, and I indicated very early on that if a solution could be found to this that pardoned the individuals then that is what I wanted to happen.[4]

By early 2006 the Farr case had given the Shot at Dawn campaigners much hope. Some activists believed that the government was now worried that the Farr family would win their case and rumours began to circulate that an announcement about pardons was likely.

In late May the new Minister for Veterans' Affairs, Tom Watson, was reminded of the Farr case when he travelled to Staffordshire to visit the National Memorial Arboretum. It was one of his first engagements as a Minister, and he had made the journey to talk to veterans of the Suez campaign. The grounds at Lichfield contain some sixty thousand trees, and the site is also home to a memorial for the executed soldiers. The centrepiece is a ten-foot statue modelled on seventeen-year-old

Private Herbert Burden of the Northumberland Fusiliers, who was shot in 1915.

When Watson took a walk through the grounds he paused to examine the statue and then walked along the lines of wooden crosses that have been placed in the ground to mark each of the men who were shot at dawn. Understandably, he made a beeline for one particular cross.

> I went to look for Harry Farr's post. I found it and got emotional and thought, God, we killed this guy, and then I thought of everything he had gone through and the horror of what went on, and it reminded me that we had got to get on with the pardons.[5]

In mid-summer the plans to pardon the executed soldiers were being worked out. Andrew Mackinlay was unaware of the detail and coincidentally used Prime Minister's question time in the House of Commons to question Tony Blair about the subject. Days later he received a sympathetic letter from Downing Street informing him that the Secretary of State for Defence would make a decision shortly.

By now Des Browne was preparing to do something his predecessors had resolutely refused to do. On 1 July he found himself on French soil as politicians, heads of state and veterans' groups gathered to mark the ninetieth anniversary of the Battle of the Somme. The trip gave him a chance to think over his solution to the pardons question. Surrounded by the memories of conflict, the place where thousands of British soldiers had fought and died provided a most poignant backdrop. As he walked past the neat lines of headstones and read the ages of the soldiers who had been killed, Browne was struck by the high number of young men who had lost their lives.

The son of a Second World War soldier, Browne was now convinced that what he was about to do regarding the pardons was correct:

> It wasn't a defining moment but it definitely reinforced the view that the way in which I was thinking was the right way.[6]

As thousands gathered in France from throughout Britain and Ireland, many others marked the Somme anniversary by attending memorial days and parades. In a moving ceremony the President of Ireland, the Taoiseach and veterans' groups assembled at the National

War Memorial at Islandbridge in Dublin to mark the Irish contribution at the Somme. As Peter Mulvany left the service he bumped into a politician who was a supporter of the pardons campaign. When the subject was raised Mulvany was told, 'The pardons are on their way.'

In August the rumours and speculation turned to fact when the Ministry of Defence contacted the Farr family to inform them that Harry Farr and 305 other servicemen would be pardoned. As this was happening, Andrew Mackinlay and Gertie Harris, two people who had been central to the pardons story, were in different corners of the world. Gertie Harris, the daughter of Harry Farr, was at her home in Harrow in north-west London. When John Dickinson, the lawyer representing the Farr family, unexpectedly phoned her he simply said, 'Gertie, you've got it.' Puzzled by what he meant, the 93-year-old replied that she didn't understand. Dickinson then made it clear. 'You've got the pardon for Harry.' Stunned, Gertie Harris simply could not believe that her father was at last being pardoned. That night she was unable to sleep, so she listened to radio bulletins throughout the evening: and slowly the news began to sink in.

Andrew Mackinlay, in Australia as a member of the House of Commons Select Committee on Foreign Affairs, was asleep in his hotel room in Canberra. He was woken from his slumber and, like Gertie Harris, he tried to take in what he was being told. Frustrated at being so far away from home, he abandoned any idea of going back to sleep and spent the next few hours talking to campaigners and journalists back in Britain. Within minutes the news was making headlines around the world.

The next day the full details of the government's proposals became clear. The pardons would not cancel convictions or sentences and would apply only to servicemen convicted of battlefield offences—such as cowardice and desertion—where the actions may have been influenced by the stress of battle. In line with the campaigners' demands, the pardons would not apply to those who had been convicted of murder. The pardons, which would have to be endorsed by MPs, would be included as an amendment to the Armed Forces Bill that would shortly be presented to Parliament.

Des Browne later explained that the move was about righting a wrong:

I believe a group pardon, approved by Parliament, is the best way to deal with this. After ninety years the evidence just doesn't exist to assess all the cases individually. I do not want to second-guess decisions made by the commanders at the time, who were doing their best to apply the rule and standards of the time. But the circumstances were terrible and I believe it is better to acknowledge that injustices were clearly done in some cases—even if we cannot say which—and to acknowledge that all these men were victims of war.[7]

The news that pardons were forthcoming was greeted with delight by the Irish government and those behind the Irish Shot at Dawn campaign. In Dublin, Peter Mulvany was both thrilled and stunned when the news finally came through:

Even though I had a sense that something was happening, I was stunned when it happened and I simply could not believe it.[8]

That disbelief and joy was shared in many homes in Britain and Ireland. 92-year-old Muriel Davis heard the news at her house in Warwickshire. Her brother-in-law Tommy, from Ennis, Co. Clare, was a member of the Munster Fusiliers who was executed in 1915 for quitting his post in Gallipoli. When news of the execution reached Ireland Tommy's mother, Margaret, was heartbroken. She had then called his siblings together and asked each one to keep the detail secret. For decades the family say they lived with the stigma of the events of Gallipoli; and in August 2006, ninety-one years later, Muriel Davis said that this stain on the family name was finally lifted.

We are delighted, absolutely delighted. It means everything. Tommy's mother would have been so relieved. She had led a life of grief, she couldn't talk about it. Even when she did talk about him she filled up with tears. She knew he was not a coward.[9]

Similar emotions were felt in the Walsh household in Dublin. Christy Walsh is the great-nephew of Patrick Downey, a private in the Leinster Regiment who was shot in December 1915. His death was a landmark in the history of military executions, as he became the first soldier to be executed for disobedience during the First World War. At nineteen years of age the Limerick soldier was also one of the youngest Irishmen to be placed before a firing squad. When Walsh heard that his great-uncle had been pardoned he was naturally delighted:

> I was elated when he was pardoned. The stigma has been removed from this family. It is now accepted that Irishmen went and fought for the British, and at the time many of them were not seen as Irish—but now we can call them Irish. We owe it to the Irish executed to show they were victims of an injustice. They went to fight for freedom and they gave their lives for freedom.[10]

As the news of the pardons made headlines the Minister for Veterans, Tom Watson, was hundreds of miles from his desk in an apartment in the west of Ireland, overlooking the Atlantic. The Minister and his wife and young son were enjoying a family holiday in Westport.

> I knew the announcement was coming but I didn't know when. That night as I watched the television news I saw Gertie Farr and I felt really pleased for her and knew we had done the right thing. I was drinking Guinness, so my wife and I toasted Harry Farr, and my wife turned to me and simply said, 'Well done, love.'[11]

When Watson returned to London, the parliamentary plans to get the pardons on the statute book were well advanced. However, the internecine politics of the Labour Party meant that his days as a Minister were numbered. In September he publicly called on Tony Blair to end the uncertainty over his leadership and step down as Prime Minister. Watson, a supporter of Gordon Brown, came under pressure to withdraw his comment or resign and he chose the latter path. Tony Blair was reported as saying that Watson had been disloyal and discourteous and that he planned to sack him from the government for his behaviour. Watson's career as Minister for Veterans' Affairs came to a crashing halt after four months.

In November 2006, the most appropriate of months, it was the job of Watson's successor, Derek Twigg, to lead the debate in the House of Commons when the pardons amendment was proposed. A number of Conservative MPs opposed the government's plans, and Derek Twigg was accused of 'rewriting history' and letting rogues off the hook. Despite the limited opposition, Twigg reminded his parliamentary colleagues that the pardon was about removing the dishonour of execution and not about quashing convictions or sentences.

For Andrew Mackinlay the debate in the House of Commons was the pinnacle of his political life and after fourteen years of campaigning he was enjoying his proudest moment as an MP. He told his fellow-parliamentarians that there had been a 'cry from Heaven for this wrong to be remedied.'

On a November evening, four days before Armistice Day, Mackinlay's plea and that of the families was answered when MPS agreed to pardon the men who were executed at dawn. Coincidentally, the Irish Minister for Foreign Affairs, Dermot Ahern, was in London when the bill received the Royal Assent, and he took the opportunity to ring the Secretary of State for Defence, Des Browne, to convey his appreciation. Ahern was pleased that a resolution had been found and told Browne that the Irish campaign had been an example of how people from different traditions had come together to campaign on an issue of shared history.

Ninety years earlier, at the outbreak of the Great War, Protestants and Catholics, unionists and nationalists, had joined forces to fight for a common cause. Now that unity of purpose had been repeated when every political party on the island of Ireland endorsed the pardons campaign. As a former Northern Ireland Office Minister, Browne understood the subtleties of Ahern's comments and was pleased that the Irish government now accepted that the issue was resolved.

For the Secretary of State for Defence there was still some important work to be done. Des Browne had agreed to sign an individual pardon for each of the executed soldiers, which would be placed in their court martial files at the National Archives in London. However, the task of signing 306 pardons was time-consuming, so each day over the next few weeks at his desk in Whitehall an official would present him with a batch to endorse.

One by one, the reputations of the forgotten soldiers were slowly being restored.

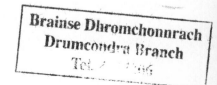

NOTES

Chapter 1: Ninety years on (p. 1–12)
1. Interview with author, February 2007.
2. Interview with author, February 2007.
3. Interview with author, February 2007.
4. Interview with author, February 2007.
5. Interview with author, February 2007.
6. Department of Foreign Affairs press statement, 2003.
7. Interview with author, February 2007.
8. Jeffery, *Ireland and the Great War*, p. 114.
9. Jeffery, *Ireland and the Great War*, p. 135.
10. *Freemans Journal,* August 1914, quoted by Denman, *Ireland's Unknown Soldiers,* p.28.
11. Jeffery, *Ireland and the Great War,* p. 16.

Chapter 2: The clash of the Croziers (p. 13–31)
1. Crozier, *A Brass Hat in No Man's Land,* p. 57.
2. Crozier, *A Brass Hat in No Man's Land,* p. 57.
3. Crozier, *The Men I Killed,* chapter 2.
4. Crozier, *The Men I Killed,* chapter 2.
5. Crozier, *A Brass Hat in No Man's Land,* p. 52.
6. Crozier, *A Brass Hat in No Man's Land,* p. 62.
7. Crozier, *A Brass Hat in No Man's Land,* p. 131.
8. Public Record Office of Northern Ireland, 3835/e/2/5/20a.
9. Crozier, *A Brass Hat in No Man's Land,* p. 64.
10. Crozier, *A Brass Hat in No Man's Land,* p. 69.
11. National Archives (London), WO/71 450.
12. National Archives (London), WO/71 450.
13. National Archives (London), WO/71 450.
14. National Archives (London), WO/71 450.
15. Crozier, *A Brass Hat in No Man's Land,* p. 86.
16. Crozier, *A Brass Hat in No Man's Land,* p. 87.
17. Crozier, *A Brass Hat in No Man's Land,* p. 88.
18. Crozier, *A Brass Hat in No Man's Land,* p. 88.
19. Crozier, *A Brass Hat in No Man's Land,* p. 88.

20. Starrett, 'Batman', p. 57.
21. Crozier, *A Brass Hat in No Man's Land,* p. 89.
22. Crozier, *The Men I Killed,* chapter 2.
23. Crozier, *The Men I Killed,* chapter 2
24. Department of Foreign Affairs Report, 2004.
25. Crozier, *The Men I Killed,* p. 40.
26. Crozier, *The Men I Killed,* chapter 2.
27. Starrett, 'Batman', p. 57.
28. Crozier, *The Men I Killed,* chapter 6.
29. Crozier, *The Men I Killed,* chapter 6.
30. Crozier, *The Men I Killed,* chapter 6.
31. National Archives (London), personal file of F. P. Crozier.
32. National Archives (London), personal file of F. P. Crozier.

Chapter 3: The new front (p. 32–48)

1. Carver, *Turkish Front,* p. 32.
2. A. P. Herbert, quoted by Barnett, *The Great War,* p. 74.
3. National Archives (London), WO71/431.
4. National Archives (London), battalion war diary.
5. Department of Foreign Affairs Report, 2004.
6. Barnett, *The Great War,* p. 74.
7. Interview with author for BBC Radio Ulster, 1992.
8. Letter to author, 1992.
9. Interview with author, July 2006.
10. Carver, *Turkish Front,* p. 69.
11. Johnstone, *Orange, Green and Khaki,* p. 172.
12. National Archives (London), WO71/441.
13. National Archives (London), WO71/441.
14. Corns and Hughes-Wilson, *Blindfold and Alone,* p. 125.
15. National Archives (London), WO71/441.
16. *Letters of Professor J. J. Mackenzie,* 1933.
17. Corns and Hughes-Wilson, *Blindfold and Alone,* p. 126.
18. Department of Foreign Affairs Report, 2004.
19. Interview with author, July 2006.
20. Interview with author, March 2007.
21. *Seanad Debates,* March 2006.
22. Interview with author, July 2006.

Chapter 4: Side by side (p. 49–65)

1. National Archives (London), battalion war diary.
2. National Archives (London), WO71/394/395.
3. National Archives (London), WO71/394/395.

4. National Archives (London), WO71/394/395.
5. Department of Foreign Affairs Report, 2004.
6. Babington, *For the Sake of Example.*
7. Putkowski and Sykes, *Shot at Dawn.*
8. Oram, *Worthless Men.*
9. Interview with author for BBC Radio Ulster, 1992.
10. Corns and Hughes-Wilson, *Blindfold and Alone,* p. 39.
11. Interview with author, March 2007.
12. National Archives (London), WO71/453/454.
13. National Archives (London), WO71/453/454.
14. National Archives (London), WO71/453/454.
15. Department of Foreign Affairs Report, 2004.
16. National Archives (London), WO71/453/454.
17. Interview with author for BBC Radio Ulster, 1992.
18. Interview with author, March 2007.
19. Interview with author, March 2007.

Chapter 5: Dying for Ireland (p. 66–76)
1. Drury, 'War Diary'.
2. Lucy, *There's a Devil in the Drum,* p. 352.
3. Lucy, *There's a Devil in the Drum,* p. 356.
4. Denman, *Ireland's Unknown Soldiers,* p. 145.
5. Francis Ledwidge, *Selected Poems,* p. 17.
6. Gregory and Paseta, *Ireland and the Great War,* p. 207.
7. Francis Ledwidge, *Selected Poems,* p. 57.
8. Denman, *Ireland's Unknown Soldiers,* p. 129.
9. Lucy, *There's a Devil in the Drum,* p. 93.
10. Putkowski, 'Shot at Dawn' web site.
11. Putkowski, 'Shot at Dawn' web site.
12. *Canadian Parliamentary Proceedings,* 2001.

Chapter 6: Death on the Somme (p. 77–93)
1. Brown, *Tommy Goes to War,* p. 134.
2. National Archives (London), WO95/2301.
3. National Archives (London), battalion war diary.
4. National Archives (London), WO71/498.
5. National Archives (London), WO71/498.
6. National Archives (London), WO71/498.
7. National Archives (London), WO71/498.
8. National Archives (London), WO71/498.
9. National Archives (London), WO71/498.
10. National Archives (London), WO71/498.

11. National Archives (London), WO71/513.
12. National Archives (London), WO71/513.
13. National Archives (London), WO71/513.
14. National Archives (London), WO71/513.
15. National Archives (London), WO71/513.
16. National Archives (London), WO71/513.
17. National Archives (London), WO71/513.
18. Putkowski, 'Shot at Dawn' web site.
19. Department of Foreign Affairs Report, 2004.
20. Interview with author, February 2007.

Chapter 7: The shock of battle (p. 90–102)
1. National Archives (London), WO71/529.
2. National Archives (London), WO71/529.
3. National Archives (London), WO71/529.
4. National Archives (London), WO71/529.
5. National Archives (London), WO71/529.
6. National Archives (London), WO71/529.
7. Haig, *War Diaries and Letters,* p. 259.
8. Department of Foreign Affairs Report, 2004.
9. Brown, *Imperial War Museum Book of the Western Front,* p. 165.
10. Corns and Hughes-Wilson, *Blindfold and Alone,* p. 144.
11. National Archives (London), WO71/484.
12. National Archives (London), WO71/484.
13. National Archives (London), WO71/484.
14. Department of Foreign Affairs Report, 2004.
15. Johnstone, *Orange, Green and Khaki,* p. 212.
16. National Archives (London), WO71/500.
17. National Archives (London), WO71/500.
18. National Archives (London), WO71/500.
19. National Archives (London), WO71/500.
20. National Archives (London), WO71/500.
21. National Archives (London), WO71/500.
22. Department of Foreign Affairs Report, 2004.
23. Department of Foreign Affairs Report, 2004.

Chapter 8: Looking for hope (p. 103–13)
1. Hansard (*Parliamentary Debates*), January 1916.
2. Hansard (*Parliamentary Debates*), March 1916.
3. National Archives (London), WO71/401.
4. National Archives (London), battalion war diary.
5. National Archives (London), battalion war diary.

6. Brown and Seaton, *Christmas Truce*, p. 153.
7. National Archives (London), WO71/401.
8. National Archives (London), WO71/401.
9. Department of Foreign Affairs Report, 2004.
10. Haig, *War Diaries and Letters*, p. 96.
11. Department of Foreign Affairs Report, 2004.

Chapter 9: Heading for home (p. 114–27)

1. Brown, *Tommy Goes to War*, p. 161.
2. National Archives (London), WO71/432.
3. National Archives (London), WO71/432.
4. Department of Foreign Affairs Report, 2004.
5. National Archives (London), WO71/412.
6. National Archives (London), WO71/412.
7. National Archives (London), WO71/550.
8. National Archives (London), WO71/550.
9. Department of Foreign Affairs Report, 2004.
10. National Archives (London), WO71/563.
11. National Archives (London), WO71/563.
12. National Archives (London), WO71/563.
13. Department of Foreign Affairs Report, 2004.
14. Putkowski, 'Shot at Dawn' web site.

Chapter 10: Not in my name (p. 128–40)

1. Haig, *War Diaries and Letters*, p. 267.
2. National Archives (London), WO71/557.
3. National Archives (London), WO71/557.
4. National Archives (London), WO71/557.
5. National Archives (London), WO71/557.
6. National Archives (London), WO71/557.
7. National Archives (London), WO71/557.
8. Siegfried Sassoon, *The War Poems*, p. 28.
9. National Archives (London), WO71/571.
10. National Archives (London), WO71/571.
11. Haig, *War Diaries and Letters*, p. 298.
12. Quoted by Philip Gibbs, *Now it can be told*, p. 470.
13. Department of Foreign Affairs Report, 2004
14. Interview with author, July 2006.
15. Interview with author, July 2006.
16. National Archives (London), WO71/613.
17. National Archives (London), WO71/613.
18. National Archives (London), WO71/613.

19. Department of Foreign Affairs Report, 2004.
20. Interview with author, July 2006.
21. Interview with author, July 2006.

Chapter 11: A class of their own (p. 141–54)

1. Scott, *Dishonoured,* p. 54.
2. Scott, *Dishonoured,* p. 54.
3. Scott, *Dishonoured,* p. 57.
4. Babington, *For the Sake of Example,* p. 8.
5. Crozier, *A Brass Hat in No Man's Land,* p. 68.
6. National Archives (London), WO339/14160.
7. Starrett, 'Batman', p. 56.
8. Crozier, *A Brass Hat in No Man's Land.*
9. National Archives (London), WO71/506.
10. National Archives (London), WO71/506.
11. National Archives (London), WO71/506.
12. National Archives (London), WO71/506.
13. Corns and Hughes-Wilson, *Blindfold and Alone,* p. 359.
14. Department of Foreign Affairs Report, 2004.
15. Department of Foreign Affairs Report, 2004.
16. Corns and Hughes-Wilson, *Blindfold and Alone,* p. 93.
17. Oram, *Worthless Men,* p. 101.
18. Public Record Office of Northern Ireland, 3835/e/2/5/20a.
19. Interview with author for 'Spotlight', BBC Northern Ireland, November 2005.
20. Oram, *Worthless Men,* p. 61.
21. Department of Foreign Affairs Report, 2004.
22. Bowman, *Irish Regiments in the Great War,* p. 20.

Chapter 12: One last chance (p. 155–67)

1. National Archives (London), WO71/611.
2. National Archives (London), WO71/611.
3. National Archives (London), WO71/611.
4. Putkowski, 'Shot at Dawn' web site.
5. Department of Foreign Affairs Report, 2004.
6. National Archives (London), WO71/679.
7. National Archives (London), WO71/679.
8. National Archives (London), WO71/679.
9. National Archives (London), WO71/679.
10. National Archives (London), WO71/679.
11. Department of Foreign Affairs Report, 2004.
12. National Archives (London),WO71/659.
13. National Archives (London),WO71/659.

14. National Archives (London),WO71/659.
15. National Archives (London), WO71/659.
16. National Archives (London), WO71/659.
17. Department of Foreign Affairs Report, 2004.
18. Haig, *War Diaries and Letters*, p. 440.

Chapter 13: The final executions (p. 168–78)

1. Williamson, '*Happy Days' in France and Flanders*, p. 158.
2. Williamson, '*Happy Days' in France and Flanders*, p. 159.
3. Williamson, '*Happy Days' in France and Flanders*, p. 160.
4. Williamson, '*Happy Days' in France and Flanders*, p. 158.
5. National Archives (London), WO71/667.
6. Walkinton, *Twice in a Lifetime*, p. 156.
7. Williamson, '*Happy Days' in France and Flanders*, p. 157.
8. Walkinton, *Twice in a Lifetime*, p. 157.
9. National Archives (London), WO71/661.
10. National Archives (London), WO71/661.
11. National Archives (London), WO71/661.
12. National Archives (London), WO71/661.
13. National Archives (London), WO71/661.
14. National Archives (London), WO71/661.

Chapter 14: The fight for change (p. 179–92)

1. Brown, *Imperial War Museum Book of the Western Front*, p. 344.
2. Denman, *Ireland's Unknown Soldiers*, p. 181.
3. Falls, *History of the 36th 'Ulster' Division*, p. 51.
4. Babington, *For the Sake of Example*, p. 251.
5. *Report of the War Office Enquiry into Shell-Shock*, London, 1922.
6. *Daily Express*, 1928, quoted by Moore, *The Thin Yellow Line*.
7. *Daily Express*, 1928, quoted by Moore, *The Thin Yellow Line*.
8. Babington, *For the Sake of Example*, p. 275.
9. Hansard (*Parliamentary Debates*), May 1972.
10. Moore, *The Thin Yellow Line*, Introduction.
11. Interview with author, February 2007.
12. Interview with author, February 2007.
13. Interview with author, February 2007.
14. Hansard (*Parliamentary Debates*), July 1998.
15. Interview with author, February 2007.

Chapter 15: Ireland's call (p. 193–203)

1. Government source.
2. National Archives (London), WO71/509.

3. Interview with author, December 2006.
4. Interview with author, December 2006.
5. Interview with author, February 2007.
6. Interview with author, December 2006.
7. Press statement, August 2006.
8. Interview with author, February 2007.
9. Interview with author, February 2007.
10. Interview with author, February 2007.
11. Interview with author, February 2007.

SOURCES

Primary sources
Personal interviews
National Archives, London
Public Record Office of Northern Ireland, Belfast
'Shot at Dawn' web site (www.shotatdawn.org.uk)

Publications
— Babington, Anthony, *For the Sake of Example: Capital Courts-Martial, 1914–1920,* London: Leo Cooper, 1983.
— Barnett, Correlli, *The Great War,* London: BBC, 2003.
— Bowman, Timothy, *The Irish Regiments in the Great War: Discipline and Morale,* Manchester: Manchester University Press, 2003.
— Brown, Malcolm, *The Imperial War Museum Book of 1918: Year of Victory,* London: Pan, 2001.
— Brown, Malcolm, *The Imperial War Museum Book of the Western Front,* London: Pan, 2001.
— Brown, Malcolm, *Tommy Goes to War,* London: Tempus, 2001.
— Brown, Malcolm, and Seaton, Shirley, *Christmas Truce,* London: Pan, 1999.
— Carver, Field Marshal Lord, *The National Army Museum Book of the Turkish Front, 1914–1918: The Campaigns at Gallipoli, in Mesopotamia and in Palestine,* London: Pan, 2002.
— Chielens, Piet, and Putkowski, Julian, *Unquiet Graves: Execution Sites of the First World War in Flanders: Guide Book,* London: Francis Boutle, [2000].
— Corns, Cathryn, and Hughes-Wilson, John, *Blindfold and Alone: British Military Executions in the Great War,* London: Cassell, 2001.
— Crozier, F. P., *A Brass Hat in No Man's Land,* London: Jonathan Cape, 1937.
— Crozier, F. P., *The Men I Killed,* London: Michael Joseph, 1937.
— Crozier, F. P., *The Writings of F. P. Crozier,* Belfast: Athol Books, 2002.
— Denman, Terence, *Ireland's Unknown Soldiers: The 16th (Irish) Division in the Great War, 1914–1918,* Dublin: Irish Academic Press, 1992.
— Drury, Noel, '1914–1918: My War Diary' (private papers).
— Falls, Cyril, *A History of the 36th (Ulster) Division,* Belfast and London: McCaw, Stevenson and Orr, 1922.
— Gibbs, Philip, *Now it can be told,* London: Dodo Press, 2007.

— Gregory, Adrian, and Paseta, Senia (editors), *Ireland and the Great War: 'A War to Unite Us All'?* Manchester: Manchester University Press, 2002.
— Haig, Sir Douglas, *War Diaries and Letters, 1914–1918* (Gary Sheffield and John Bourne, editors), London: Weidenfeld and Nicolson, 2005.
— Hargrave, John Gordon, *The Suvla Bay Landing,* London: Macdonald, 1964.
— Hindenburg, Paul von, *Out of My Life,* London: Cassell, 1933.
— Jeffery, Keith, *Ireland and the Great War,* Cambridge: Cambridge University Press, 2000.
— Johnstone, Tom, *Orange, Green and Khaki: The Story of the Irish Regiments in the Great War, 1914–18,* Dublin: Gill and Macmillan, 1992.
— Ledwidge, Francis, *Selected Poems,* Dublin: New Island, 1992.
— Lucy, John F., *There's a Devil in the Drum,* London: Faber and Faber, 1938.
— Mackenzie, John Joseph, *Number 4 Canadian Hospital: The Letters of Professor J. J. Mackenzie from the Salonika Front: With a Memoir by Kathleen Cuffe Mackenzie,* Toronto: Macmillan of Canada, 1933.
— Moore, William, *The Thin Yellow Line,* London: Wordsworth Editions, 1999.
— Oram, Gerard (edited by Julian Putkowski), *Death Sentences Passed by Military Courts of the British Army, 1914–1924,* London: Francis Boutle, 2005.
— Oram, Gerard, *Worthless Men: Race, Eugenics and the Death Penalty in the British Army During the First World War,* London: Francis Boutle, 1998.
— Orr, Philip, *The Road to the Somme: Men of the Ulster Division Tell Their Story,* Belfast: Blackstaff Press, 1987.
— Pretani Press, *The Great War: A Tribute to Ulster's Heroes,* Belfast: Pretani Press, 1991.
— Putkowski, Julian, and Sykes, Julian, *Shot at Dawn: Executions in World War One by Authority of the British Army Act,* London: Leo Cooper, 1992.
— Sassoon, Siegfried, *The War Poems,* London: Faber and Faber, 1983.
— Scott, Peter T., *Dishonoured: The Colonels' Surrender at St Quentin: The Retreat from Mons, August 1914,* London: Tom Donovan, 1994.
— Sheffield, Gary, *Forgotten Victory: The First World War: Myths and Realities,* London: Review, 2002.
— Starrett, David, 'Batman' (unpublished manuscript).
— Terraine, John, *The Great War, 1914–1918: A Pictorial History,* London: Wordsworth Military Library, 1965.
— Walkinton, M. L., *Twice in a Lifetime,* London: Samson, 1980.
— Williamson, Benedict, *'Happy Days' in France and Flanders with the 47th and 49th Divisions, etc.,* London: Harding and More, 1921.

Documentaries
— 'In the Firing Line', BBC Radio Ulster, November 1992.
— 'Burden of Shame', 'Spotlight', BBC Northern Ireland, November 2005.

APPENDIX

Irish-born soldiers and members of Irish regiments executed, 1914–18

Name	Regiment	Date of execution
Thomas Cummings	Irish Guards	28 January 1915
Albert Smythe	Irish Guards	28 January 1915
Thomas Hope	Leinster Regiment	2 March 1915
John Bell	Royal Field Artillery	25 April 1915
Thomas Davis	Royal Munster Fusiliers	2 July 1915
Peter Sands	Royal Irish Rifles	15 September 1915
James Graham	Royal Munster Fusiliers	21 December 1915
Patrick Downey	Leinster Regiment	27 December 1915
James Crozier	Royal Irish Rifles	27 February 1916
James McCracken	Royal Irish Rifles	19 March 1916
James Templeton	Royal Irish Rifles	19 March 1916
James Wilson	Canadian Infantry	9 July 1916
James Cassidy	Royal Inniskilling Fusiliers	23 July 1916
Joseph Carey	Royal Irish Fusiliers	15 September 1916
Albert Rickman	Royal Dublin Fusiliers	15 September 1916
James Mullany	Royal Field Artillery	3 October 1916
Bernard McGeehan	King's (Liverpool)	2 November 1916
Samuel McBride	Royal Irish Rifles	7 December 1916
Arthur Hamilton	Durham Light Infantry	27 March 1917
Thomas Hogan	Royal Inniskilling Fusiliers	14 May 1917
James Wishart	Royal Inniskilling Fusiliers	15 June 1917
Robert Hope	Royal Inniskilling Fusiliers	5 July 1917
Stephen Byrne	Royal Dublin Fusiliers	28 October 1917
George Hanna	Royal Irish Fusiliers	6 November 1917
John Seymour	Royal Inniskilling Fusiliers	24 January 1918
Benjamin O'Connell	Irish Guards	8 August 1918
Henry Hendricks	Leinster Regiment	23 August 1918
Patrick Murphy	Machine Gun Corps	12 September 1918

INDEX